BHAVAN'S BOOK UNIVERSITY

Beyond Destiny

The Life and Times of Subbudu

Lada Guruden Singh

BHAVAN'S BOOK UNIVERSITY

Beyond Destiny

The Life and Times of Subbudu

Lada Guruden Singh

BHARATIYA VIDYA BHAWAN
Kulapati Munshi Marg
Mumbai - 400 007

First Edition : 2005

ISBN : 81-7276-369-7

Price Rs. 275/-

Published by
Bharatiya Vidya Bhavan
Kulapati Munshi Marg, Mumbai - 400 007

Designed, printed and bound by
Bibliophile South Asia, New Delhi

Subbudu
dedicates his biography
to
Sh. R. Venkataraman
Former President of India
for protecting and preserving
Kalakshetra
from becoming a victim of cultural politics

General Editor's Preface

Bharatiya Vidya Bhavan's Book University had brought out several biographical accounts and some autobiographies of eminent persons, scientists and thinkers. Bhavan has also published several books on the great Indian Heritage in Arts, Music and Dance. The Delhi Kendra of Bharatiya Vidya Bhavan took the initiative in preparing the manuscript of this biography of Subbudu, the respected and well known critic of Carnatic classical music and Bharatanatyam. The author of the book, Lada Guruden Singh is a young writer, a performing artiste and an admirer of Subbudu and has indeed succeeded him in *The Statesman*, as one of its critics writing on dance and culture. Bharatiya Vidya Bhavan is privileged to offer this biography to the discerning readers who, I am sure, will find the book full of insights and illuminating the life and work of Subbudu and also on several aspects of life and works of artistes and critics. I wish to express our heartfelt thanks to all those who have made this book possible and congratulate the Delhi Kendra on this initiative.

Dhiru S Mehta

Bharatiya Vidya Bhavan
Mumbai 400 007
July, 2005

Subbudu thanks...

Subbudu owes a deep sense of gratitude to the following people who have afforded him the status of loco-parentis right through his career as a critic...

T.K. Tyagarajan, Former General Manager, *The Indian Express*

A. Natarajan, Former Director, Doordarshan, Chennai

R. Krishnaswami, Secretary, Narada Gana Sabha

R. Suryanarayanan, Treasurer, Narada Gana Sabha

M. Krishnaswami, Deputy General Manager, *The Indian Express*

Justice Bhaktavatsalam, Retd. Judge, Madras High Court and Chairman, Bharatiya Vidya Bhavan, Chennai

Shanta Serbjeet Singh, Eminent Critic and Chairperson, Asia Pacific Performing Arts Network

Leela Venkataraman, Veteran Dance Critic, *The Hindu*

Anjana Rajan of *The Hindu*

I am Indebted

I owe this book to Subbudu.

But for his faith in my ability to capture the varied shades of his life, I wouldn't have found my name attached to his own.

I have felt terribly guilty for pushing him to relive his life even when he was advised complete rest especially since the pace of the work depended entirely on the frequency of my interactions with him.

I am grateful to J. Veeraraghavan, Director, Bharatiya Vidya Bhavan, New Delhi for being extremely encouraging and remarkably patient with me and to my original mentor, Shanta Serbjeet Singh, Chairperson, All India Performing Arts Network for always understanding my *dasha* (condition) and showing me *disha* (direction).

I also thank Ashish Mohan Khokar, editor, *attenDANCE*, for being the first person to have confidence in my writing abilities.

I thank all the musicians, dancers, critics, Subbudu's friends and enemies and members of his family, for allowing me an insight into their relationship with him and for being generous with their time.

I am thankful to the staff of the Sangeet Natak Akademi Library.

A special word of thanks for Subbudu's siblings, Pattammalji, Ramamoorthy *mama* and Krishnamoorthy *mama*, and to Subbudu's assistant, A. Kandaswamy for taking my endless phone calls at odd hours and for patiently clearing my doubts each time.

I am grateful to Lalitha Venkat, editor, *Narthaki.com*, for all the help she extended during my trip to Chennai.

I express my gratitude towards my friends for putting up with my mood swings.

I have no words for my sister and my maternal grandparents for their endless prayers and innumerable blessings.

Finally my parents, especially *Ma*, thanks for distinguishing between my tears of agony and ecstasy as I tried to live through *Beyond Destiny*.

Lada Guruden Singh

Pilgrimage

Foreword

Nearly three years ago a suggestion was made to me that Bhavan should bring out a collection of Shri Subbudu's articles published in *The Statesman* and elsewhere and also a biographical account of his life and work. I responded enthusiastically to this suggestion on account of the great admiration I have for Shri Subbudu, both as a person and as a professional. But the project got delayed despite my best efforts, as those who were selected for taking up this assignment could not continue the work for one reason or another, though they were admirers of Shri Subbudu and committed to their assignments. It was then Shri Subbudu himself came to our rescue by suggesting that the task could be assigned to a most unlikely person, Shri Lada Guruden Singh, in age a very much younger person. Of course, his being a dancer qualified him partly for the job and after a few discussions with him and after seeing some of his writings, I was convinced that he would be able to take up this project and complete it in reasonable time.

Not unreasonably, Shri Subbudu himself was getting impatient. Hence, the idea of having a collection of his writings in *The Statesman* and elsewhere in English was dropped. Fortunately his Tamil writings have already been compiled and published.

I am happy to say that Shri Lada Guruden Singh has fully justified the faith reposed in him. He has worked hard and with enthusiasm and after many interviews with Shri Subbudu and his colleagues, he has given us a reasonably full account of Shri Subbudu's life and work and makes us familiar with the measure of his contribution to classical music and dance criticism.

We must thank *The Statesman* and *The Hindu* who have provided valuable space in their Delhi editions for music and dance criticisms. I wish the *Hindustan Times* and *The Times of India* would emulate this example and provide similar space, which they used to do in earlier times. Thanks to these newspapers, leading critics of classical dance like Subbudu (P. V. Subramaniam), Shanta Serbjeet Singh, Leela Venkataraman and Sunil Kothari (among others) have enhanced the understanding and appreciation of our great classical heritage in dance.

Some years ago, I had participated in a function organised by Shri Garg of the Indian Cultural Society to honour another reputed dance critic, Shri V. V. Prasad. On that occasion all the speakers eulogised one particular aspect of Prasad's writings that he never hurt anyone's feelings. Obviously Prasad believed in the Sanskrit dictum सत्य ब्रूयात्प्रिय ब्रूयात् न ब्रूयात् सत्यमप्रियम्। Tell the Truth, Say the Pleasant but do not tell the Unpleasant Truth. There is also the famous observation of the novelist Sarat Chandra that in telling the bitter truth, it is the love of bitterness rather than love of truth that prevails.

But surely we must distinguish the injury caused by a bludgeon from the pain caused by a skilful surgeon's scalpel. The latter heals and accelerates the growth of the healthy tissue, while the former leads to gangrene and destruction. Subbudu often hurt the feelings of artistes and even more of the admirers and friends of artistes. (The artistes who saw the value of the truth in the criticisms often overcame the hurt faster than their friends.) I believe that the hurt he caused most often helped the growth of art.

As it is, serious artistes have a difficult task in meeting the diverse expectations of audiences and critics with different tastes and levels of understanding. Further, as Ruskin observed, great artistes always work beyond their powers of execution. Much of what they do is "unfinished" and there is the ever present search for perfection and excellence, which is never ever attained. Their own "inner voices" are often the most strident critics and it is not surprising that any criticism whose truth or validity does not carry conviction to the artiste can rankle their minds with a continuing sense of unfairness. It is in this context that it is absolutely necessary for critics to have a certain depth of knowledge of the particular art about which they write.

Bharatanatyam as an art form is centred on classical music and could be described truthfully as visual music. In his book, *Facets of Indian Culture* Prof. R. Srinivasan quotes Leopold Stokowski:

> "One of the great characteristics of the music of India to my mind is its flexibility and freedom. While giving due consideration to traditions stemming from the past, Indian music is free and improvised so that all powers of imagination in the musician are brought into play. In this way the music of India is always creative, never a reproduction of what is written or played, as sometimes happens with the music of Western countries."

So too with the Indian classical dance; it allows the individual artiste's "soul to express itself" in a combination of discipline and freedom, tradition and creativity that makes every single performance — even an oft repeated one — a new choreography on each occasion.

Subbudu's masterly knowledge of classical music undoubtedly makes him an outstanding music and dance critic.

Born in Madras in 1917, Subbudu spent his early years in Yangon (Rangoon). I was born fifteen years later, spent some of my early years near Tiruvarur (of Saint Tyagaraja fame) but mostly at Chennai. Despite this time and space difference, the great Tamil writer Kalki was a common formative influence on both of us. I was an avid reader of Kalki absorbing every line he wrote week after week — story, essay, dance or music criticism, in all of which he set a tradition.

In the 1940s, every middle class family in Madras invariably had a visiting music teacher training the girls in Carnatic classical music. The boys who were not formally taught had the incidental benefit of exposure to the music and if they were more musically inclined and talented did better than the girls. In the post-war era after 1945 all this changed. The 'home' became more crowded and visiting teachers more expensive. Music and dance schools took the place of visiting teachers and as the girls went there to learn, the boys lost the exposure. That gave the opportunity to Radio Ceylon (Sri Lanka) and Radio Goa, then under Portuguese rule, to attract them to Hindi film songs which became the rage. (All India Radio did not then enter in this game of film music.)

It is no wonder that Subbudu strides like a colossus among critics because of his deep knowledge and mastery of both music and dance. But beyond this, his greatness lies in the simplicity of his living, his courage and fearlessness and his commitment to the art he espouses so well and spiritedly.

Shri Lada Guruden Singh deserves our thanks for this endeavour. We in the Bhavan's family also wish to place on record our sincere and deeply felt gratitude to Subbudu for giving us the privilege of publishing this biographical account. Prof. N.N. Pillai, Shri Manna Srinivasan, Dr. G.R. Sundar and Justice Viswanatha Iyer read through the manuscript and made several suggestions for which I would like to express our grateful thanks.

J. Veeraraghavan

My Impressions

With sixty-five years floating between us, measuring the flight of Subbudu's life was an ambitious thought but the task became easier because we met at a crucial phase of our lives. While the child in me was slowly disappearing, the child in him was gradually reappearing.

The City Still Burns...

The actual process of discovering Subbudu started when I tried to defocus him and collected memories of his influence on others, from those who fell on either side of his ink. To know that, I reached out to his *karam bhoomi*, Chennai (or Madras). Having spent nearly two weeks in Chennai interviewing dancers, musicians and *sabha* secretaries, I left the city in a confused state of mind. As my flight took off for Delhi, I just prayed for the successful completion of the book because Subbudu had grown beyond the power of my imagination and the capacity of my vision. The web of words that I built around him before leaving for Chennai had been replaced by newer ones. The mellowed and emotional man, who seemed more paternal than a legend, had become a larger-than-life figure who, apart from having knowledge and wisdom, had allowed others to nourish his ego even as he thrived on his passion and ambition to serve the arts.

As each artiste, in his/her carefully etched canvas drew a personal version of Subbudu, my task was to try and sift through his/her greatness and to spot his/her vulnerability which made him/her respect Subbudu, willingly or unwillingly. It was tough to understand the agendas behind the impressions, but the linear thought emerging from my interactions with them was, that Subbudu had made and marred artistes with rare courage and faith in his own strength. Though he was never the only reason behind the success or the failure of an artiste, he was surely a catalyst in bringing either shame or fame to an artiste.

He had refused to be pusillanimous like his predecessors or contemporaries in what he wrote and played the role of a king-maker with joy and impatience because, he did not allow an artiste to claim greatness if he/she had fallen from grace in his eyes.

His mercurial writings, unadulterated humour and tough mental make up made it impossible for artistes to bend him and tame his terror. He ravaged through the streets of the Indian performing arts, beating his chest and roaring stridently till artistes followed his path or were hunted down. His attacks, personal and offensive, were never limited to the talent a person possessed but sought to prick the skin that adorn the talent. As he repeatedly said, "Art is what an artiste is, not the other way round." Subbudu blazed through all the boundaries between the public and the private that defined any artiste.

Chennai still burns under Subbudu's fury. There may not be any visible spark now but the fire, confined under the layers of time, needs a mention of his name to re-invigorate. He reverberates in the strange corners of the *sabha* halls, in the foyer of the Music Academy, at the tea stall outside Narada Gana Sabha, in Maris and Woodlands Hotels. His name brings a glint and dismay with equal intensity proving that he has lived his life the way he wished to, without caring if he could improve his appearance before others.

The Sensitive Maverick

Much of Subbudu's tough exterior is a result of the hyper sensitive mind he has been bestowed with. Having lived a life akin to that of a seasoned political journalist, Subbudu survived controversies, lawsuits and verbal and physical death threats to tell the tale of a man who sought a personal touch at the end of every battle, from his opponents. For him every thing he did was for a purpose, which extended beyond the emotions of the artistes.

For someone who created pits and pinnacles to test an artiste's level of endurance, Subbudu became the focal point around which the power of media, the fate of the artistes and the relationship of our arts with the bourgeoisie concentrated. Just as he demolished the wall between the private and the public space of an artiste's life, he also allowed artistes to enter his private world. His interactions with the families of talented artistes, his impressions of the hardworking prodigies and his ability to push an artiste to test his/her own limits allowed him to gain the status of a family elder, where the family included all the artistes. But more than being a writer, Subbudu was an artiste because his writing was driven from the heart not head. He sought to perform even through words. Perhaps, his love for acting influenced his writing as well and that's why he loved hyperbole.

Subbudu was accused of magnifying issues but what saved him was his sense of purpose and his sensitivity to the fact that artistes and the audience also shared a sacred relationship. At a time when critics and artistes love to keep a safe public distance, Subbudu pushed ahead to establish a personal rapport with the artistes in order to gain access to their life beyond the visible. He still feels, "If you are a genuine person, you will be a genuine artiste." He sought people beneath talented artistes, so that he could teach and also learn. How would otherwise, anyone explain his personal interests in the right growth of child prodigies like Alarmel Valli or U. Srinivas, who are now masters in their fields or his legendary fights with the doyen of Carnatic music, Semmangudi Srinivas Iyer or with Veena S. Balachander?

In his time, Subbudu did not allow any artiste to build his/her ivory tower. He was always seeking to invade the boundaries that an artiste created around himself/herself because for him an artiste is always answerable to his audience and as a critic, he is the bridge between the two. However, Subbudu made sure that he kept his distance from the artistes who carried the bureaucracy in their pockets. He met them after their performances if only to clarify a point. He made sure that no one ever found him among many people surrounding an artiste backstage after the performance. He survived on the idea of identity, which in his case was a combination of knowledge, skill and obsession. Be it the accusations that Subbudu was a sell out to a market-driven tabloid media, led by magazines like *Idayam Pesukirathu* or the sophisticated taunts and sneers of his contemporary dance scholars, who while mentioning Subbudu did not fail to hint at their own superiority over the man. He wished to be different and he ended up being more than that.

Each time, a new talent was discovered, Subbudu was on the forefront promoting it, everytime a legend showed his/her worth, Subbudu humbly rose and saluted. Once at the end of a vocal recital by M.L. Vasanthakumari in the Music Academy in the 1980s, He declared on stage that if he were a day younger, he would have prostrated before Vasanthakumari. And he did prostrate himself before M.S. Subbulaskhmi, when they met for the last time.

For the youngsters who debuted on the scene of art writing, he made sure, he kept track of their work, and showered them with words of praise. In my own experience with him, Subbudu came across as someone who was conscious of his role in the bigger world order. What he has acquired here, he must pass it on, so that he dies with no burden except the satisfaction that he created his own image. But he demanded his due in as many words and therefore hurt himself in the process. However, Subbudu's search for *eklavya* continues and till this day, he remembers popular Tamil writer Kalki and says with pride, "Kalki was a mentor to me."

The Karma Yogi

"I want to be born as a musician now because I want to sit on the other side of the fence. I just want to be lost in the world of *dhvani*, in the power of sound." Subbudu looks forward to the next life with a strange sense of excitement. His intense encounter with death during his escape from Burma to India, was perforated with episodes where he threw dead bodies of the fellow travellers down the steep valleys. As he later said, "That is when I realised death is the only certain thing in life." The exodus of Indians from Burma was the largest recorded migration during the Second World War and Subbudu, considered himself fortunate to have survived the journey which taught him that one must carry on regardless of what others say because they are not aware of personal tribulations and triumphs. He did not care what people thought of him as long as they did not question his integrity.

A second generation leading Bharatanatyam dancer from Delhi attributed Subbudu's "acerbic" writings to his own sense of frustration, at the hands of fate. Her understanding of Subbudu's no holds barred writing is that he wrote to hurt, or may be to just direct the attention of the artistes and the masses to himself. "Look at his contemporaries, they were at all national and international festivals while he merely continued making rounds of the *sabhas*," she remarked.

But then, that is what he wanted to do. He saw himself as the caretaker of the roots.The deeper the roots, the deeper his level of satisfaction. One wished, someone could explain the insanity of the man who did that for more than five decades and in the process became the favourite writer with auto rickshaw drivers on one hand, and the President of India, on the other. And why go further, the dancer in question too invoked her destiny by seeking his blessings.

For Subbudu, what mattered was his own image in front of the mirror kept in his bedroom. If he could face himself there, he could face anyone else in the world. In his career as a critic, he walked against the direction of the crowd not to gain novelty value but because he felt a personal need to do so. His remarks on the decay of the Tanjavur's cultural richness exposed him to violent protests in Tiruvaiyyaru on his visit to the city. But even today sitting in his faintly lit drawing room, he feels the same.

The only incident that has changed him has been the death of his life partner of sixty-five years, Chandra in 2003. Her death pushed Subbudu into a state of confession. He feels that she died because of him and that he is suffering because she is no longer there for him. That is the price he has had to pay for serving the world of dance and music.

Subbudu believes that had it not been for his Good Karma he wouldn't have found a woman like Chandra who gave him space and fought with him only for his own good. Whether she disapproved of his weakness for betel leaves and *supari* or his erratic eating habits, Chandra surrendered herself to managing her home and limited her ambitions to let Subbudu live his life the way he wished to.

The Naïve Egoist

During one of our last meetings, Subbudu, lying down on his bed with his face tilted towards me, whispered in my ears, "My golden period still continues." For others however, Subbudu reigned supreme between the 1960s and 80s. Kalki's unexpected death in 1954 gave him an opportunity to capture the space vacated by him in the realm of music criticism and as the cliché goes, the rest is history. Kalki and later Subbudu's rise was perhaps the finest example of the democratisation of our arts. With the public becoming the patron, people like Kalki and Subbudu became vital links between the masses and their protégés — the artistes. Much of this also snowballed into instances of sycophancy around these figures. As Subbudu confesses in hindsight, "Fame got into my head." For those who love to hate him, this confession is a proof of his callousness towards their years of dedication but in the larger context, Subbudu by saying this, stripped himself of any facade. He, therefore, could afford to be more human than any artiste I have met in the course of his biographical journey.

Popular people require two qualities to become influential. First, a sound knowledge of the subject they deal in and the ability to flaunt it and second, lack of personal agenda. Subbudu fulfilled both the conditions. In a world which moves forward largely due to symbiotic relationships, Subbudu chose not to seek anything so that people could value what he gave. In this process however, he became a larger than life figure for many, especially for those who gained a sense of their talent in the 1970s and 80s. As such, one of the first instances of the media's relationship with the arts was the portrayal of Carnatic singer, M.S. Subbulakshmi as Meera. In her case too, she had the talent and was equally diffident in terms of nursing her personal ambitions. It is a different matter that her husband, freedom fighter T. Sadasivam, had taken up the task of making her a household name. So, Subbudu's fame was a result of the growing intimacy between the media and the artistes, because both depended on the masses for their survival. His mesmeric style of writing and his ability to write for the masses helped him grow into a celebrity with the people waiting for him to show the direction and artistes trying hard to impress him so that he could create an audience for them.

It is well known that he has a clear distaste for contemporary dance. His famed rhetoric that he would drive eminent contemporary dancer and feminist Chandralekha out of Madras with the might of his pen, is an example of the critic's remarkable sense of self-belief which concealed his supposed myopic viewpoint on the evolution of dance. Till date both agree to disagree on the notion of puritanism in dance. Nearly two decades after Subbudu launched his diatribe against Chandralekha, both have continued to exist at the opposite ends of the dynamic mechanism monitoring the evolution of our dance.

People have often misconstrued his attack on a particular artiste as an example of motive-driven malicious writing. But then Subbudu has not moved from his stand and has refused to question his idea of dance. For many of his contemporaries, Subbudu has been unable to re-invent himself with the changing world of performing arts. But as he has always stressed, he did not seek people to read him or to revere him, he sought them to remember him for what he said, did and believed in.

The Aging Lion

Famous Bharatanatyam exponent, Sudharani Raghupathy, while commenting on the later years of Subbudu's writing felt that sometimes he unnecessarily lavished praise on an artiste. Once when she asked him if he genuinely felt that way about a particular artiste, Subbudu told her, "Sudha, my child, I have grown old now and people have always said nasty things about me. Even I need some flattery in this old age." In the last few years, Subbudu's trip to *kutcheris* have become far and few but that hasn't stopped artistes from making personal visits to his home to request his attendance. Subbudu today represents the dilemma facing our arts — rich in heritage but with weak resistance! The critical space for the arts has been overtaken by reportage and Page 3 culture.Today, a dancer has to compete with a model to feature in a newspaper or television. With changing preferences, Subbudu's "golden period" seems like an old world fable.

Few belonging to my generation are aware that Subbudu was a central government employee who wrote on music and dance just because he wanted to. He did not depend on it for his bread and butter and that is also why he did not fear anyone on anything. Could anyone be so tactless to invite trouble by writing caustic articles which brought editorial pressures on one side and death threats on another? Well, Subbudu was.

A self-assessed misfit in the changed world, Subbudu seeks solace in the fact that he turned the world upside down when he wanted to. With artistes missing him all the more and even his contemporaries asserting there will be no one like him, Subbudu looks back at the world where he mattered most with a sense of detachment. His wife's death has brought him face to face with the truth that he does not even know how to dress for an occasion. Her death made him question if he had been fair on her at a time when the world took notice of his fearlessness and integrity.

For me, it was difficult to understand which Subbudu I should place before the readers. The one who was passionate and impulsive or imaginative and knowledgeable or fearless and cunning or sensitive and lonely or emotional and humorous or vulnerable and weak or religious and liberal. I decided to let the readers pick that Subbudu whom they could relate with. For me, he was an imposing figure before this journey, an icon midway and a *Thatha* or a grandfather at the end of it all.

Since Subbudu could not recall the time line of events with much confidence, the biography had to be anecdotal. As someone, who has written about Hindustani and Carnatic music, all classical dance styles, has staged and acted in drama productions and has written scripts and produced documentaries, Subbudu felt that it was not possible for him to talk about all the shades of his personality. Therefore, he was more comfortable with the idea that his biography should mainly concern his critical intervention only in the realm of Bharatanatyam and Carnatic music.

New Delhi, 2005 **Lada Guruden Singh**

The Dawn

Subbudu turned 88 on March 27, 2005. On receiving a bouquet of flowers from a well-wisher, he said, "you should have brought a wreath."

On April 4, 2003, Subbudu had lost Chandra, his life partner of 65 years. Her death changed him forever. Chandra's death had defeated the critic. Let's rewind.

His first victims were his two uncles. Both were neither musicians nor dancers. Born under Rohini *nakshatra*, which was also the birth star of Krishna (who killed his Uncle Kamsa), Subbudu jokingly blamed himself for the death of his uncles, because they saw the new born with naked eyes and not his image in a metal utensil filled with oil, as the practice was in case a child was born under the influence of that *nakshatra*. Fortunately, the third uncle was more conservative in glancing at him and hence he survived. But by then, Subbudu had gained notoriety as Uncle Slayer. That he would turn out to be as brave and fearless as Krishna, was not known to the world then. But, while Lord Krishna was diplomatic, Subbudu was going to be brutally honest.

The Scorpio sign was in the ascendant when the fourth child and the second boy was born to Padi Venkataraman Iyer and Saraswati on March 27, 1917, at C-104, Ramaswamy Street in George Town, now one of the old faces of Chennai. The three-month-old boy made his first ever journey overseas with his mother to Yangon (then Rangoon) on a steamer. He was to stay there for another twenty-four years.

> ***In Andhra they added "Uddu" to the name, so from Subramaniam, I became Subbudu.***
>
> *— P.V. Subramaniam on how he became Subbudu.*

Two decades before Subbudu touched the shores of Burma, his father, Padi Venkatarman Iyer had been put to the test by fate, which forced him to leave his own country and seek his destiny in an alien land. In 1896, at the age of seventeen, Venkataraman lost his father. While his elder sister had been married, the teenager had to support his mother, two brothers and two sisters. Venkataraman's father was a Revenue Inspector and according to the laws then, he became eligible for a compensatory job. He got a job in the Revenue Office of Chingalpet at Rs. 20 per month but the salary was not enough to sustain his entire family. The family's financial condition was a cause of concern for their relatives as well.

Venkataraman had been on that job for a couple of years when his maternal uncle, M. Subramaniam Iyer, who was a Theosophist based in Rangoon, asked his sister to send her son to him. He felt the young man had the potential to do more and, like many educated migrants in Rangoon, he could also strike gold overseas. His mother agreed to the proposal but before Venkataraman left for Rangoon in 1899, he was married to petite Saraswati, who was ten years younger. The marriage was a five-day affair but the young bride was so engrossed in playing with her friends that on the wedding day, her parents had to hunt for her. Immediately after marriage, Venkataraman left for Rangoon. Saraswati, whose father was a Tehsildar in Guntoor district of the Madras Presidency, was still living in her paternal home. She was to be sent to her husband's home after she attained puberty.

Incidentally, Venkataraman left for Rangoon at a time, when migration from India to alien shores was at its peak. Figures reveal that between 1852 and 1937, nearly forty million Indians crossed over to different parts of the world. The migration was the result of the expansion of the British colonial empire and the abolition of the slavery system from a number of colonies, due to which the plantation owners pressurised the British to allow and encourage labour flow from South Asia in general and India in particular. However, Burma, which was also known as the rice bowl of Asia, was the most sought after destination for the rich and the poor but for different reasons. Most Indians who crossed over to Burma were shopkeepers, contract workers, bankers, merchants, entrepreneurs and professionals. The upper class merchants and professionals migrated freely and voluntarily. They were self-absorbed individuals who took advantage of opportunities abroad to improve their career prospects and business profits.

But, concealed beneath the stories of Indian success in other parts of the world were sordid tales of indentured labourers. According to a report on the migration effect on different classes, the condition of the lower castes was made worse because of a hostile work environment where they had to compete with the local population and also face the harsh treatment of upper caste Indians comprising largely Baniyas from United Province, Marwaris from Rajputana, Chettiars from Madras Presidency, Pathans from the Northwest, Gujaratis from Bombay and Punjabis from Punjab.

Although Burma had been on the trade route of Indian merchants for centuries, the real Indian occupation of Burma began after the Third Anglo-Burmese War in 1885.

The last Burmese king was deposed by the British army, which comprised mainly Indian soldiers. Subsequently, a guerrilla revolt spread and a new military force of 35,000 was raised, largely from the Punjabi ex-soldiers. By then, Indians had firmly entrenched themselves in Burma. Interestingly, it is said that Burma at the turn of the 20th century had the best infrastructure in South Asia and that the Indian migrant population was the main reason behind it. Large numbers of these men and women migrated to work in the railways, posts and telegraphs, customs and other government departments.

In those days, ships from Madras used to take two days to reach Rangoon. Such was the demand for educated Indians that, as soon as they landed at the harbour, they were made to stand in different groups depending upon their qualifications, so that the employers could hire them immediately. To do away with any confusion at the harbour, agents of the employers used to ring a bell and shout "Jobs ready for SSLC passed". The educated 'visitors' were immediately taken to the Secretariat. Venkataraman's uncle had already found a job for him in Magwe, three hundred and thirty-one miles away from Rangoon. Minbu and Magwe were the two most beautiful cities in Southern Burma separated by the Irawati river flowing between them.

Venkataraman joined government service as an upper division clerk in the Prison's Department at a salary, which was way beyond his expectations — Rs. 300 per month.

Life in Magwe was very different from that in India. Though there was the same distinction between the British and the Asians, the climate and facilities of the city made life pleasant for Venkataraman. Moreover, it was home away from home, as the areas around Rangoon had been virtually invaded by South Indians.

To support the family and fund the education of his brothers and sisters, Venkatarman sent Rs. 200 home every month and kept the rest with him. In this respect he mirrored the aspirations of the educated bourgeoisie. This class was not afraid of taking risks and accepted challenges to improve its future. It also became a source of coherent socio-national bonding abroad. Of course, the intra-level socio-cultural differences existed even then. For most migrants, inculcating their own regional and national values in their children was the major concern.

Venkataraman had been in Magwe for four years when Saraswati joined him. Soon the couple shifted their base to the capital Rangoon which in Burmese means the end of strife. Venkataraman also asked his two brothers to come to Rangoon but only one of them crossed the sea.

Once in Rangoon, Venkataraman took the job of a branch clerk in the Prison's Department. Meanwhile, his interactions with the Indian community, particularly with the Tamilians made him realise the need for an Indian system of education. Those days, schools in Burma taught in Burmese and made it compulsory for the children of the immigrant population to learn that language.

Ironically, since there were 53 per cent Indians in Rangoon at that time, the Burmese had to learn Hindi, Punjabi, Tamil and Telugu to trade with the Indian merchants and businessmen. It must be noted that as Indians filled important government posts, and Indian businessmen began dominating the Burmese economy, the relationship between the two communities soured. However, because of their shared antipathy for the British, matters never flared beyond minor and sporadic incidents of rioting and looting till the late 1930s.

To carve out a niche for their Indian identity, Venkataraman along with other members of his community got together and established the Burma Educational Trust or BET. This trust undertook the responsibility of imparting Indian education to the children of the immigrants and established two schools in Rangoon for girls and boys separately.

The foundation stone of the schools was laid by Theosophist Annie Besant in 1906, the same year when Venkataraman and

Saraswati were blessed with their first child, Rajeshwari. Saraswati delivered the baby in Madras. Rajeshwari's untimely death in 1935 cut short a brilliant music career. The talented girl got a beautiful sister named Pattammal in 1912, and a brother, Chandrashekaran in 1915 before Subbudu made his debut in 1917.

Meanwhile, Venkatarman pursued his dream for Indian education. He was sure that he wanted his children to study in an Indian school. Since the members of the community, most of whom held government posts, made the contributions, the government readily recognised the trust and facilitated its functioning. Interestingly, the schools were situated on the ground floor while Venkataraman and his family stayed on the top floor. The schools continued functioning on the ground floor till Venkataraman moved to government accommodation when Subbudu was six years old and had been succeeded by two brothers, Ramamoorthy in 1919 and Krishnamoorthy in 1922. These two were going to be highly sensitive to Subbudu's genius throughout their lives.

> ***The old fellow is a genius. I have no better word to describe him.***
>
> *— 86-year-old Ramamoorthy talking about his brother Subbudu's abilities*

Meanwhile BET sponsored qualified teachers from Madras to work in Rangoon. The schools started with one student each, C. Rajagopalachari and Rajalaskhmi. When they grew up, Venkataraman got the two married. C. Rajagopalachari went on to become the Headmaster of the school. Later, he became involved with the freedom movement of India and and evolved into one of the most influential leaders of his time. BET schools along with Bengal Academy run by the Bengalis and Reddiar School managed by the Telugus were the only Indian schools at that time. Venkataraman was one of the founder trustees of the BET.

There is a popular saying that, wherever a few South Indian familes gather, a temple, a school and a *sabha* come up. After they settled down, thanks to the sponsorships provided by the Chettiars, the South Indians in Rangoon started inviting artistes from the Madras Presidency for dance dramas and music *kutcheris*. With more people crossing the sea than ever before, some Tamilians began settling for local matches for their children and weddings started taking place in Rangoon.

Incidentally, Brahmin priests considered crossing the sea inauspicious. Since there were very few of them in the city, Subbudu's father took on the mantle of binding the prospective couples in holy matrimony. A special booklet, presumed to be published by Madras-based P.T. Pani Company, was printed every year. This book mentioned auspicious dates for family functions, including marriages. The book also contained the Tamil translation of Sanskrit *slokas*, meant for such family occasions. Since Subbudu's father was more comfortable with Tamil, he worked on his diction and decided to indulge in community help by getting people married. From a clerk to a Brahmin priest, Venkataraman reflected the versatility and strength of character, which was to distinguish Subbudu from the rest of the crowd in years to come.

But, love for music was common to all in the family and that explains why young Rajeshwari was encouraged to learn Carnatic music at an early age.

While these changes were taking place in Rangoon, Madras had been witnessing a huge turnaround or volte face in its cultural space. According to certain records, post-1895, there is evidence of Madras having its *sabhas* though it took more than seven decades for the *sabhas* to gain the status and power they enjoy now. Unlike Bharatanatyam, Carnatic music did not go through a period of renaissance and resurrection, due partly to it being a Brahmin domain.

That was also the reason why, when *sabhas* were first formed, they only catered to classical music and not dance. The need for *sabhas* was felt because they led to greater social interaction among small groups and helped sustain and develop the interest for music within the family and the neighbourhood.

But it all began with the arrival of the British. After the fall of the Thanjavur court, artistes sought shelter in small neighbouring states and estates of Pudukkottai, Ettayapuram, Mysore, Travancore and Manali. The rulers of these states provided shelter to the artistes and helped them to sustain their arts. While musicians did not suffer from any social stigma, the future of *devadasis* had become precarious. But the changes were not peculiar to South India only. In the North, the imminent fall of the Mughal empire forced the artistes to relocate themselves in smaller centres of arts such as Gwalior, Rampur and Lucknow.

However, by the turn of the century, the artistes had to again search for new patrons and it is here that growing metropolises like Madras played a significant role.

One of the three cities founded by the British, Madras had grown to be a commercial centre with bankers, financiers and merchants calling the shots. Along with this new class, the Chettiars and the Mudaliars replaced the kings and the feudal lords to provide sustenance to Carnatic music. They set up new temple trusts to invite renowned *vidwans* and also took a lead in starting chamber concerts, by requesting private performances in their palatial homes. Since these classes were the main beneficiaries of the migration movement, they ensured that the same patronage and sponsorship was extended to facilitate the growth of Carnatic music abroad.

The Padi family. Subbudu standing at extreme right.

The Errant Star

Subbudu was sent to school informally for a year before he was officially admitted at the age of five. His parents and the teacher expected him to sit in the class quietly and learn the ways of school life. Subbudu did all of this and more. He sat, stared, got bored and decided to run away. Technically, he did.

Subbudu's first friend at school was Pattabhi, a six-year-old boy who lived nearby and was also studying in the first standard. He sold the idea of playing truant at the school to Subbudu, who reasoned that he wanted a break from the monotony of school life. Vacillating between a sense of anxiety and a desire for adventure, he decided to opt for the latter.

Since the teacher knew that Subbudu's father was one of the founder-trustees of the school, he did not bother to monitor his movements. A day before the boys played truant, Pattabhi met Subbudu and told him to be prepared the next day.

Subbudu feared getting caught but Pattabhi dispelled his apprehensions by informing him that they would be spending their day at the Tirupati shop nearby. The shop was not very far from the school and had a playground next to it. Often, small children would swarm the place hoping to get free sweets from the shop owner. Pattabhi invited Subbudu to join him and the little rebel agreed to spend the next day playing on the two tables kept outside the shop for customers.

Though it is not clear how the owner of the Tirupati shop allowed the boys to miss school, it seems he did not care as long as they did not steal anything or asked him endless questions. Subbudu and Pattabhi continued their rendezvous with freedom at periodic intervals for nearly six months. As their morning visits to the shop became a routine, the shop owner grew suspicious and asked them if the two were attending school regularly. Fearing an expose, the boys did a survey of the area and selected a tank a few blocks away from the shop as their next best haunt.

Blessed with an incisive sense of reasoning, the boys were smart enough to reach home in time for lunch because their ears were trained to notice the school bell indicating closing time. But, as all good things must come to an end, Subbudu and Pattabhi too ran out of luck. The BET had different timings with the girls' school closing before that of the boys. Once Subbudu mistook the closing bell of the girls school as that of his own and rushed home half an hour early. Incidentally, Subbudu's sister Pattammal reached home five minutes after Subbudu. Seeing him there, she questioned him. The poor boy could not manage a convincing answer and the matter was reported to Saraswati.

Finally, Subbudu's dare-devil deeds had been exposed and the time had come to mete out justice. He was duly awarded for his 'bravery and valour' with a broom beating and as the beautiful boy cried and apologised, he learnt the first lesson of his life — to be smarter in future.

Though Subbudu always yearned for a sense of freedom in one way or another, he never went against his parents, perhaps more out of a sense of respect and gratitude than as a matter of principle. However, once he got officially admitted to the school, he made sure he paid attention to what the teachers taught, not because he was a serious student but because he did not wish to study once he reached home.

His tremendous memory power helped him remember everything he read and his ability to recall facts and incidents was going to surprise the world of dance and music because, at thousands of recitals that he attended, Subbudu never took any notes.

While he was toying with different ideas to keep himself busy after school hours, his older sisters were getting lessons in Carnatic music from Guru Krishnamurthy Bhagavatar. Incidentally, by the time Subbudu was born, Rajeshwari had already given a concert and had become the favourite child prodigy for the Chettiar community. Subbudu's interest in music developed by default. Sometimes, when he had nothing to do, he would sit in a corner and listen to the Guru's teachings. Little did he know that one day he was going to see gurus bowing before him.

Venkataraman and Saraswati were driven by a sense of duty to inculcate a finer understanding of their own culture and tradition in their children. They devised various ways to expose them to music and theatre which they believed, represented their rich cultural heritage.

Interestingly, Venkataraman's father had done the same with his children and he found himself emulating his father's role. Apart from encouraging their daughters to learn Carnatic music, he also organised dramas to collect funds for the school. Running the school and imparting education had become his lifelong passion.

Being a migrant himself, Venkataraman was conscious of the condition of the indentured labourers who were suffering because of their illiteracy. He knew that education could make a world of difference to the lives of these people. His work was cut out. He spread the word around that he was going to take free night classes for labourers. The initial response was lukewarm but soon the numbers grew so much that Venkataraman had to ask other people to help him. Many students of the night school went on to become postmen and peons while others gained knowledge of their rights as labourers and ended their exploitation. As the years elapsed, Venkataraman was joined by his children in this noble effort.

Meanwhile, Subbudu began spending more time with his sisters whenever Guru Krishnamurthy came to teach them. Guruji found the young boy alert and curious. The fact that he was also cherubic in appearance got him extra attention from the Guru who often put him on his lap and listened to his 'wise' remarks on his sisters' talent. Once, Guruji asked Subbudu to sing an *alaap* and notate it. The youngster did it with rare accuracy for someone so raw. The Guru immediately hugged and kissed the boy and proclaimed that he must have been an eminent musician in his previous life. Though Subbudu had been anointed for a life as a musician, he chose to be a critic and decided to enact the role of a musician in his next life.

Venkataraman and Saraswati realised their son's talent in these music classes. They were amazed with his power of comprehension and decided not to pressurise Subbudu to study hard as long as he remained an above average student.

Now, Guru Krishamurthy took a special interest in Subbudu's growth as a musician. However, Venkataraman informed Guruji that he did not wish his son to have a career in music because musicians were looked down upon during those days.

Each time an artiste from Madras visited Rangoon, Guru Krishnamurthy brought them to the Venkataraman household to meet the family. Often, these singers taught Rajeshwari and Pattammal the subtle nuances of music that they probably learnt the hard way but Subbudu always monopolised the attention of the visiting artistes because of his unique talent at such a young age. The time soon was approaching when he was going to accompany some of these artistes to the *kutcheris* in Rangoon. Even as a young boy, Subbudu never missed a chance to witness the performance of any visiting artiste. He recalls that every visiting artiste was given a grand reception at the Karthik Temple which had a silver temple car.

Before Subbudu set out on his musical journey, he had already showcased his talent in another field-mimicry. One of the main reasons behind his decision to attend school was his insatiable need to exhibit his talent in acting. Discovered by his siblings, Subbudu's talent brought him praise and recognition from his peers and helped him to carve out his own identity. What had begun as a hobby turned into a passion as he became a natural choice for any comic role in the plays staged by his father and later by others.

Even now, at eighty-eight, sitting on the bed in his dimly lit drawing room, Subbudu's mimicry and imitative skills still hold sway not only for family but also visitors. As he gesticulates and twitches every muscle of his face, he leaves little scope for the imagination. From musicians, to dancers, to even his contemporaries, Subbudu can masquerade in any *avatar* and leave you wondering if he does the same behind your back.

Subbudu's passion for mimicry came in handy when he began acting in the plays staged by his father to collect funds for the school. In fact, Venkataraman's close friend, Venguswamy Iyer, an auditor at the Accountant General's office, used to double up as the scriptwriter and acting coach. Subbudu was the most enthusiastic participant and his love for theatre increased after he witnessed his first ever drama at the age of eight. The fascination with the stage and the instant rapport with the audience excited him no end. There was no question of stage fear because he sought the spotlight with an obsessive zeal.

As time elapsed, Subbudu graduated from mimicking people to imitating the sounds of birds and animals. Be it a pigeon or an elephant, He imitated with élan and astonished everyone around him. Incidentally, Subbudu's entire family participated in dramas because for Venkataraman, social duty was more important than anything else. As soon as Subbudu began acting in plays, his family realised their talented musician boy was a natural actor. However for some co-actors, he was too natural and spontaneous for comfort.

Subbudu's younger brother Ramamoorthy once became a victim of his brother's scene-stealing. Subbudu was playing the role of Hanuman with Ramamoorthy enacting the part of Vibhisana. Subbudu was so passionately involved in the scene that he started speaking impromptu and did not allow Ramamoorthy to deliver a single piece of the dialogue, till the scene ended. For once in the history of drama, talkative Hanuman had silenced wise Vibhisana.

While Subbudu intimidated his fellow actors with his natural flair, he became the most notable presence in any drama. He imagined himself to be the king of humour with the world looking to him to break its tedium. In the process, he derived energy from his audience and began devising new ways to keep its interest alive. He realised he had to surprise everyone and do the unexpected. Subbudu wanted to keep the element of anticipation alive in anything he did. This was going to become a forte of his writing style in the coming years.

The young boy was so restless that as soon as one production ended, he started waiting for the next one. After learning to make sounds of birds and animals, Subbudu tried to even imitate the sound of musical instruments. One fine morning, he surprised his brothers and sisters by playing the sound of Nagaswaram through a betel leaf which was found in plenty at his home since his mother Saraswati loved eating *paan*. Though he cannot digest *paan* any longer, Subbudu manages to demonstrate his imitative skills by making the sounds of a peacock.

Subbudu's family lived in the suburbs dominated by South Indians. Anyone visiting the area for the first time could mistake it for a scene captured from Madras, with angular roads cutting at right angles and neatly structured houses sporting a *rangoli* at the entrance. *Mamis* in their bright coloured silk *sarees* used to sit in the courtyard gossiping and matchmaking with the sounds of *supari*-cutters punctuating their sentences. The days used to begin early in Rangoon with parents visiting the temples early in the morning while their children slept.

But during the month of Margazhi (between mid-December and mid-January), even children used to wake up in the early hours to participate in *Namasankeertanam* which meant singing hymns or *bhajans* in the glory of God collectively. The occasion used to provide Subbudu with an opportunity to observe every one attending the procession. Often, he would pick up a particular mannerism of someone and repeat it during the day, entertaining his friends. However, even as a child he was cautious not to be indecent and disrespectful to his seniors, a trait which was common to all the brothers and sisters. But, at times, while mimicking his own friends, Subbudu crossed limits and paid a heavy price.

In the third grade, He became friendly with Srinivasan, a fellow student who used to stammer while speaking. In his partly naive and partly wicked behaviour, he tried to mimic this handicap. In order to please his friends, Subbudu used to stammer throughout the day. Though he became popular, Srinivasan was deeply hurt.

Subbudu, oblivious of the consequences, understood his insensitivity when he realised he could not stop stammering. His art produced a handicap in him. Subbudu has not stopped stammering since then. He rues his act but still thanks God for he can sing *bhajans* without stammering.

Another instance which left a lasting impact on Subbudu's mind was when, in an effort to trumpet like an elephant, He plugged his ears with the thumbs and put his little fingers in the nostrils. He exhaled forcefully but forgot to unplug his ears. The incident left a ringing sound in his head and became a part of his existence from that day onwards.

Before these incidents, Subbudu had been warned not to make fun of helpless people. A hawker had caught him by the nape of his neck and had held him mid-air, about two feet above the ground. He was the first person to get back at Subbudu and made him realise what it feels to be cornered.

Encouraged by his friends and by the spirit of showmanship, Subbudu began following pushers, vendors and hawkers through the streets of Rangoon. As they strained their vocal chords to reach the inner chambers of the quarters to sell their fruits, vegetables and other items, Subbudu made sure he copied them verbatim so much so that a heavy rough voice was followed by a squeaky voice each time. Initially no one knew where it came from. As Subbudu gained popularity among his peers, these men also noticed him. They tried to catch him on many occasions but Subbudu evaded them each time. However, this particular hawker who must have noticed Subbudu's movements caught him red-handed when the young fellow was busy mimicking another vendor walking in front of him. The naughty child was so engrossed in his approach that he forgot that someone could be following him as well. As soon as the vendor tried to chase Subbudu, the boy turned around and started running with his eyes closed and bumped into the man who was observing and following him. The law took its own course and despite a failed mimicry show, Subbudu's friends had a great laugh at his expense.

Though his antics continued to entertain his friends, amuse his parents and bother innocent folk, his talent as an actor on stage touched new heights. In fact, his role as Hanuman, the monkey God devotee of Lord Rama marked the arrival of Subbudu, the actor.

When he first played the role of Hanuman, he discovered that unlike anyone else, he could unlock his jaws. He would open his mouth and detach his jaws near his ears and then shut his mouth in such a manner that it resembled a monkey. Dialogues were specially written for Hanuman Subbudu. Sometimes walking on the streets, people would forget his name and instead call him Hanuman. Except for sporting a customary tail, Subbudu never put on any make up to enact the role of Hanuman. He was naturally endowed.

Once, essaying the role, Subbudu impressed the Chief Guest at a play so much that he expressed his desire to meet him again. This particular gentleman was Mr. Pearson and he was a representative of Steel Brothers & Co. dealing in rice and teak with business interests in south Burma. He had imagined Subbudu's face to be a stroke of a genius make up artiste but later discovered it to be otherwise.

When the performance ended, he met the actors and as soon as he met Subbudu, Mr. Pearson could not fathom the way in which his make up was done. He expressed shock when the make up artiste told him that he had merely attached a tail behind Hanuman Subbudu.

Mr. Pearson was so impressed with the boy's talent that he invited him for a cup of tea. Subbudu was exicted at the prospect of visiting an Englishman's house. When he visted his home, Mr. Perason introduced him to his wife who thought Subbudu was an adorable child. But soon, the lady was to change her opinion.

When Mrs. Pearson went to the kitchen to bring tea, Mr. Pearson asked Subbudu to immediately make a monkey face. When the innocent woman came to the drawing room, she was so shocked to see a monkey sitting next to her husband that she dropped the tray.It seemed to her, the boy had suffered an epileptic attack and his brain had lost control over his body. She was so stunned that it took Mr. Pearson a week to convince her that Subbudu was healthy and mentally sound. He was just a gifted artiste.

When not impressing his friends and elders with his acting abilities, Subbudu spent his time practising on the harmonium. His father had brought a mohan flute harmonium and Guru Krishnamurthy taught Rajeshwari and Pattammal to play on it with the eight-year-old boy watching intently. In spite of amazing confidence, Subbudu was sensitive to the presence of others around him. So, instead of practising with the harmonium in the presence of his sisters and brothers, Subbudu used to take it to the storeroom to practise. He began by polishing his fingers on India's National Anthem, *Jana Gana Mana*, penned by Rabindranath Tagore. Unlike his sisters, Subbudu did not have any formal learning under anyone and used the trial and error method to achieve perfection. Music and mimicry were maddening the man.

As he grew old, both the arts became an integral part of his identity. So much so that Subbudu took his studies seriously so that his parents could never fault his love for music and acting. Subbudu had a canny ability to convince and lead people and this helped him take the director's seat and organise mock dramas at home with his siblings. He wrote dialogues for his actors and indulged in a set designing activity by tying a huge bed sheet horizontally against a wall and creating a small raised platform to stage his plays. By the time he turned twelve, he had composed his first drama — *Prahalada* — and by the time he turned fifteen, he had finished writing his second drama, *Sita Kalyanam*.

In his early years, Venkataraman greatly influenced Subbudu's outlook towards life be it, having faith in destiny or inculcating self-discipline. It was this discipline, which pushed Subbudu to learn yoga on his own. He developed his own style of praying and recited *slokas* while performing yoga. That habit has continued to this day without a break except on occasions when he has fallen sick. Venkataraman believed that listening and reciting *slokas* created positive energy around human beings and provided them with the strength to lead an honest life.

With misty eyes, Subbudu remembers that at ten in the night his father used to lull the children to sleep by reciting *slokas*. Interestingly, all the children used to sleep on one huge mattress and every morning, after a bath, they had to report to their father who used to check if they had bathed properly. Since there was no iron at home, Subbudu and his siblings used to fold their clothes and keep them under their pillow while sleeping. In the morning, they had neatly 'ironed' clothes ready.

In fact, children had to wash their clothes on their own, which in itself was an intelligent way of preventing them from soiling their clothes, and every month for one rupee, a barber used to give the young boys a haircut.

Subbudu's interest in *Namasankeertanam* was also a result of Venkataranam's efforts to make his children not only God-fearing but God-loving. The practice of singing *bhajans* was a natural extension of Subbudu's interest in music and was to make him the centre of attention among the South Indians in Delhi when he shifted his base from Rangoon in his mid-twenties.

The practice of *Namasankeertanam* was yet another part of the revivalist movement. In the 17th century South India, the Bhagavata Trinity of Sadguru Bodendra Swamigal of Kanchi Kamakoti Peetam, Sadguru Sridhara Venkatesa Ayyaval of Thiruvisainallur and Sadguru Swamigal of Marudanallur propagated the concept of *Namasankeertanam*, or singing the glory of God in chorus. This trinity along with Sri Sadasiva Brahmendral and Swami Narayana Tirtha, were the founders of the Bhajana Sampradayam in the southern part of the country. These five pillars were therefore highly vital in the Renaissance of the Bhakti Movement in the 17th and the 18th centuries. The *Namasankeertanam* practice came into existence much before the trinity of Carnatic music — Saint Tyagaraja, Muthuswami Dikshitar and Shyama Sastri. After a lull, it again resumed popularity among the masses owing to the efforts of saints like Pudukkottai Gopalakrishna Bhagvathar. In the latter half of the 20th century, Swami Haridas Giri led the movement. Swamiji also left a deep impact on Subbudu in his later years.

Apart from observing the behaviour of people every year during the month of Margazhi, Subbudu also accompanied the congregation as a musician. He would alternate between playing the harmonium and the *mridangam*. As Subbudu grew older, his dexterity at playing the harmonium became an asset and this helped him to accompany some of the great artistes of their time.

Apart from these two instruments, Subbudu loved playing the violin. But, that did not continue for long because he felt he was not as proficient compared to his eldest sister. Somewhere deep down, Subbudu wanted to be a master of anything he did and refused to make an effort for things he could not. Moreover, Rajeshwari categorically told Subbudu to just train his ears for the violin because that is all he could do with the instrument!

For the migrants who had left the Indian shores decades earlier, creating a sense of community must have been one of the most important goals of their lives. Carving their own identity and then developing a familial bond with those who belonged to their own culture and shared history was a defining moment for them and to achieve that they had to fight a three-pronged war.

On one side they had to deal with the Burmese culture while on another they had to fight against the British influence. The third angle was provided by the challenges from within the community, mostly dealing with the conflict between the liberals and the puritans. But almost all of them agreed on the vital need to lend a voice to their own identity and it is here that the idea of *kutcheris* in Rangoon gained prominence.

The musicians and dramatists who travelled to Burma from Madras Presidency were the most dynamic link between the migrants and their motherland and its culture. Over a period of time, people collectively sponsored the trip of the artistes who reached Rangoon on Monday mornings and left for Madras on Friday mornings. The contribution made by the wealthy Chettiar community was extremely significant in supporting and sustaining the growth of *kutcheris*. These became a regular feature in the social calendar of any South Indian and they provided a platform for an exchange of thoughts on issues of art, culture and even politics. Theatre was the most popular branch of entertainment and it explains why Subbudu was lured to the medium in his youth. Incidentally, the observation made by the school authorities on Subbudu's high school certificate read: "An extraordinary comic actor."

He felt that the theatre acted as a great leveller during those days. Though all the men belonging to the medium hailed from economically weaker sections of society, they represented all the castes that comprised the social structure of the time. However, theatre ranked low among some Brahmins as a medium of entertainment especially because the artistes were not exclusively Brahmins. But the case was entirely different when it came to the music *kutcheris* where only Brahmins were vocalists while accompanists hailed from other castes. Kanniah Company, Madurai Original Boys Co. and Sewa Stage were some of the popular drama companies whose theatre productions had impressed Subbudu.

Though Subbudu had a lot of energy and was extremely restless, his erratic eating habits affected his health repeatedly. In 1929, He fell sick because of jaundice. When the doctor checked him he told Saraswati and Venkataraman that their son had been eating too much *supaari* as well because of which his body had developed weak resistance. The couple became greatly worried about their son's health and habits.

Venkataraman decided to send Subbudu to Besant Theosophical School. He was in the seventh standard at that time. Though the surroundings of the school and its Gurukul like atmosphere inspired Subbudu to regain his health, he could not concentrate on his studies because he missed his family terribly. In a few months time, he became popular in the school as a great mimic. And while he enjoyed receiving compliments for his mimicry from boys of other standards, he soon realised that he still had a long way to go in the acting department.

Subbudu hated playing outdoor sports. Even when he was in Rangoon, he used to while away his time gossiping with his friends every evening. But here things were different. He knew that he had to follow the rules of the school. Soon he discovered that he was going to have compulsory sports class. He began to panic. The day he had his sports period, he went up to the school's medical superintendent and complained of chest pain. Subbudu told the doctor that he was a heart patient. It seems the doctor was smarter than him for he could see through his acting.

He told Subbudu, "No problem. When you come next, show your heart on the left side! You can go and play hockey."

Within a year, Subbudu was back home in Rangoon and rejoined BET Boys School. However by the time he returned, he had become even more serious about his studies and by the time he turned thirteen, he had cleared his high school, two years in advance. But before he did his family proud by completing high school so early, he had tasted fame as the union leader of the students.

It so happened that Subbudu and his friends used to rehearse for the plays in the school premises. The rehearsals used to take place between 4:30 pm and 6:30 pm and while most of the boys sweated it out without having any food, three boys were fortunate enough to get tiffins from the school itself. Subbudu noticed the trend for a few days before he took up the matter with the school Headmaster, K.R. Chari. Mr. Chari refused to take any action against the supposed discrimination and ended up getting threatened by Subbudu who spread the word around that if the other boys did not get tiffin too, they would go on a strike. Chari reported the matter to Venkataraman who chided Subbudu. Not one to give up easily, he narrated the entire incident and got his father's support. The headmaster buckled under pressure and all the boys were privileged to have tiffin.

On his music front, Subbudu was a teenager when he began accompanying the musicians as their escort-cum-page boy. As soon as the artistes disembarked at the harbour, Subbudu offered his services and tagged along with them. In that capacity, he had the chance to serve great musicians such as Muthiah Bhagavatar, Saraswati Bai, Musiri Subramaniam Iyer and others. It was not that he could be on equal terms with the *vidwans* but, he was happy enough to fetch *paan*, *supaari* and tobacco of the Madras variety available at the Mohul Street near his home. He also got their clothes laundered by the best pinmen and ensured hot water for their baths and a constant supply of coffee and snacks for them. Often while doing all this, Subbudu looked forward to learning something from them by just observing them closely. If he was really fortunate, he ended up having a conversation with them. If the musicians were impressed with the boy, they also allowed him to accompany them on stage but only after Subbudu proved that he was the best attendant they could have asked for.

He began accompanying artistes first as a substitute and later as an added attraction for the local *rasikas*. He still recalls that on one occasion when Muthaih Bhagvatar visited Rangoon, he found that the harmonium player accompanying him had fallen sick. When Subbudu came to know of this, he wondered if he could accompany the great singer. Amused with the boy's confidence, Muthiah Bhagwat asked him to demonstrate his talent first.

When Subbudu finished playing, the singer remarked, "You will not spoil my performance." As he had foretold, Subbudu did not spoil his performance but performed so well, that he was awarded Rs. 50 for his feat by the organisers. The effect of Subbudu's performance was such that the very next day, Muthaih Bhagvatar's violinist reported two hours before his music concert. He feared the young boy playing the violin as well!

Most of the *sabhas* that flourished at that time were being financed by the Chettiars. But, even as the migrant population was gaining cultural space, the local population had started resenting the marginalisation of its culture and ambitions. In 1930, Chettiar moneylenders collectively accounted for Rs.750 million which was equal to the entire British investment in Burma. Incidentally, in the same year, the annual Chettiar loans were pegged at Rs.120 million, which was equal to 70 per cent of all lendings in Burma. In the late 1920s, a steep decline in the commodity prices as a prelude to the Great Depression brought about a large-scale transfer of agricultural land to the Chettiars.

The transfers accelerated in 1930s and so did the collective anger among the small-time Burmese farmers. Land alienation was creating a feeling of national outrage with the 'patrons of arts' Chettiars coming across as swindlers and oppressors.

Meanwhile, Subbudu continued serving the *vidwans* and as the years went by, he became a part of their family. By the time he turned sixteen, he had mastered the art of playing "Mohan Flute Harmonium". He had already dabbled with playing the pedal harmonium during the theatre productions. His mastery on the MFH instrument helped him gain confidence as an artiste and instilled in him the belief that he could have his share of fame too.

Saraswati Bai and Bhagwat were some of Subbudu's favourite musicians whom he had a chance to accompany on stage many times. All the *vidwans* were amazed by the young man's talent and his ability to match up with their trained voices. Interestingly,

Subbudu never showed his virtuosity when the singer displayed his talent. Rather, he kept himself under wraps till his turn came during the *thani avarthanam* or the solo sequence and then played to capture the limelight.

Because Subbudu was ambidextrous, he would deliberately play with both hands to gain more attention than the *vidwan* himself. For the migrant community settled in Rangoon, it was gratifying to see their local boy sharing the stage with renowned musicians. From mimicry to music concerts, he had invaded the cultural space available to the Tamilians in Rangoon but it was time that he did something different again.

Apart from serving the musicians, Subbudu had developed a keen interest in reading and in his free time, he kept himself busy with Tamil magazines. As a child, he had been exposed to the power and the beauty of the Tamil language. In fact, he fell in love with the language and excelled in it to the extent that he won a gold medal from the Chettiar community for securing maximum marks in the language in the entire country in his high school. T. Janakiraman, Devan and Thumilan were some popular Tamil writers who influenced Subbudu.

From *Ananda Vikatan* to *Swadesh Mitran*, Subbudu virtually lived off these magazines. One of the Tamil writers, who was going to change the way Subbudu thought, also wrote at that time. He was a craze among the readers. In fact as soon as the copies of *Ananda Vikatan* would be offloaded at the Rangoon harbour, there used to be a stampede to get the first copy of the magazine so that people could read his article. His name was Kalki Krishnamurthy and he was destined to be a mentor to Subbudu in the coming years.

But before Subbudu turned to writing, his fortitude was tested by nature. In 1934, Venkataraman retired and decided to move to Bauktaw, six miles away from Rangoon. By then, Subbudu's elder siblings had been married and Rajeshwari and Pattammal had already become mothers. While Rajeshwari had an arranged marriage with a corporation councillor, E. Ramanathan Iyer, Pattammal, who had turned out to be the beauty of Rangoon, had a love marriage with one of the best lawyers of his time, G.R. Rajagopal. And Subbudu had a role to play in getting the two married. When the astrologers matched the horoscopes of the young couple, they found that both belonged to the same gotra. So every Brahmin priest in the city refused to marry the two. Though Venkataraman was prepared to solemnised the marriage, Subbudu and one of his uncles, spread the word around among the priests that whoever attended and conducted the marriage, would be given a gold coin. Hearing that, all the priests of the city came and solemnisd the marriage. However, no one was presented with gold coin. Pattamal's marriage was a historic affair because for the first time in Rangoon, two people, in love with each other but belonging to the same *gotra*, were married. And, that too by all those priests who had refused to solemnise the marriage because of planetary conflicts in the natal charts of the bride and the groom.

Soon after marriage, Rajagopal introduced Subbudu to Swami Ranganathanananda who was the head of the Ramakrishna mission. Subbudu was deeply influenced by the teachings of the saint. Soon he was asked to sing after the Geeta lecture every day. His interactions with Swami Ranganathanananda helped him to see matters rationally in life. Since Subbudu was extremely emotional by nature, his dialogue with the saint helped him develop the ability to detach himself from everything negative around him.

I was told not to waste time on the mirror, so in order to avoid it, I started combing backwards.

— *Subbudu on how he learnt to be beautiful from the inside*

Subbudu's eldest sister Rajeshwari

Sadly, the artistes in the sisters died a slow death post- marriage. The worst was yet to come. On August 31, 1935 Rajeshwari passed away shortly after she gave birth to her eighth daughter, who also died a few days after her birth. Earlier also, she had lost a daughter during delivery. Just before dying, Rajeshwari had requested Venkataraman and Saraswati to take care of her daughters. Subbudu's father had spent his entire earnings in building a new house and an elementary school. With six young girls, the eldest being ten years old to look after, the couple experienced their worst financial crisis.

It is not that Rajeshwari's husband was not around to help or take care of his children, but the family felt a need to reach out to the young girls on its own but there were no earning members. In fact the couple's eldest son, Chandrashekaran, a geologist had left for the Mawchi mines in South Burma with his wife.

Ramamoorthy and Krishnamoorthy were still in school while Subbudu was studying the intermediate. Without notice, Subbudu gave up his studies and opted out of college. He decided to immediately take up a job. Within a few days, he got a job as a clerk with the Imperial Bank. His first salary was Rs.75. A few months later, Subbudu got a better offer from the Auditor General's office at Rs.90 per month. The young man had moved up the financial ladder. Each rupee earned had a value for the Venkataraman family. In some ways, Subbudu had become the head of the family.

A few years into the job, Subbudu realised that his love for writing, music and theatre had turned into an obsession and now, to sustain his space in the world of music and theatre, he had to work so that he was economically independent and secure. Sometimes, while going to the office, Subbudu would take his *dhoti* in a bag and after work, he would change clothes to attend a music *kutcheri*. Though, he had saved his father from going bankrupt, he never took credit for what he did.

By the time Subbudu turned twenty, he had already started writing short reports on the cultural events taking place in Rangoon for *Rangoon Times* at Rs.2 per article. Before that started, he had been contributing articles to the BET school magazine. Though Subbudu enjoyed writing for the paper, he had fallen under Kalki's spell. *Ananda Vikatan* was the magazine he wanted to write for.

In 1928, film magnate S.S. Vasan had acquired *Ananda Vikatan* and in a few weeks time the circulation of the magazine had increased threefold. By the time Subbudu started following it religiously, Kalki had consolidated himself as the editor-in-chief of the magazine.That was the first time, when Subbudu admitted to himself that he wished to be someone, like Kalki. But he was to discover later that God willed him to be different and in this difference, Subbudu's destiny and longevity as a writer lay.

While Subbudu continued writing for *Rangoon Times*, he also started contributing letters to the editor to *Ananda Vikatan*. Just like in *Rangoon Times*, he wrote about the happenings in the capital in *Ananda Vikatan* as well.

Though he loved talking about everything and anything happening in the city, Subbudu never talked about his own talent as an artiste and as a prankster who was shaping into an unconventional writer. What made Subbudu unconventional was his ability to bring out humour through his writing and his amazing audacity to take to task anyone who failed to live up to his expectations.

While Subbudu wrote in Tamil for *Ananda Vikatan*, he wrote in English for *Rangoon Times*. This bilingual activity would continue for the rest of his life. Subbudu had the advantage of learning English from an Englishman who used to rap the boys on the knuckles whenever they made a grammatical mistake.

However, none of the letters that Subbudu wrote was printed in his name. They were all from a certain "well-wisher from Rangoon". Perhaps, Kalki wanted to test how long this well-wisher could continue without having the volition of having his name printed.

Subbudu was to survive the test and become the most influential critic of Carnatic music and dance. Through *Ananda Vikatan*, Subbudu got exposed to the vibrant cultural scene in Madras. Since he wrote regularly to *Ananda Vikatan*, he soon caught Kalki's attention. Slowly, his letters started getting more space in the magazine. Sometimes, they were printed with incisive observations made by Kalki himself. Each time, Subbudu's letter found its way to the pages of *Ananda Vikatan*, he tightened his grip on his dream to have an article in his own name in the magazine. Little did he know that over the next two decades, his name was to become a catalyst in augmenting the circulation of the magazines.

Meanwhile, destiny had brought him to the doors of his first controversy. It so happened that he and his friends thought of playing a prank on the TTE while travelling on a train. Though Subbudu had a train ticket, he pretended that he was travelling without one. When the TTE was about ten feet away from Subbudu, he looked at him and found his behaviour suspicious. Before the TTE could blink his eye, he started running.

The chase on the running train, must have continued for about five minutes before the TTE was able to apprehend him. He was nearly going to beat him up but Subbudu managed to produce his ticket. When the TTE asked him why he was running, Subbudu replied that his face scared him.

Unable to find a befitting reply, the TTE let him go, though with a warning that if he repeated the act, he would be put behind bars.

Certainly, the event was not controversial. It snowballed into a controversy after Subbudu narrated the incident with great humour in an article he wrote for the school magazine. Unfortunately, a senior railway official read the article and got so infuriated that he lodged a complaint with the Railway Board of Burma. Apprehending damage to the image of the Railways, the board issued a warning to the school and to its special former student Subbudu. The message was loud and clear: "You can be prosecuted, if you repeat your unscrupulous behaviour." The young musician had suddenly become a rogue but then that was just the beginning of a journey punctuated with amusing titles and disturbing incidents.

Meanwhile, the first overseas controversy introduced itself when Subbudu reviewed the performance of Gotuvadyam Narayana Iyengar, the court musician of Mysore. Kalki published his review in his Karnatakam column (Karnatakam was the pseudonym Kalki used to review music) with an introductory note written by himself on Carnatic musicians going abroad, under the heading *Kalai Kappalerigiraudu* or "The art takes ship".

Yet again Subbudu was named as a well-wisher. This was the first review which reflected his contempt for the old and the decadent. It also gave a glimpse of his fertile imagination and ready wit. The review also became the first example of Subbudu's progessive mind, where talent mattered more than experience. It would be interesting to reproduce the English translation of the review. The following is the review as it appeared in *Sruti*, a Madras based magazine on music and dance.

"It must be said that along with many sins of which they are guilty, the people of Rangoon may have acquired some merit (*punyam*). Otherwise how could they, who have been sick and tired of the toothless old *Bhagavatars* and the wailings of the novice lady disciples, have had the good fortune of listening to the concert of Bharmasri Gotuvadyam Narayana Iyengar that was nectar to their ears? I cannot describe the grandeur of his playing. But I can say this, he operated not only on the strings of the *gotuvadyam* but also on the heartstrings of the audience. I realised that day the truth that those listening to the music of his instrument will have years added to their life."

For someone so young, the review carried the tone of a veteran and this particular article was the reference point to the coming years of Subbudu's writing. Though there were still some years before he formally became a music critic, this particular article marked his birth as a critic.

Your habit of punning will kill you.

— Venkataraman scolding his son for his habit of punning on everything

The review was printed and when one of the "toothless old *bhagavatars*" read it, he decided to sue *Ananda Vikatan*. Fortunately, Subbudu's name was missing and the review was attributed to a *rasika*. Moreover, Subbudu had not mentioned the name of the "toothless wonder". The young man had been saved but now the question was, for how long.

Beyond reporting on events in Rangoon, Subbudu still wished to be a musician, even if it meant constructing a music instrument exclusively for himself. After Narayana Iyengar left for Madras, Subbudu asked a Chinese carpenter to help him to make a *gotuvadyam* out of plywood. He was so interested in playing the instrument that he began practising it on the terrace every night. After three days, the lady next door visited Subbudu's house and asked his mother to take care of her child who had been crying for three nights continuously. She said she had been unable to sleep properly because of the child's wailings. Subbudu's long pending dream to be a musician suffered another jolt.

Meanwhile, his deftness on the harmonium had taken its toll on his youngest brother Krishnamoorthy's individual talent. So intimidated was the young boy with his brother's mastery on the instrument that he would practise the instrument surreptitiously in his absence. In fact, Krishnamoorthy was haunted by a persistent dream of Subbudu chasing him through the streets of Rangoon in his early years. Did he feel that Subbudu was metaphorically eating into his space for creative exercise? Certainly, both would have disagreed. However, Krishnamoorthy knew from the beginning that he had little scope in Carnatic music with his elder brother gaining prominence in his teens. It is interesting to note that as Subbudu and his siblings were growing up, they showed signs of healthy competition among one another. Be it Subbudu's attempt at the violin after being inspired by his eldest sister Rajeshwari or Krishnamoorthy's love for the harmonium thanks to Subbudu, they all followed one another and never stopped short of even criticising each other, all in good humour.

But one incident that made Krishnamurthy aware of Subbudu's growing clout and pushed him to carve his identity beyond the looming shadow of his elder brother was when he won a prize in a school music competition. Subbudu had accompanied him on the harmonium. Krishnamurthy's detractors proclaimed that Subbudu had covered up his brother's shortcomings. The joy of winning an award came under the shadow of baseless accusation and from that day onwards, Krishnamurthy decided to prove his critics wrong.

> ***Even today when I sit with my keyboard to compose or play, I mentally imagine that Subbudu, with his characteristic closed eyes and twitching fingers is listening to me. I draw my inspiration from his imaginary presence like Ekalavya.***
>
> *— 84-year-old P.V. Krishnamoorthy*
> *on his elder brother Subbudu*

Subbudu with cousin Padmasini

Tossed by the Storm

The period between 1935-1939, was one of the most crucial phases of Subbudu's life. He had crossed the imaginary boundary line that distinguished a youth from a man. No longer under his parents' shadow in any form, Subbudu was set to continue his father's legacy.

On June 9, 1938, at the age of twenty-one, Subbudu's marriage with fourteen-year-old Chandra was solemnised in Madras. When Chandra travelled to Burma to join Subbudu and her in-laws, Subbudu observed, "now I have a seventh niece!"

While his parents chided him for a rather poor sense of humour, Chandra was to address Subbudu as Appa because she wanted their children to address Subbudu as Appa the moment they started speaking. Subbudu's marriage brought happiness back to the household. But no one was prepared for the events that were to unfold in a short span.

Around the same time, Burma witnessed one of its worst ever communal clashes recorded in its modern history. The roots of the riots lay in the socio-economic changes the country had witnessed in the two previous decades. The Burmese were generally known to be spendthrifts. With the economy firmly in the hands of the Indians, they had turned to gambling and drugs. Ever since their migration, Indians had virtually taken over the whole of Rangoon and the natives were relegated to the rural areas of the city. The demographic change was so apparent that Indian languages, especially Hindi had become the means of communication.

In 1938, a survey conducted to ascertain the hold of the community on the agricultural land came up with a staggering figure. Almost 90 per cent of the land had changed hands and was now under direct or indirect control of the Chettiars. The brewing anger among the Burmese turned into nationwide protests after newspapers and magazines owned by the Burmese started giving vent to anti-Chettiar sentiment. The then editor of a Burmese magazine, *Thuria,* laid the foundation of such propaganda. The protests took a political turn amidst the changing international political situation with the world staring at the possibility of outbreak of a second world war. Meanwhile, the local Burmese leaders began preparing the ground to introduce and pass the "Land Alienation Bill". The bill sought to debar the non-Burmese from acquiring land in Burma. The anger against the Chettiar community eventually became anti-Indian because of their success in the foreign land and also because the income generated in Burma flowed to India. An example of Indian invasion was Raja Sir Annamalai Chettiar's Chettinad Bank which had its branches in every Burmese city.

In the midst of all this, the country witnessed communal riots in 1938-39. To this day, different versions have been offered to explain the reasons behind the riots which also led to the fall of the government of the time. While the riots broke out between the Buddhists and the Muslisms, there were reports that they were primarily a result of the brewing tension between the wealthy Chettiar community and the local Burmese, which was a spillover effect of the Burmese revolt engineered by Saya San.

But for most people, the riots started when some 'mischievous' Muslims distributed pamphlets denouncing Buddhism and accused it of being base. The writings condemned Buddhism and understandably enraged the Buddhist population. Various reports put the total number of casualties to anywhere between 25,000 to 35,000. Over a hundred mosques and temples were set on fire during this period of instability and turmoil. Subbudu observed the incidents that took place in Rangoon during this time and sent a report on the riots to *Ananda Vikatan*. Unfortunately, the cartoon accompanying the article depicted a Buddhist killing a Muslim near a foothill even as Lord Buddha could be seen crying, standing on the hilltop. Though the article stressed the facts of the riots, the cartoon gave an impression of a bias against the Buddhists.

When the copies of the magazine reached Rangoon, which was still in a state of chaos, there was immediate panic in the city. The authorities confiscated three thousand copies of the magazine to prevent any more rioting. Meanwhile, Kalki was contacted to ascertain who had written the article because the Government of Burma wanted to charge the writer with an act of sedition. Fortunately, the article did not carry Subbudu's name and Kalki too refused to reveal the identity of the writer as part of the magazine policy. Subbudu had been saved but he became sceptical about the future of Indians in the country.

The community had become over-visible because of its ostentatious display of wealth and the changing international situation only exacerbated the crisis. Interestingly at this time, Burma was witnessing two kinds of sentiments, one against the Indians and the other against the British. Both were viewed as invaders. However, given the cultural proximity between the Burmese and the Indians, the latter was looked upon as a lesser evil compared to the whites.

The riots were not only a revolt against the economic domination of the 'outsiders' but also their cultural domination. But the Indian community had become such an integral part of Burmese politics and economy that hurting it was nothing short of inflicting self-injury. At another level, Indians controlled the major centres of power — be it politico-economic or socio-cultural. There was no escaping Indians, especially when they were involved in ruling the country in connivance with the British.

Another example of continued Indian hegemony was the beginning of broadcasting in Burma. After a decade of tattered growth in India, All India Radio finally came of age in 1935 after the government took it under its control in order to counter the adverse propaganda of Radio Moscow.

Remember, the entire period post-1935 was dominated by a fear of outbreak of a second world war. But nobody expected that the arrival of AIR would lead to democratisation of Carnatic music. The musicians were forced to come out of the *sabha* halls in search of new audiences, strangers, i.e. common men and women that they would never have any direct contact with. While the reason for starting broadcasting in Burma was the need to protect British interests, soon the radio became a vehicle for the musicians to reach out to the masses. Interestingly, Subbudu along with his youngest brother Krishnamoorthy, who was working on a Bachelors in English at Rangoon University started producing fortnightly music programmes for the Indian community. Ever since the incident in school, Krishnamoorthy had decided to divert from Carnatic to light music. By the time he reached college, he had formed his own multinational and multilingual orchestra.

Meanwhile, the Second World War broke out after Germany attacked Poland, and France and Britain declared war on Germany in 1939. Incidentally, much of the 1930s had seen a steady rise of the Fascists and the Nazis in the West and Japan's militaristic ambitions in the East. Many believed that the conquests made by these countries just before the outbreak of the war not only represented a will to establish a new world order but also a desire to create a new market because of the impact of the Great Depression on the world economy. By the time the war officially broke out, Japan had already overrun parts of China. However to conquer the whole of China, it had to take control of Burma. The Japanese knew that if they could cut the overland access to China via the Burma Road, they would be successful in stifling any military aid being provided through Rangoon and could then overwhelm the Chinese army. The other factor behind invading Burma was the fact that it had rich resources of oil, tin and rubber. Ironically for the Indians settled in Burma, Japanese invasion meant doom even though Subhas Chandra Bose had tied up with the Japanese to drive out the British from mainland India. For the Burmese however, Japanese were looked upon as Asian Tigers who took the British head on.

Apart from winning over parts of China, the Japanese had annexed Hong Kong and Philippines. The Japanese forces crossed river Salween to invade Burma in January 1942. They faced a weak opposition from the British with two regular British battalions, two Indian Army infantry brigades and the local Burmese army defending the country. The Japanese invasion was successful, partly because of their ability to infiltrate into the British army and the support extended to them by the locals. As time passed, the British forces began to arrive but they could not prevent the fall of Rangoon and Mandalay. With the Japanese moving northwards, Indo-British forces under Generals Alexander and Slim began a painful withdrawal to India.

But the worst was in store for the Indian migrants, who not only left their lifelong earnings behind but also had to endure a journey punctuated by tales of separation, torture and death. Most Indians feared being treated as aliens in mainland India because some of them had stayed in Burma for at least three generations. The situation was awful for the poor Indians who had come to

Burma in search of a better future. The most painful exodus in the history of colonised South Asia began with the fall of Rangoon.

As Subbudu was to reveal later, a shrewd Japanese dentist, eulogised by all those who aspired for Burmese independence, had devised the strategy for the capture of Rangoon. The defence installations around the city were bombarded by Japanese fighter planes before the army moved in. The British were demoralised owing to the stunning victories of the Axis Powers and they lost all courage to counter the aggression and passion of the Japanese. Before the Japanese entered Rangoon, the British had left the city. Their arrival was celebrated by the local Burmese who danced in the streets.

Meanwhile, at the same time, Subhas Chandra Bose held discussions with the German Propaganda Ministry and soon the Ministry spokesperson announced the creation of the Indian National Army. The British who were facing revolt in India feared a collusion between the Japanese and the Indians and hence on February 18, 1942, ordered all the Indians to vacate Rangoon.

There was complete chaos at Subbudu's home. Venkataraman had to make the toughest decision of his life. He did not know who was willing to receive his huge family in India. He wrote letters to his brothers but because of the breakdown of the postage system, he did not receive a reply from them. However, the family was fortunate to hear from Subbudu's father-in-law C. Vishwanath Iyer in Coimbatore.

The entire family prayed before Balaji for help and guidance through the testing times. Meanwhile, Subbudu's older brother Chandrashekharan rushed back home. Being a senior geologist, he was told by the government to destroy Mawchi mines completely since it produced raw material used for making gun powder. As soon as he completed his task, Chandrashekharan was relieved from his duty. He reached Bauktaw the following day and promptly made arrangements to send his parents, women of the household and children to India because men were not allowed to board the steamers.

Subbudu's neighbour, J.D. Bagchi, who was the manager of Scindia Shipping Company, sought more ships to ferry passengers to India when they received orders from the Japanese forces that they could take only the old, women and children apart from arms and ammunition. Since Krishnamoorthy was still young, he was allowed to travel to India with the parents.

Meanwhile, it was decided that Ramamoorthy would travel to India with Pattammal's husband, Rajagopal, who was the chief metropolitan magistrate at that time. On March 9, 1942, they left Rangoon for India.

As a child, whenever Subbudu or his siblings dropped four *annas*, they would search for hours together. If they were unable to locate the money lost, they would assume, Lord Krishna had taken it. Similarly, they believed that now the Lord wanted them to part with all that their family had earned. But Subbudu was unable to leave their four cows and their calves. When his mother had made her first journey across the sea, Lakshmi, her cow, was sent along with her. Within a year, Laskhmi had given birth to a calf. Before the family left Rangoon, Lakshmi was bathed and adorned with vermilion on its forehead. The cattle were sent to a farm even as prayers were made to the cowherd God to protect them. As soon as Subbudu and his brother-in-law, Ramanathan returned home from the harbour, they heard that the Accountant General's office had been bifurcated. Subbudu was still working as he was the only earning member of the family staying with the parents. While Chandrashekaran (who died in 1988) made some trips between Burma and India to help migrants, and went through a different land route, Subbudu reported back to the job where he learnt that the two deputy accountant-generals had moved the offices to their respective mothers-in-law's places.

One was in Pakkaku and the other in Mimamiya. Subbudu was shifted to Pakkaku along with some other office colleagues. Workwise there was less burden even though the Accountant General's office never had much work to do. Things had became normal and everyone present there would talk about their family with much love and some apprehension. Subbudu was the youngest in the group but he was always the centre of attention with his indomitable sense of humour even in the hour of crisis. Those who later discovered Subbudu realised that it was a veneer which concealed a sensitive and sentimental man.

He discovered Pakkaku completely unaffected by the devastation that was taking place elsewhere. He spent his days there bathing in the river, eating delicious food and entertaining everyone. And then came the dreadful news that the Japanese had captured a town north of Pakkaku through the land route. At that time, the Deputy Accountant General told Subbudu and others to leave the city immediately. They were given three months' salary and a job certificate and were asked to carry the records of the Accountant General's office as well. Four buses were provided to them for a safe passage till Kalaivai. Even before Subbudu could think what had happened, he was on his way to Kalaivai. The scene on the outskirts of the city overwhelmed him and his colleagues.

Thousands of grim faces waited for their destiny to lead them to safety. Subbudu was surprised to see women in the group. He later discovered that most of these women came from poor families and lower castes and therefore could not travel through the sea route. People stood there with packed baggage waiting for the officials to announce when and how they could start their journey — the journey to India, their own country which looked more alien than ever. Along with Subbudu, there were eighteen other middle-aged officers. Subbudu had carried just one bag full of clothes and food from Rangoon when he had left for Pakkaku. He used the bag as a pillow to get some sleep before their march to India. The exodus began, early next day.

On their way, there was going to be no water for a stretch of fifteen miles. Subbudu surrendered himself to God, not out of choice but reason. He was apprehensive of the journey and therefore sought the protection of the Almighty. He suggested to his fellow colleagues that they should also chant the name of God. The message was passed to fellow travellers and as the caravan made its way through, the air was filled with the echo of a thousand sounds each chanting the name of God and shouting — "Ram Lakshman Janaki, Bolo Jai Hanuman Ki".

The tropical weather suited the long journey and in the first day, the group covered nearly eighteen miles. Finally people stopped next to a ration camp set up by the Burmese government for the migrants. Rice, pulses, jaggery and oil were distributed among people. Subbudu decided to be the cook for his group. He collected wood and used it to boil rice with cereals. While serving the food, he spread jaggery on top of the rice. Incidentally, to this day he has been unable to forget the taste of that food —*Devamritham*, as he was going to refer to it for the rest of his life. Though the camp was located next to a forest which appeared to be an invitation to the den of Hades, with wild animals making ominous noises, everyone was prepared to face any eventuality. After thanking God for protecting them, Subbudu went to sleep.

The next morning, he prepared himself for the journey once again. The haste to complete the journey had overshadowed the anxiety of attempting to re-start life from scratch. People were silent and tried to strain their ears to listen to the sounds of wild animals. The optimists began to think that if they continued in this fashion, they would reach India in a matter of a few days.

Even though, they were into the second day of the jouney, there were some who were already wearing themselves out, searching for their family members, who went through different routes. Because the road was surrounded by forest area on both sides, the progress of the group was slow which led one of the men in Subbudu's group to observe that at this rate no one would be able to reach India alive. This man from Palghat in Kerala had been saying inauspicious things since the beginning of the journey and despite warnings from the group he did not relent.

Subbudu had steeled himself to mend the old man's ways and he achieved the task by slapping him. No one came to the rescue of that man or questioned Subbudu. The man, bewildered by the slap across his face, muttered something and became silent. Subbudu was beginning to turn inwards and could not bring himself to find humour in the situation. He was staring at the stark reality facing them all.

The caravan stopped again at another camp and this continued for four nights. Soon the migrants crossed into India.

Subbudu imagined that the following day they would reach Dimapur in Nagaland from where the buses would take them to Calcutta in a matter of ten hours. From Calcutta he would catch a train to Madras. He believed his motherland awaited him.

But he was yet to become a battleground between his powerful destiny and the ferocity of nature. He was going to witness death up front. That incident was to signal the birth of a fearless individual, who eventually became a fearless critic.

The caravan which was beginning to look for a place to rest, found itself surrounded by the images of Japanese airplanes flying dangerously low. Just when people thought they were under the line of fire, the planes became invisible. But before any one could thank God, there was a deafening sound of bombardment in the area. People took time to realise that they were still alive. Strong-willed men saw death flirting with them and prayed fervently. The Japanese had bombarded Imphal. Curfew was imposed and war emergency was declared. As a result, the authorities opened the gates of Spade Raja Jail and the zoo near Imphal. In times of war, it is an international pact that prisoners and animals in the zoo should be set free. As people tried to huddle together and made sure that they walked in groups of twenty to thirty, they were told that only the British and Anglo-Indians had the right to use the road which was to lead them to Dimapur. Perhaps, this was the most vulnerable moment of Subbudu's life where he wished he was an Anglo-Indian. Meanwhile, the path had changed and the ominous predictions of the Palghat man rang in Subbudu's ears. It was raining heavily and the seven hills of Cherrapunji, covered with thick forests echoed the sound of the blinding rain.

Subbudu had vowed to visit Tirupati temple but he could not complete his vow before he undertook the arduous journey from Burma to India. As the seven hills stood before him, he begged God to show his mercy and sought his forgiveness for not keeping his word.

The entire stretch passing through Cherrapunji was a single pathway which reached Assam via Lakhimpur. But nobody knew the new route. Tears rolled down Subbudu's cheeks as he confessed, "O! Lord of seven hills. We used to reach you in vehicles, without the customary traversing of the seven hills. So we are being punished for that."

Pregnant women were crying inconsolably since they feared delivering their children in such inhuman conditions. The new route was meant for cattle only and at that time, it was too flooded with rain. There was going to be no camp till Silchar so people were advised to take as many rations as possible. At this time, the old man from Palghat who was addressed as Palaghat Iyer could not control himself and ended up saying, "I have already told you there there will be no town on this road." For a minute, Subbudu remained numb and then laughed hysterically. He had reached a state of emotional turmoil and could not gather enough strength all over again to silence the old man.

Meanwhile, the convicts freed from the prison had set their eyes on these people, who were now walking in groups.Just before the group began its journey, the government sent a message across saying that on the new route it would not be able to protect anyone. Everyone in the group was asked to keep sticks handy. The leader of the caravan gave three to five sticks to each group, which now had eight to ten people. He said that if anyone tried to attack, just kill them. And as feared, the convicts attacked Subbudu's group. As men fought to save their lives and savings, Subbudu got hold of a stick and chased one of the attackers. The chase which took him away from his group ended with Subbudu injuring the thief on his head. Till this day, he is not sure if the man died or survived his attack.

The rain was showing no signs of letting up but no one could wait any longer. Taking the stick in one hand and holding their bags in another, the group started the second leg of the journey praising the Lord:

"Ram Lakshman Janaki, Bolo jai Hanuman ki."

Their own strength had saved them and they thanked God for giving them courage to survive and smile through the most excruciating period of their lives. Subbudu imagined the power of their voices to be such that no wild animal could come near them. Fear had given way to a feeling of freedom and with new found enthusiasm the caravan continued moving through the entire stretch of night, till the rain subsided for sometime.

With water no longer running down their bodies, people felt severe pain in their legs. They looked down and saw leeches covering their legs till the hips. The white *dhotis* which had turned brown due to the muddy water were soaked in blood now. Unable to grasp the situation, few older members of the group died of fear in a matter of a few hours. Death was not in a mood to relax and was manifesting itself in various forms. Subbudu along with some others, began throwing dead bodies, down the steep valleys in order to prevent animals from attacking the caravan in search of dead meat.The friends and relatives of those who died, were wailing and threatening to commit suicide even as Subbudu discovered that human life has the most fragile existence.

He heard a middle-aged man saying, "O God! what sin have we committed? Have we killed a cow or a calf?"

Time had turned its head again.There was no freedom from death. With great nervousness people removed the leeches with the help of salt stone.The joy of being on the last leg of the journey had once again given way to the fear of not reaching the end of it at all.

Even if men and women walked 10 metres, they felt weary. Meanwhile, a man was unable to walk after the first leech attack. Just when everyone lost all hope of surviving till the end of the journey, the group encountered a tribesman walking nearby. Seeing the condition of the group, he offered his assistance and in a rare gesture, he picked up the injured man. The local man trudged the single path barefooted carrying the man nonchalantly in the severe cold. He walked at twice the speed and stopped near a cave where he collected some wood and prepared the tea in a utensil offered by one of the travellers. The tea was without milk and sugar. *Gur* (jaggery) was added to the tea which looked like liquor. People consumed it.

From here on, the man walked with the group and decided to be with them, till their next halt.

For once, it seemed time had grown weak in the presence of these mortals. Its movement had no impact on their moment of trial and tribulation. Even though there was no resting place in sight and no food to eat. There was pitch darkness in what appeared to be the longest night in the lives of the travellers. If people stopped, it was only to remove leeches from their bodies. The sight did not horrify them any more with leeches appearing to be the only other sign of life.

Meanwhile, using sign language, the local guide suggested that the area was filled with wild animals and with such fatigue it might be tough for people to protect themselves. He pointed to a light shining on the opposite hillock and signalled, going there and resting was the only alternative.

No one knew how to react to the tribesman's invitation. At this time, Subbudu conceived a brilliant idea. He used his mimicry skills to tell the man that though everyone was prepared to come, they feared that he would hack them. Even though the man had been helpful, people were extremely fearful because of the incidents that had marked their journey of survival. He understood the people's apprehensions and removed a cross hanging around his neck and stayed still. His faith reassured them.

As Subbudu made sense of what was happening, he expressed his confidence in the intentions of the man by holding his hand and touching the cross. Subbudu was astonished to find that even in that dense forest the Christian missionaries had arrived and had shown a different world to these people.

Within no time, people had agreed to follow the man. Though the place appeared close, it took them quite a while to reach there. The sun was about to rise and the birds started chirruping. The man had taken the entire crowd to the church, which was made entirely out of wood.

Next to the church was a small house where the Father stayed. He had been serving there for the past 40 years. The tribals in the area hung the skull of the previous Father on their walls. This Father knew that fact. Keeping social service in mind, he came here, learnt the language, translated the Bible into their language, established a school, a hospital and a weaving unit and rehabilitated people.

The tribesman knelt before the house and shouted in his language. The next moment a French Father came out carrying a lamp and an umbrella and received everyone warmly. He did not ask the visitors any questions. However, Subbudu and his friends entered the church after much hesitation. The Father brought heavy clothes woven by the native people. Finally, the people got a chance to change into dry clothes. Everyone was thanking God for sending the local tribesman who got them to the church.

Some people cried out of sheer joy. Subbudu didn't know what was happening to him. He felt a strange connection with the Father and wished that he had been a Christian.

The Father appeared again with a drum full of tea. After everyone had drunk it, he prepared rice and served it with jaggery for his visitors. The sun shone brightly after many days and the group was again ready to march forward. The Father too cautioned the group about the wild animals in the area especially the cheetahs.

He suggested that everyone should move in a group. Incidentally, he gave an interesting interpretation on why some animals are afraid of man.

He said, "Because men stand vertically and animals tend to grow horizontally, they are afraid of men. Unless they are hungry, they will not kill anybody. Man has no principle and therefore he kills animals as a pastime. Don't go alone, even if you are delayed, go together. God will save you. Amen." With these words, the Father bid farewell to everyone.

After the group crossed the Cherrapunji mountain, they began descending. Everyone was hungry but despite that, they continued walking.

Subbudu and his friends must have walked for a couple of hours when the aroma of mint filled the air. Palghat Iyer was very happy, "It's mint. No fear, we will reach a town very soon."

For the first time through the journey, he had spoken positively. He danced like *Nandanar*, who received Thillai Nataraja's darshan. Palghat entered the forest and brought two sprigs of mint. Someone had a leftover lump of salt. Iyer got into the business, he spread the salt over a rock, finely ground the mint and served it. Everyone licked the paste. Though mint is good for the digestion, it can lead to dysentery in case the stomach has become used to light eating. Subbudu fell ill with dysentery. Meanwhile,Babu Iyer, the man who was carried by the tribesman, could not walk a step and his leg resembled an over ripe banana.

He had to be carried again. Others however managed somehow. Their walk had a certain urgency. Subbudu knew that if he stopped now, he would never see his family again. That was not going to be.

In a matter of a few hours everyone was at Lakhimpur. A steamer was waiting to take people to Calcutta. However, it could not accommodate everyone but the locals were very generous and arranged food for those who had to wait for another steamer.

Finally the journey through the river started and Subbudu fell in love with the silence around. The noise of the rain beating down on the ground, the shrill voices of fearful pregnant women and the cries of old men were ringing in his ears. Subbudu prayed for his peace of mind. Soon he and other members of his group reached Calcutta but by then, he had developed symptoms of malaria as well.

Meanwhile, the entire group was received by the editor of *Indian Finance*, K. Rangaswamy Iyengar who arranged food, shelter and medical assistance for everyone. On reaching Calcutta, Babu Iyer was sent to the government hospital. Subbudu flatly refused to be treated in the government hospital because he feared dying there.

On seeing his condition, Rangaswamy Iyengar kept Subbudu at his own place and provided him with the necessary medical treatment but he did not respond to the medicines at all. A few days later, he was diagnosed for cholera. The situation seemed grim because he was continuously losing weight. Meanwhile, he was always thirsty and no matter how much water he drank, he felt his lips and tongue were dry. Once, at midnight, Subbudu felt so thirsty that he drank nearly half a bucket of water. Meanwhile, Mrs. Rangaswamy prepared cereal soup for Subbudu and forced him to drink that every six to eight hours.

He was worried he would die without seeing his parents and his wife. To make matters worse, he heard that Babu Iyer had died. All this enervated his body and he cried out of fear. His body had given up and his mind was cluttered with horrifying images of the journey. There seemed little hope of his recovery. But Mrs. Rangaswamy was still hopeful. Seeing his condition, she brought two large cups of buttermilk and cajoled him to drink them. After having buttermilk, Subbudu slept well and in the morning, he woke up with vigour. He felt that Mother Goddess Alamelu Mangai had appeared in the form of that woman and saved him.

At Calcutta's refugee camp, Subbudu's brother-in-law, Ramanatha Iyer acted as a camp commander. One of his jobs was to deliver tickets to each refugee to their home town. He had come into contact with Rangaswamy Iyengar while making the arrangements for the refugees. Three days after Rangaswamy had brought Subbudu home, he bumped into Ramanatha Iyer who asked him if he had come across a man called Subbudu. Since Iyengar didn't know that P.V. Subramaniam was also known as Subbudu, he said, he had not. On the fourth day, Rangaswamy casually told Ramanatha Iyer that there was a young man called Subramaniam staying at his residence. "He is weak and says that his father's name is Padi Venkataraman."

Ramanatha Iyer rushed to meet Subbudu and took him to the house of the Accountant General, Sh. Parthasarthy, and had him treated by Dr. M.S. Rao. Within three days, Subbudu's health improved remarkably. Parthasarthy's wife used to play the violin very well. She discovered that Subbudu too had an interest in music and so the two developed a special bond. In a few days, Subbudu proceeded to Madras by train. The dream of going to his native place, meeting relatives, parents and wife and eating drumstick sambar haunted him. Subbudu's family waited for him in Coimbatore at his father-in-law's residence.

Later, he discovered later that during the journey to India he had suffered a black out. While crossing the fourth mountain on his way to Cherrapunji, he had fainted because of extreme weakness. The people accompanying him had tried to revive him but were unable to do so. Thinking, he had died, they had left him there. The rule at that time was that each person should look out for his own safety. On his way, Subbudu had seen people dying but he and everyone else had become immune to the fear of death.

As people passed by, no one cared to ascertain if he was still alive or not. At that moment, Ramaswamy, who had worked in Subbudu's house and had studied under Venkataraman, came that way. On seeing Subbudu, he started crying. He rubbed mustard oil on his palm and chest and tried to revive him. Fortunately, Subbudu regained consciousness but when he tried to rise, he again fainted. Ramaswamy carried him on his shoulders and walked one and a half miles before he handed him over to the people in his group. Subbudu had been saved.

Before Ramaswamy found Subbudu, Venkataraman's family friend, Parangasa Muthaliar had tried to see if Subbudu was alive or not but since he did not wake up, he imagined the worst and left his 'body'. When he went to meet Venkataraman in

Coimbatore, the latter asked him if he had seen Subbudu. Muthaliar remained silent and instead went to the puja room where Subbudu's mother was praying before Lord Venkatajalapathi.

She asked him the same question, "Have you seen Subbudu?."

Very cautiously, Muthaliar said he had only seen Subbudu. Hearing this, an eagerness gripped Subbudu's mother. She took out her *mangalsutra* and threw it on Alamelu Mangai's statue.

"Alamelu, If you want to live as a Sumangali, you should bring back my son." In the next ten days, Subbudu had reached his home.

Subbudu and his family stayed at his in-laws, place for some time before his parents moved to Madras and he left for Shimla where the Burmese government had re-located. Chandra joined him six months later.

As Subbudu regained his health, he again started taking a keen interest in music and drama. Shimla was very different from Rangoon or Madras, with its cool climate and mountainous terrain. However, with the Burmese government functioning from there, a large number of Indian officers settled in Rangoon moved to the hill station as well. Within a few months, *sabhas* began functioning and invitations were sent to the artistes in Madras.

For the first time, he lived independently off his parents. His journey from Burma to India had changed him. Flashes from the great escape haunted him, which have continued to this day, though the frequency has drastically reduced. He was more apprehensive of those nightmarish dreams than of the fear of death. He had seen people dying, and had also been one among hundreds who chose to move on leaving the dead behind. He had witnessed men and women losing their life partners, their brothers and sisters and even their new born babies. It was not about losing out at the hands of death but surviving through the death of others, a challenge that has always stood before human kind, which bothered Subbudu now.

The company of people from Rangoon in Shimla helped him divert his mind and he decided to start his own theatre group and named it South Indian Theatre. Apart from his friends from Rangoon, a few Punjabis and Bengalis also joined his initiative. The drama group continued for the next forty years. Meanwhile, Subbudu's brother Krishnamoorthy had joined All India Radio. Soon he became the Tamil incharge of the External Services Division of All India Radio. While he was there, Krishnamoorthy shied away from giving any contracts to Subbudu in fear of being accused of nepotism. But, Krishnamoorthy's boss assured him that Subbudu was an artist in his own right. He told him to give him contracts. Subbudu became famous in a series called "Kuppuswamy in Kudumbam". He played a cook's role with *élan.* Subbudu's long-term associate Poornam Viswanathan had written the script.

In the meantime he had also caught up with his Tamil magazines. *Ananda Vikatan* was no longer his favourite ever since Kalki and Sadasivam had started their own magazine, *Kalki* in 1941. Ironically, *Kalki's* increasingly nationalist writings had created sharp differences between the then owner of *Ananda Vikatan*, S.S. Vasan and Kalki, and had led to the latter's exit from the magazine. Sadasivam was the advertising manager of *Ananda Vikatan* when *Kalki* was at the helm of affairs. Sadasivam's wife and leading Carnatic singer and actress M.S. Subbulakshmi played a side-heroine to popular Marathi actress Shanta Apte in a film called *Savitri* only to raise money for the *Kalki* magazine.

Subbudu sent his first full-fledged review to *Kalki* in early 1943. The magazine had taken up the arduous task of covering the music recitals at most places. Indian dance was a new phenomenon in the public domain and it did not qualify for a critical intervention. But dance was going to overtake the world of music in terms of the visibility factor in the coming decades. Subbudu who saw himself as an observer of music was to become its celebrated and shrewd critic before gaining unimaginable fame and notoriety as a 'queen' maker in the world of dance.

The man felt a strange attack of nervousness overwhelming him as he impatiently waited for a response from Kalki. In a couple of weeks, Subbudu received a two-line letter from Kalki, in which he had written: "You write well. Write often, whether we publish or not."

Ironically, there was never a moment in Subbudu's life when a piece written by him was rejected. As soon as the next copy of the magazine was out, Subbudu rushed to buy it. He wanted to see how his name looked on top of an article. It wasn't narcissism but inexplicable excitement which can only be experienced by a writer.

Subbudu read his article repeatedly and showed it to his wife, who had limited her concern to seeing him happy and satisfied. Much as Subbudu wanted to write, Shimla did not offer him too many opportunities to witness music concerts because there were hardly any events taking place. Meanwhile, his drama company began staging plays ranging from mythological episodes to enacting pieces by famous writers.

Since the hill station was a small town, there was a greater interaction among people. Talk of Indian independence dominated the morning conversations with Subbudu often encouraging people to wear khadi since he loved wearing it too. But he never took part in any demonstrations. Subbudu was sure of two things, his religion and his nationhood are extremely personal matters and they shouldn't be flaunted to either whip up a sentiment or to demonstrate one's loyalty.

Staying away from his parents also meant that Subbudu thought of them increasingly now and like his father, he took the lead in ensuring a sense of community bonding. He moved a step ahead of his father and reached out to the people of other communities as well. Whenever anyone known or unknown died in the hilly town, he along with five of his friends, offered themselves to make arrangements for a proper funeral and cremation of the dead. These young men did that because they knew that in the moments of grief the family members were not in a position to take care of the arrangements. Just as Subbudu helped people in distress, he and his friends also assisted during wedding ceremonies. Right from cooking to overseeing the flower arrangements, Subbudu and his team attended to everything.

The Sprouting Spirit

War was still raging and there were fears that the Japanese might overrun India. War time recruitment was going on in the Indian government and since India and Burma were under the British empire, there was little difference in their administrative set up. After being uprooted from Rangoon, Subbudu did not want to return to the city of his childhood memories. He was prepared to forget his memories in order to provide his wife and children with a secure future and therefore, he decided to shift his base to Delhi and joined the Revenue Department of the Finance Ministry on December 16, 1943.

There were about 2,000 South Indian familes in Delhi at that time. It was a comfortably large number to seek a cultural identity in the country's capital. Even as India was discovering its different shades and trying to understand the complexities of its diversity, the slow but steady invasion of South Indian culture in the North had begun. A few *sabhas* catering to the interests of the connoisseurs of music had already started functioning. Among them, the Karnataka Sangeetha Sabha was prominent. The *sabha* was always looking for popular as well as new musicians visiting North India. Many of these musicians were selected from holy places like Benaras and Haridwar when they were on a pilgrimage. Those days the concerts used to be four to five hours long. Even though the shows were ticketed, there was no dearth of audience.

Meanwhile the audiences that attended the *kutcheris* even in the 1940s when *sabhas* were a new found phenomenon, indicated the growing confidence of the *rasikas* as the new patrons for the art and they demonstrated their power by sometimes applauding the accompanists and ignoring the main artiste.

As Indira Menon also observes in *The Madras Quartet : Women in Karnatic Music*, the new system of patronage did not compare with the royal patronage of yesteryears. Moreover, even among the rich merchants there were different castes at play thus making the patrons a less homogeneous mix. Artistes, accustomed to royal patrons, had to therefore make alterations in their music to suit individual tastes. The temple festivals gave them an opportunity to display their virtuosity and expertise in music. But some artistes, blessed with the farsight to notice the social changes that were taking place, began to think in the direction of having concerts for common people. The revolution in technology which resulted in the arrival of the gramophone, the microphone and cinema hastened the arrival of new patrons of art.

The Karnataka Sangeet Sabha in Delhi was registered in 1936. By 1939-40 eminent musicians like G.N. Balasubramaniam, Madurai Mani Iyer, Ariyakudi Ramanuja Iyengar, Dwaram Venkataswamy Naidu and young M.L. Vasanthakumari had been invited to give music recitals.

Meanwhile, Harikatha congregations ensured that South Indians interacted with each other regularly. Subbudu soon came into the limelight with his talent on the harmonium and his ability to introduce humour into every occasion. As in Shimla, he offered his services during the family functions of South Indians, be it marriages or funerals. His office had also begun to take note of him because the man wrote for *Kalki*, which had emerged as a strong representative of the Tamil voice. As Subbudu again picked up his pen to cover Delhi's music circles, he also became a familiar figure among the South Indians, most of whom were part of the establishment at that time.

Subbudu's uncle, P. Doraiswamy Iyer had moved to Madras long before his brother Venkataraman. Doraiswamy's son and daughter had strong theosophical leanings and his family had developed a close bond with Rukmini Devi, theosophist, animal welfare activist and the first Brahmin woman from the upper class to aggressively take-up the cause of pruning Sadirattam and rechristening it as Bharatanatyam. As the time passed, Doraiswamy also got involved with Rukmini Devi's efforts to give a new identity to Bharatanatyam and to establish Kalakshetra, a premier institution for performing arts especially Bharatanatyam. The institute got its present address because of the untiring efforts of Doraiswamy who slowly bought small pieces of land next to the sea over a period of four to five years. The land where Kalakshetra stands today was covered with just sand and the Iyers was the first family to extend all help to Rukmini Devi in constructing and building the institution. Incidentally, Doraiswamy's daughter, Dr. Padmasini gave her entire life to Kalakshetra. Meanwhile when Venkataraman and his family shifted their base to Madras, he took up the job of a manager in the institution. Both the brothers continued working for Kalakshetra for some time. Over a period of time, Dr. Padmasini became the right hand of Rukmini Devi and she remained with her till the latter's death in 1986.

In the early days, Dr. Padmasini used to often sing for Kalakshetra's productions. However, as the institution grew, she shifted to administrative work and went on to become the institute's medical officer and the hostel warden. Given the context, it was interesting to note that the first meeting between Subbudu and Rukmini Devi was not exactly cordial, even though they developed mutual admiration for each other in years to come. As luck would have it, Subbudu also met his mentor Kalki the same day he met Rukmini Devi. This happened when Subbudu had come down from Shimla to meet his family.

He wrote a piece on a play he witnessed in Madras which was presided over by Kalki. In his characteristic fashion, Subbudu said, that if people missed the rumblings of the Bihar earthquake, they should have been present to experience them again. He was referring to the effect of Kalki's oration on the audience. On reading the review, Kalki wrote a letter to Subbudu asking him why he had not met him that day. He told Subbudu to meet him the following Monday evening. And that Monday turned out to be the one when Rukmini Devi also sought Subbudu's attendance at her residence. One had to rely entirely on Subbudu for what transpired at the two meetings.

Subbudu arrived at Rukmini Devi's residence and was stopped by Peter Hoffman, who told him that Athai was busy and that he would have to wait a little longer if he wished to meet her. Subbudu stared at Peter uneasily. As the young man rose to leave, he was stopped by Hoffman, who requested him to wait for a minute outside as he went and told Rukmini Devi that someone called P. V. Subramaniam had come to meet her. In a couple of minutes, Peter came out and ushered Subbudu inside. Already agitated because he was asked to wait, Subbudu was unsually aggressive throughout the meeting while Rukmini Devi, it is believed, was condescending. It is open to surmise if both were being egoistic about their respective stations in life. Rukmini Devi had emerged as the new face, or rather the alternative face of Sadirattam, which had been rechristened as Bharatanatyam by E. Krishna Iyer. The other face of the dance form was Balasaraswati who was going to bring international recognition to the art. Since Subbudu had secured a permanent job with the Finance Ministry and was writing for *Kalki*, he did not care much for what Rukmini Devi had to offer. On her part, Rukmini Devi wanted to rope in efficient people for Kalakshetra so that she could ensure the longevity of the institution. Subbudu, however, was never going to be a part of the institution.

At the very outset, she asked Subbudu to sing his favourite *kriti* which he flatly refused. It is relevant to add here that people are not born great, they become great and on that journey, they reveal their weaknesses. Rukmini Devi or Subbudu's behaviour must be interpreted in that context.

Meanwhile, Subbudu asked her, "Why must I sing?" According to Subbudu, Rukmini Devi observed, "Because I want you to sing." The angry young man immediately retorted, "That is why I do not want to sing." Subbudu replied in the manner which became typical of him as the years set on the horizon.

He always refused to do anything that he was asked to. As the two came dangerously close to having a full blown argument, Rukmini Devi told Subbudu that she would not mind if he wanted to join Kalakshetra. Subbudu's reply was, "I am not temperamentally suited for the job since I have my own views on every subject." It is interesting to know that while Subbudu remained largely apolitical in his career as a government servant, he could not help being controversial as a critic. In his own understanding, he had to be firm and unyielding with artistes who lived in their own ivory towers.

As he emerged from her residence, he felt a strange rush of excitement. He wondered if they had both been genuine in approaching each other. But before he could think further, his mind was diverted to the second meeting of the day. His rendezvous with Kalki. That meeting changed everything Subbudu stood for. Kalki fashioned his mind in such a manner that he was forced to over-extend himself every time he wanted to write. That was the time, when Subbudu stopped writing because he liked to write and began writing because he wished to be remembered.

Kalki had been in the thick of a controversy over his latest article but he surprised Subbudu with his relaxed and composed demeanour. As the two men sat down to have lunch, Kalki said something, which Subbudu never forgot. He gave him a talisman. "You must write in such a manner that after the performance, people forget about the artiste and start talking about you."

Even though Subbudu internalised those words, he could never be sure if Kalki was serious or just joking. In one stroke, he had told him to perform through his writing. By the time Subbudu reached home, Rukmini Devi had sent a word to his father that the young fellow was rude and discourteous. Later, Venkataraman told Rukmini that she should have consulted him before offering him a job because he would have advised her not to do so. He knew his son's temperament too well.

You can spot a Kalakshetra student from the first step.

—Subbudu

While Rukmini Devi immersed herself in bringing glory to Bharatanatyam and institutionalised it so as to ensure its longetivity, Carnatic music was witnessing a revolution with a number of female vocalists demolishing the male dominance. M. S. Subbulakshmi was first such singer. In 1944, she gave her first performance in Delhi. The same year she performed at the All India Dance Conference held in Bombay where top artistes took note of her talent. The following year, she was going to catch the imagination of the entire nation in her title role in the Tamil and Hindi feature film *Meera*. She came into the national limelight attracting the attention of Mahatma Gandhi, Pt. Nehru and others. In fact, Gandhiji asked her to sing the Ramdhun and two of his favourite *bhajans*— "*Vaishnava jan to...*" and "*Hari tum haro jan ki bhir...*". However, M.S. Subbulakshmi ran the risk of getting typecast as a *bhajan* singer, and Subbudu had to caution her through his writings in the following years. The relationship between *Kalki* magazine and M.S. Subbulakshmi is the first instance of a symbiotic relationship between the media and the artiste. With a shift in patronage, the artistes had to reach out to the common man and the media proved to be the most effective tool on hand.

Post-1945, at the suggestion of Rajaji, MS and Sadasivam announced that MS would sing only for charity concerts and that any earnings made through her singing would go to charity institutions that the couple was associated with. With her talent and her husband's unstinted support, contacts in the political circles and the indomitable promotion by *Kalki* magazine, MS became a symbol of national pride in the pre-independence era.

With All India Radio, gramaphone companies and magazines such as *Kalki*, artistes reached out to complete strangers and in the process, invested them with the power to choose the best from the lot. Writers like Kalki and later Subbudu, by virtue of being critics, found themselves endowed with the role to be the messengers. What they heard and liked percolated down to their writings and later helped the common man, oblivious of the talent of a particular singer, in making his judgement. But, what began as a conversation turned into a monologue, with the media playing into the hands of certain influential artistes. Subbudu, in his enviable long career, did not allow that and hence ended up intimidating the artistes. The fearless critic, was therefore not only bold in his style, but also in the impression he left on those who sought to challenge his impartiality in any way possible.

M.S. Subbulakshmi's performance was highly appreciated by the audience in Delhi and was followed by D.K. Pattammal's debut in Delhi in 1946. DKP arrived on the scene when the Self-respect Movement was at its height. The movement targeted the Brahmin community.

DKP, being a Brahmin may have had initial difficulty during this time, but her arrival on the scene was crucial because a lot of leading men debuted almost at the same time. DKP with her powerhouse performances broke the myth that *Ragam-Tanam-Pallavi* in Carnatic repertoire was an exclusive male bastion.

The *sabha* culture was catching on in Delhi. With ticketed shows and concerts exceeding the duration of four hours, the audience wanted the best entertainment for their money and they were willing to devote as much time, to hear their favourite singers. The mike had already debuted on the scene in the mid-1930s. It is believed that the coming of the microphone increased the career span of the Carnatic singers who either lost their voices or died young while trying to keep up with the strain of singing. Maha Vaidyanatha Iyer, Kancheepuram Naina Pillai and Konerirajapuram Vaidyanantha Iyer were some refined Carnatic voices that were lost because of this. Subbudu who gave equal importance to the quality of voice felt that the coming of the mike was particularly helpful to the likes of Semmangudi Srinivasa Iyer who, according to Subbudu, had an errant voice. For the female vocalists, the mike added volume to their voices.

By this time, the Gramaphone companies like HMV and its rival Columbia Gramaphone Co. had created stars out of M.S. Subbulakshmi and D.K. Pattammal respectively. DKP was said to be the first Brahmin woman to enter the arena of Carnatic vocal music. However, some scholars mention that C. Saraswati Bai was the first ever Brahmin woman to sing Harikatha in public. In fact, M.S. Subbulakshmi attended her recital as a child when in the middle of the concert, Saraswati Bai started singing an English song which advocated freedom.

Studio stars were born during this period as well, which later led to the fall in the standard and the sales of the recorded music. But the slow rise of All India Radio enticed the music lovers, who got the opportunity to listen to their favourite artistes live. The thrill and excitement was unimaginable and for Subbudu it was the first step towards complete public patronage.

In terms of the change of patronage, Subbudu's rise as a critic became a crucial turning point. He represented the first generation of *rasikas* who had the power to choose the musician they wanted to listen to. Subbudu, more than Kalki, used the pen as a symbol of democratisation of art. As the years went by, the role of the critic, especially someone like Subbudu, became vital as the distance between the musicians and their audience widened. And it is here that Subbudu's personal tastes affected the choices of the audience and the ambitions of the musicians.

After Independence, both Carnatic and Hindustani music flourished because All India Radio used to conduct a national programme for music every Saturday. The government policy was to have one Carnatic music recital against three Hindustani music recitals. And whenever a Carnatic musician came to Delhi to perform, he or she was invited to perform at *kutcheris.*

The year DKP descended on Delhi was the same year when Subbudu got into trouble but again not because of his own doings. Subbudu was writing off and on for *Kalki* magazine when his theatre group decided to stage Kalki Krishnamurthy's *Kalvanin Kathali* or the *Sweetheart of the Dacoit,* for charity for the National College in Trichy. Three days before the play was to be staged, a leading newspaper, *Dawn* carried an editorial criticising the play because it was supposed to be a lampoon on Mohammad Ali Jinnah. Liyakat Ali Khan of the Muslim League who was the then Finance Minister and Subbudu's de facto boss pulled him up through his secretary even as he tried explaining matters to him. Meanwhile, Rajaji who was to preside over the play at the South India Club asked Subbudu for the script to know the facts first hand. Upset over the lack of responsibility shown by the editor of *Dawn,* he telephoned him and chided him for a false accusation. Just a day before the play was staged, *Dawn* carried an apology and retracted from its earlier claims. This was Subbudu's first victory against his political bosses. Many more were to follow...

All these people could have crushed me officially and financially but I rose with my sheer knowledge and fearlessness.

— Subbudu on the political pressures he faced throughout his career

Meanwhile, India gained independence on August 15, 1947. The period was marked by communal riots between Hindus and Muslims, which created maximum havoc in the border areas of India and Pakistan. Subbudu too could not escape a mob of rioters in Delhi when he returned home from his job one evening.

Every young Hindu boy has to get his ears pierced as part of a religious ceremony. However, Subbudu's father did not believe in the custom and therefore, neither Subbudu nor his brothers had their ears pierced.

Ironically, the Hindu rioters who caught hold of Subbudu saw Subbudu's ears and concluded that he was a Muslim. At that very moment, Subbudu showed his scared thread and began reciting the Gayatri Mantra. This convinced the rioters and they let him go. The incident, which occurred exactly a decade after Subbudu's first brush with riots in Burma, made him critical of those religious and political leaders who fanned the sentiments of the masses for their own good. Subbudu was still trying to come to terms with the latest episode when he heard the shocking news of Mahatma Gandhi's assassination. He realised that one should always be prepared to face the consequences and challenges of leading a public life with honesty and fearlessness.

In 1948 itself, All India Radio set up its centre in Cuttack. Under Subbudu's brother P. V. Krishnamoorthy's leadership, a number of talented musicians, writers and dancers were brought together on one platform.

As Orissi dancer, Ileana Citaristi wrote in Orissi Guru, Kelucharan Mohapatra's biography, *The Making of Guru*, PVK also roped in the three leading lights of music, who "generated a revolution in the dance music scene: Bala Krishna Das, Bhubaneshwar Mishra from Gunjam district and Hariprasad Chaurasia from Uttar Pradesh. With the support of the versatile Surendra Mohanty, the talented scriptwriter and dance teacher attached to All India Radio, as producer, Krishnamoorthy promoted both drama and dance drama productions with the aim of improving the level of performing arts in general and to stimulate creativity among the artistes."

Meanwhile, a core group of writers and intellectuals like Mayadhar Mansingh, Kalicharan Patnaik and Satchi Routray were trying to create a cultural identity for their state. While PVK was in Cuttack, he also came across Annapurna Theatre which was controlled and managed by Pankaj Charan Das, who belonged to the Mahari community (and performed Orissi's parent dance Gotipua). At Annapurna Theatre, PVK saw the young couple Kelucharan and Lakshmipriya. All these people became responsible for the 'birth' of Orissi dance. Later, PVK made Subbudu aware of Orissi but Subbudu still felt that nothing could beat Bharatanatyam.

Shortly after independence, sitar maestro and music composer Ravi Shankar staged two productions based on Pt. Nehru's *Discovery of India*. The young sitarist was appointed the music director of All India Radio's first national orchestra, Vadya Vrinda in 1949.

In the years that were to follow, he was reminded of Gandhi each time he was attacked physically or otherwise. Once while composing music for a programme, Ravi Shankar found that the *ghatam* player had fallen sick, so he asked Subbudu's brother, P. V. Krishnamurthy, who was a programme executive at AIR, if he knew anyone who could play the *ghatam*. Krishnamoorthy told him that his brother could play the instrument and he introduced the two. Like everyone, Subbudu had a two-minute part in the entire programme but he enjoyed playing an instrument different from the harmonium. Little did they know that a chance incident a year later involving both of them, would land him with a job at *The Statesman*.

It so happened that once, attending the performance of G.N. Balasubramaniam organised by the Karnataka Sangeeta Sabha, in Wavell Theatre in Delhi, in 1950, the former Director General of AIR, Narayana Menon and Ravi Shankar, got somewhat confused about the *raga* being rendered by G.N. Balasubramaniam. Subbudu who was sitting behind both the men, overheard their conversation. Suddenly, Ravi Shankar turned around and asked Subbudu if he knew which *raga* G.N. Balasubramaniam was singing. Subbudu immediately said, it was Padi. After the performance ended, Dr. Menon asked G.N. Balasubramaniam whether he sang a particular *kriti* in Padi *raga*. His positive reply became the starting point of Subbudu's association with *The Statesman*. Dr. Narayana Menon who was the music critic for the paper, was so impressed by him that he offered him the job of a music critic for the paper on the spur-of-the-moment. Subbudu was unable to react to the offer but he managed to inform Dr. Menon that he was unsure about his writing skills in English. However, Dr. Menon argued saying *The Statesman* only wanted facts.

He was so firm in his offer that he could not refuse any further. Dr. Menon asked Subbudu to see him at his residence the next day. When Subbudu reached Dr. Menon's house, he was introduced to Mr. Brooke who was the news editor of the paper. Dr. Menon categorically told Brooke that Subbudu would be covering the Carnatic music recitals hence onwards. Interestingly, while G.N. Balasubramaniam's music recital landed him with an offer to be a music critic with *The Statesman*, the musician's disciple, Vasanthakumari was the first artiste Subbudu reviewed for the paper. After witnessing her performance in the capital, Subbudu went home and wrote the article the same night. The next morning he rushed to meet Dr. Menon, who, after making some grammatical corrections recommended it for publication. Subbudu had arrived.

Subbudu's feat did not surprise his brother PVK but his knowledge of Carnatic music still amazes him since he did not take any formal training in music. All he learnt was by observing the musicians he served during their trips to Rangoon.

Subbudu's appointment as the music critic for *The Statesman* was going to become the turning point in the history of music and dance criticism in India. For Subbudu the new role brought increased recognition from Kalki and Sadasivam who began inviting him to cover music concerts in Bombay as well. Moreover, the fact that he was going to write in English for a leading newspaper was going to raise Subbudu's status as a critic. From now on, Subbudu was going to cater to a different readership as well. Subbudu just didn't know how to type. Whenever he had to type at *The Statesman*, he used a single finger to type the entire article.

The year was significant for Subbudu not only because he was beginning to shape his identity but also because he became the father of a bonny boy.

Subbudu's wife Chandra delivered their first child on April 6, 1950. He was named Sriram. Chandra had earlier suffered four miscarriages. To seek divine help, the couple made a trip to the historic Rameshwaram temple in Tamil Nadu where they witnessed a *devadasi* performance for the first time. Incidentally by that time, the Tamil Nadu Assembly had already passed the bill prohibiting dance in temples.

Sriram was born twelve years after marriage and his arrival was greeted with much joy and excitement in the entire family. During these intervening years, Subbudu and Chandra had discovered soul mates in each other. Understandably, this was the toughest phase in the lives of the young couple. Chandra was under tremendous emotional pressure which Subbudu deflected through his humour and enduring support. With both relying firmly on God, the birth of their first child reaffirmed their faith. Though Subbudu had tried everything, from naturopathy to yoga to treat his wife when she was suffering miscarriages, he never interfered in the way Chandra raised the children. It was clearly her domain and that is why children took pride in their father but adored their mother. In fact, Sriram feels that there would have been complete chaos had Chandra also accompanied Subbudu to performances every evening.

Meanwhile, Chandra had to sort out all the family problems on her own. Frequently she had to be the head of the family and had to take decisions for her children. Sriram's younger brother Ravi who was born on September 3, 1952, helped his mother run the household.

He was a few months old when Subbudu and Chandra decided to visit Chandra's parents in Coimbatore. At one of the transit stations, Sriram told Subbudu that he wanted to eat biscuits.

Subbudu with Chandra, Sriram and Ravi

He tagged along with Subbudu and got off the train with him. Sriram held on to his father's *kurta* and tried to keep pace with him. With some people getting in and out of the train and still others trying to look for their respective coaches, there was a lot of hustle and bustle on the platform. Subbudu, lost in his thoughts, didn't realise that Sriram had been left behind. Meanwhile, Sriram held someone else's *kurta* and started walking with that man. Subbudu bought the biscuits and entered his coach. When Chandra saw him, she asked him where Sriram was.

Subbudu had forgotten that Sriram was with him. All hell broke loose. He rushed out and started running towards the vendor from whom he bought the biscuits. Meanwhile, when Sriram realised that he was holding on to some stranger, he began crying and ran back. As luck would have it, he remembered the face of the army jawan who was standing next to his coach when he had got down with Subbudu. Fortunately the jawan too remembered Sriram and took him to Chandra. Meanwhile, Subbudu, unable to locate Sriram, rushed back and found Sriram ensconced on her lap. The couple thanked God for saving their son. Chandra once again realised that she could not trust Subbudu with their children. But before she could say anything to him, she saw his crestfallen face and his apologetic expression, and decided to let it be.

Sriram was an active child. Though Subbudu employed Mahalingam, a music teacher for him, he used to run out of the house to play with his friends whenever he had a music class. The actual reason behind employing Mahalingam was that he was an extremely poor man who had to take care of a large family. Subbudu wanted to help him and he thought he could do that by giving him an opportunity to teach Sriram. Subbudu did not want Mahalingam to have a feeling that he was being patronised. He made sure that whoever he helped, were also in a position to assist him whether or not he needed it.

Sriram recalls that Subbudu used to come home during lunch time and always made it a point to give him a ride on his cycle. Whenever Subbudu went to concerts, he used to take Sriram along with him. However, each time he took Sriram on his cycle, Chandra feared that he would leave him behind. While, Chandra had her share of tense moments each time father and son were out, she was happy to know that Sriram had developed a love for music. The young boy was a gifted percussion player and loved playing the *mridangam*.

Since he was the eldest child, he got more opportunities to accompany his father for music recitals than the other children. In fact, on a number of occasions, Sriram accompanied his father on stage as a *mridangist*. He grew up enjoying his mother's unconditional love and experiencing his father's humanitarian nature. Subbudu had a friend, Raghunatha Bhagavatar who used to often give Harikatha recitals in Delhi at that time. Since he was financially insecure, Subbudu made sure that he had Sriram as a *mridangist* while he played on the harmonium without charging any fees.

Even though Subbudu's job with the Finance Ministry and his work as a critic and his interest in *bhajan* singing kept him busy, he did not allow any of these to dilute his love for theatre. In fact Subbudu's children recall that they grew up witnessing endless drama rehearsals taking place in their drawing room. The excitement of seeing people play different characters went well with the impression they had of their father as a mimic. Sriram and Ravi took part in plays staged by Subbudu. Even though many believed that Ravi had taken after his mother, Chandra thought that her son had taken after her husband in mimicry. Subbudu on his part, considered Ravi to be more gifted in mimicry than he was.

While he continued devoting time at Hairkathas on weekends, Subbudu spent most of his evenings attending *kutcheris*. One of the singers Subbudu dearly missed in Delhi was G.N. Balasubramaniam. It is said that Balasubramaniam set exacting standards for himself and therefore always found fault with his singing style. Incidentally, Subbudu had a tiff with him at his last performance in the Capital before he died. While witnessing his recital, Subbudu was saddened to see Balasubramaniam struggling with his voice.

As Subbudu recalled about his all time favourite musician, "I was told that the maestro wanted to see me. I intimated my reluctance, citing that I was unsure what kind of reception his entourage would give me. The same evening, I received a telephone call, 'Mr. Subbudu, I may be a musician, but I am also a gentleman', said the Master."

When they met, he complimented Subbudu for having written what he wrote. He explained that age and sheer wear and tear had enfeebled his voice. But he maintained that Subbudu had done the right thing. "Keep it up", he said.

For Subbudu, this was the most powerful instance where an artiste had dwarfed a critic. He always believed that art makes a person humble. With Balasubramaniam, he experienced it.

Apart from Balasubramaniam several other talented male musicians had also made an enduring impact on the music scene. Among them were, Ariyakudi Ramanuja Iyengar (who was the seniormost in that generation), Musiri Subramania Iyer, Semmangudi Srinivasa Iyer, Magarajapuram Vishwanatha Iyer, Chembai Vaidyanatha Bhagavatar, Alathur Brothers and Ramnad Krishnan among others.

In fact, just as Rukmini Devi fashioned Bharatanatyam for the proscenium set up, Ariayakudi Ramanuja Iyengar consolidated the concert format of Carnatic music. The change in the concert pattern was actually the first sign of the shift in patronage. Before Ariyakudi made changes, the normal duration of a concert was anywhere between 5-6 hours. People would often rise in the midst of a recital, have a *paan* or even gossip outside the *sabha* hall before joining the audience again. Moreover, artistes sang as much as they liked. People had time to listen and the musicians had patience to perform. Ariyakudi, seeing the shift in patronage and the corresponding shift in the taste of the audience, reduced the duration of a *kutcheri* to three hours. On an average every concert consisted of a *varnam, kritis, raga aalapana* followed by *ragam tanam pallavi* and a *tukda*.

No one could have ever imagined that concerts on an average would run for 90 minutes as they do these days. Subbudu, who witnessed these changes first hand, has been remarkably liberal in giving primacy to change over tradition. With less time on hand and greater complexities in one's life, he feels it is justifiable to have a shorter duration but that doesn't stop him from criticising the current crop of musicians for not experimenting with newer *ragas* and unexplored compositions of the trinity.

Regarding this, he has so far only appreciated the contribution made by G.N. Balasubramaniam and Dr. Balamurali Krishna. Credited with being the most enterprising musician among his contemporaries and hailed as a visionary for having provided a perfect blend of vigour and variation in Carnatic music, G.N. Balasubramaniam was a self-taught man who found his successor in Madras Lalithangi Vasanthakumari. Incidentally, Subbudu was a mentor to M.L. Vasanthakumari's student, Sudha Raghunathan in her artistic career during the late 1980s and 90s.

M.L. Vasanthkumari's parents, who were instrumental in popularising the compositions of Sri Purandara Dasa in South India, were not keen that Vasanthkumari should learn music. Vasanthakumari, as she was popularly known, was the first disciple of G.N. Balasubramaniam and one of the pillars of the Madras Quartet. Once, narrating how she became a student of G.N.

Balasubramaniam to Subbudu she confessed that her musician parents never wanted her to follow their professional choices. However, when G.N. Balasubramaniam heard Vasanthakumari sing at her house, he prevailed upon her parents to allow him to take her under his wing. And there was no looking back.

After Subbudu reviewed Vasanthakumari for *The Statesman*, he had the chance to witness and review her performance at Shanmukhananda Hall in the early 1950s in Bombay. Sadasivam who was running *Kalki* along with Kalki Krishnamurthy, asked Subbudu to send a review of her performance. While he praised the young girl, she misinterpreted the review. Subbudu could not understand the reason behind Vasanthakumari's disappointment which was cleared after her husband intervened and rang Subbudu. Among other things, he requested him to interpret what he meant when he wrote: "She is like an Amazon who gives a full throttle rendition." Subbudu was able to reassure them.

The music in the 1940s and 50s was classically rich and vibrant. However, while G.N. Balasubramaniam's music appealed to the cerebral, the Kalpanaswarams by Madurai Mani Iyer haunted his fans. But one musician who became one of the most respected figures in the history of Carnatic music was Semmangudi Srinivasa Iyer. Subbudu met him for the first time in the mid-1950s. After his successful stint as the roving critic for the *Kalki* magazine, Sadasivam once again requested Subbudu to cover the Bombay festival.

Semmangudi and Subbudu were introduced to each other at the residence of S. Kannan who was the magazine representative in the city. Since Semmangudi was a family friend of Sadasivam and Subbulaskhmi, Kannan was asked to make arrangements for his stay. Meanwhile, Sadasivam asked Subbudu to contact Kannan for his stay in the city as well. As luck would have it, Kannan made the arrangements for both the men at his residence. Throughout his stay in Bombay, Subbudu shared his room with Semmangudi.

The singer had heard of Subbudu and had read a few of his reviews in the magazine but both men never had an opportunity to sit across each other in the proscenium space. It is believed Semmangudi checked with Subbudu on the veracity of his credentials that enabled him to cover Carnatic music.

In his distinctive manner, Subbudu answered Semmangudi by narrating an incident. He told him that once there was a man who didn't know how to cook at all. One day, tired of having food cooked by his wife, he decided to eat at a restaurant. He ordered a *masala dosa*. The moment he ate *dosa*, he shouted for the waiter. The waiter came and the man blasted him for making *masala dosa* out of rotten potatoes. Subbudu told Semmangudi that he too had a taste for *masala dosa*.

It is a different matter that Subbudu had a first hand knowledge of music and he was a musician himself but somehow, he did not feel like enlightening Semmangudi at that point of time.

While Subbudu's criticism of Semmangudi's style of music was going to become an epic affair, he found himself embroiled in a controversy as soon as he reached Delhi.

In 1952, Sh. B.V. Keskar was given the independent charge of the Ministry of Information and Broadcasting. His tenure, which lasted a decade, was witness to a number of controversies.

In his mid-tenure, the minister realised that the harmonium was a tempered scale instrument and therefore was unsuitable as an accompanying instrument for Indian music. All India Radio announced a blanket ban on the use of the harmonium for any studio recording and concerts, despite knowing that Hindustani musicians, especially the Maharashtrians, could not do without it. Even Carnatic singers protested against the move. Subbudu who had mastered the art of playing the harmonium for Carnatic vocalists raised his banner of revolt.

He along with Bade Ghulam Ali Saheb, musician B.L. Deshpande, tabla player Gyan Prakash Ghosh and others expressed deep resentment of the interference by the government in matters of pure culture.

In fact, the ban was lifted years after Keskar ceased to be a minister and not before seminars were organised by All India Radio and other bodies to review it. Unlike the violin, which enjoyed certain patronage from the government, the harmonium never found this favour even though great musicians like Perur Subramanya Dikshithar and G.S. Kasi Iyer had demonstrated the magic they could cast with the instrument. Subbudu always maintained that the notes of the harmonium were "flawless, unsagging and constant".

There was another side to the story. Even before the actual ban, harmonium players were not given permission to perform as independent artistes. At best, a harmonium player could be an accompanist. If at all there was talk to do away with that kind of partiality, a harmonium player was not given A grade at All India Radio. He or she could at best be a B+ category artiste. Among others, M.S. Subbulakshmi too strongly protested against the move, especially since Subbudu was a victim of this high handedness.

Moreover after a period of time, the harmonium had become a refined instrument with a first class harmonium having four sets of reeds, each covering three and a half octaves, encompassing sub-bass, bass, medium and female. Incidentally, Subbudu had gained fame in Rangoon as a genius at the harmonium, something he was to showcase repeatedly, while accompanying various musicians and dancers. However, in our times it seems the harmonium did lose out because of lack of professional and serious players. Today, the Carnatic vocal recitals do not have this instrument.

Subbudu is a name to be reckoned with in the field of music, fine arts and journalism. The depth of his knowledge in the intricacies of music, dance and drama is unquestionable.

— M.S. Subbulakshmi in a letter written to the DG, AIR recommending Subbudu for a top slot for the harmonium

The intervention made by the minister was just the beginning of the politicisation of Indian performing arts. In the decades that were to follow, artistes were going to use their clout with the ministers to pressurise critics on one hand, and for getting awards on the other.

India's first Prime Minister Pt. Jawaharlal Nehru, who floated the idea of having organisations devoted to art and literature, would have been dismayed at the growth of this nexus.

In May 1951, the Ministry of Education adopted a resolution to "constitute a national academy of dance, drama and music, to be known as 'Sangeet Natak Akademi'." The same year the Presidential Awards were constituted before they were renamed as Sangeet Natak Akademi awards. The Akademi came into being in January 1953. Among the noticeable members of the first General Council were Musiri Subramania Iyer and Ariyakudi Ramanuja Ayengar. Sh. P.V. Rajamannar was the first Chairperson of the Akademi.

The early 1950s were marked by a deluge of cultural events that sought to unite India's diverse cultural traditions.The first music festival was organised in 1954. The same year the first national drama festival also took place. The very next year the first national dance festival was organised.

Ariyakudi Ramanuja Iyengar was the first recipient of the award for Carnatic music while the second award went to Semmangudi Srinivasa Iyer. Maharaja Puram Viswanatha Iyer won the award in

1955. M.S. Subbulaskmi became the first woman Carnatic singer to win the award in 1956 followed by Musiri in 1957. By the beginning of the 1960s, G.N. Balasubramaniam, D.K. Pattammal and T. Brinda had won an SNA award each.

However, Subbudu could never forget the occasion when the Nadaswaram maestro T.N. Rajarathinam Pillai got his award. He had come to Delhi to receive the SNA award for his contribution to Carnatic instrumental music. Dr. Narayana Menon who was instrumental in getting Subbudu a job at *The Statesman*, told him to keep a close watch on Rajarathinam to ensure he did not have a drink. As Subbudu recalled, "Rajarathinam was an alcoholic and Menon wanted to ensure that he behaved himself in the presence of the President of India." He was staying at the Marina Hotel. At about 4:30 pm Subbudu told Rajarathinam that his car had arrived.

"Is it a pleasure or a van ?", he asked Subbudu. In Tamil Nadu, pleasure means car. Subbudu told him that two vans had arrived. One for him and one for the orchestra. Rajarathinam lost his cool and shouted back, "Do they think I am dead that they have sent a van to pick me up? This is an insult, I will not attend the function."

Subbudu tried to pacify Rajarathinam and rang Narayana Menon to bail himself out of the crisis. Menon scolded Subbudu and asked him to get two air-conditioned cars. Subbudu was greatly relieved when Rajarathinam relented but when they reached the venue there was another surprise waiting for them.

All the awardees were seated on impressive looking chairs but there was no chair for Rajarathinam. He got annoyed and said, "Enough is enough. I have received many awards and I don't need this." Subbudu told the organisers that unless he was treated well, he would leave.

In 10 minutes, chairs arrived for him and his artistes. Before the function began, Secretary Nirmala Joshi walked up to him and imperiously said, "Aye! Mr. Rathinam, you are famous for *Todi*, play it." He rendered *Kalyani*!

Subbudu never forgot the instance when Rajarathinam was booed by the North Indian audience when he began playing after Ustad Bismillah Khan on the Independence Day at the Red Fort. Nadaswaram is the South Indian version of the wind instrument Shehnai.

Rajarathinam was the *asthana* musician of the Tiruvaduthurai Adheenam and he even castigated the Mahadipati when he asked him to play *Todi* which he was famous for, even when he was already doing so for an hour.

Incidentally, Bala was the first Bharatanatyam dancer to win the SNA award in 1955 and was followed by Rukmini Devi in 1956-57. Mylapore Gowri Amma who also tutored renowned Bharatanatyam dancer Yamini Krishnamurthy received the SNA award in 1957-58.

By the time Mylapore Gowri Amma received her award, Subbudu was well on his way to making his mark in Madras. A catalyst in that development was Kalki Krishnamurthy's death in 1954.

The man who had been a nationalist writer, a journalist, a novelist and a music critic rolled into one, was gone, too suddenly, too soon. His colleagues and admirers felt that the void created by his death was never going to be filled again. There was a general impression that the golden age of music criticism had ended with Kalki's death. Subbudu's work as a critic had still gone unnoticed largely because as long as Kalki was alive, Subbudu did not cover the Madras season and all that he covered for *Kalki* magazine was understandably overshadowed by Kalki's own writings. To put it in another way, Kalki was a self-multiplying brand, whereas Subbudu was an innovative idea with a strong potential.

The fact of the matter was that Subbudu knew about this only too well. Much as he respected Kalki for the platform he provided, he understood that sooner than later he had to come out of his shadow to carve his own identity. Though Kalki's death devastated Subbudu because he had lost a mentor, it also posed a serious challenge before him to capture the space that had fallen vacant.

Meanwhile, Subbudu's interactions with various artistes from the South gave him a hint of what to expect during the season. Even before he met or wrote about established artistes, he had a fair idea of the circle of sycophants which almost always accompanied the artistes whereever they went and was partly responsible for the stagnation in their growth as artistes. It must be noted that because artistes had begun relying on *sabhas*, this circle of followers worked as a 24x7 PR machinery as well. However there were some artistes who despite being surrounded by such men, managed to balance it with the sanctity of their art.

Ariyakudi Ramanuja Ayengar had come to Delhi to perform at the invitation of the Karnataka Sangeet Sabha. Since he was the most influential singer of his time, *The Statesman* decided not to send Subbudu and instead asked V.S. Maniam, Chief Reporter of the paper in Delhi to cover the concert. Meanwhile, Maniam asked Subbudu to accompany him so that he could help him to understand the intricacies of Ariyakudi's performance. *The Statesman* had decided to have a special story on Ariyakudi and therefore, after the performance, Subbudu and Maniam went to meet Ariyakudi in his hotel room. Maniam asked him how the standard of the audience had changed. Ariyakudi's answer best summed up the democratisation of art. He said: "Earlier there was depth, now there is width."

On one hand, Ariyakudi referred to kings, zamindars and chieftains who were the patrons of arts and cultivated artistes because they loved and understood the arts and therefore had depth. On the other, he took a swipe at the general audience, who knew little and had its real power in the collective judgement it passed on the artiste.

Subbudu's next question to Ariyakudi led to a confrontation between Maniam and Ariyakudi's helpers and followers. He asked him if he had made any changes in his style given the fact that the audience had changed. Ariyakudi flatly refused and claimed he had maintained the purity of style.

Subbudu then asked him, how he could still be so popular given the fact that the audience, though larger in number, knew so little? Ariyakudi's men immediately warned Subbudu not to cross-question the revered musician. At this Maniam, told them that as an artiste, Ariyakudi was accountable for what he did as a musician.

Ariyakudi was perhaps the most credible artiste to give an actual account of how the change of audience had affected the style of singing and choice of songs. This is because Ariyakudi was credited with consolidating the concert pattern of the present day Carnatic music *kutcheri*. However, his Guru Ramanatha Srinivasa Iyengar was the one who invented the concert pattern after perceiving a shift in the patronage system.

Incidentally, Subbudu found another equally talented Carnatic singer Maharajapuram Vishwanath Iyer's style very peculiar. When he used to sing on the higher scale, he would gesticulate indicating he had reached the highest pitch while his voice would stop completely. Once he was supposed to give a concert in Delhi. The singer was already presenting a concert at Calcutta and could not come on time. He arrived the following day and apologised to the governing members of the Karnataka Sangeet Sabha. Furious for for not informing the *Sabha* before hand, a committee member rose and threatened the singer. Seeing the high tension level, the singer decided to sing immediately at a hurriedly called concert. However, the self-effacing singer fell out with Subbudu at a later stage when he misunderstood Subbudu's remark on his unique style of singing, which he had developed owing to a physical disability. In fact the singer appeared natural in his style but he was given to understand that Subbudu wrote about his physical disability.

In his writings, Subbudu blended the aspirations of the *rasikas* with those of his own as a critic by using everyday occurrences and events as similes and metaphors to describe the preformance and the ambience of concerts. This was accentuated with Subbudu's knowledge and his naturally vitriolic writing style. The result was a highly readable, controversial piece which further proved the growing popularity of the market as the decisive force with Subbudu acting as the instigator.

While Subbudu was able to write in English the way he wanted to with little interference from his editors, he had become conscious of his style in Tamil as he had grown closer to Kalki.

Meanwhile, Krishnamoorthy's senior boss at All India Radio recorded a duet between K.S. Narayanaswamy and Narayana Menon with another great artiste on the *veena*. The duet was recorded abroad and on listening to it a Western critic had extolled it to the skies saying that if ever he was banished to a Robinson Crusoe island and given the choice to take one precious thing, he would take that recording. On listening to that recording, Subbudu wrote, "Yes on one condition, that he should take all the copies with him." It was arguably the most embarrassing moment in Krishnamoorthy's career who had to steal the copy of the paper from his boss's office and had to ensure that he missed reading the review.

Apart from critiquing live concerts and dance recitals, Subbudu also used to write reviews of the concerts aired live on All India Radio. Since the family did not have a radio set at that point, Subbudu used to visit his neighbour's home to listen to the concerts. Chandra was not too happy seeing her husband visiting someone else's house to do his work, so she prevailed upon him, and hence Subbudu bought his first radio set in 1955. There was excitement at home when the delivery man knocked on the door. He taught Chandra how to operate the set and she later taught the children. However, Subbudu could never learn it and whenever he wanted to listen to a music concert or news for that matter, he had to seek help. In one of the most poignant moments of his life after his wife's death, Subbudu discovered that he could not operate the TV either. He has learnt it since but he still cannot escape his wife's memory each time he switches it on.

Discovering the Sting

In 1957, Sadasivam officially sent an invitation to Subbudu to cover the Madras season. There were a few *sabhas* at that time. It would not be far-fetched to say that the Madras season revolved around the Music Academy. Subbudu was extremely excited about the trip and he took a fortnight's leave from his work. Beginning that year, he did not miss his office for a single day so that he could get leave in December without any hiccups.

During this trip, he also discovered that M.S. Subbulakshmi was not only a great singer but a humble hostess who outstretched herself to keep her guests at ease. Whenever Subbudu stayed at Kalki Gardens, MS made sure that, she had her meals with him. Sadasivam was fond of flowers and took a keen interest in maintaining an impressive garden located at the entrance of their residence. Among other things, MS used to pester Subbudu to mimic other musicians before her. Since Subbudu was a well-known harmonium player, MS requested him to accompany her on a few occasions as well.

I learnt to be humble from MS.

— Subbudu on what he learnt from
Bharat Ratna M.S. Subbulakshmi

Artistes who had met Subbudu in Delhi were surprised to see him covering their recital in Madras. Subbudu's sister Dr. Padmasini was a great source of encouragement during this time since she knew that her brother had the passion and the commitment to serve the world of music and dance. Though Subbudu started out as a music critic, he was going to gather power and fame owing to his dance criticism. As long as he remained with *Kalki*, he covered Kalakshetra's dance productions with great interest. However, over a period of time, he began to feel the burden of writing for *Kalki* magazine especially since Sadasivam had asked him not to write in his style.

Subbudu was indebted to Kalki and Sadasivam for having confidence in him and therefore chose not to argue for his right to write the way he wished to. In a few years' time, Subbudu was going to distinguish himself as a caustic writer whose pungent punches full of puns were set to unnerve many prima donnas.

Incidentally, Subbudu's daughter Ragini was thirty-five days old when he made his first journey to Madas as a music critic. The year 1957 was a crucial one for the Indian performing arts as well. Sangeet Natak Akademi organised the first national music seminar on March 31, 1957 which was inaugurated by Justice T.L. Venkatarama Iyer. The seminar was significant for two things. Firstly, it brought Hindustani and Carnatic music under the same platform and secondly, it sought to revive the tradition of Drupad.

On the dance front, while seventeen-year-old Yamini Krishnamurthy gave her debut Bharatanatyam dance performance in Madras in 1957, Guru Kelucharan Mohapatra developed and presented his Orissi dance repertoire in a two hour format through thirteen-year-old Sanjukta. A year ago, young Bharatanatyam dancer Padma Subrahmanyam had her *arangetrum* under her Guru Vazhuvoor Ramiah Pillai. The same year, Rukmini Devi was honoured with a Padma Bhushan. Bala-saraswati received it the following year.

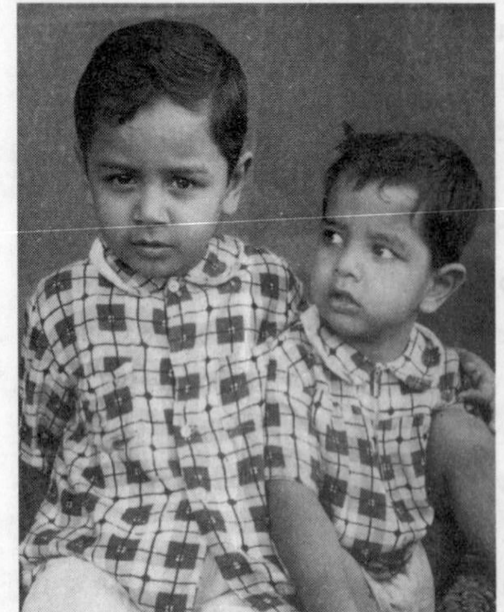

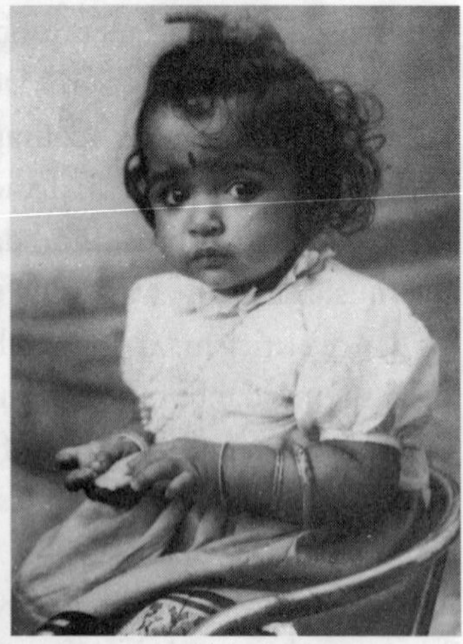

Subbudu's children Sriram and Ravi, and little Ragini

The sacred thread ceremony in the early 1960s
Subbudu and Chandra with Sriram and Ravi

Ravi with his grandfather Venkataraman

Before Subbudu left for Madras, he met Swami Hari Das Giri, who became a source of lifelong inspiration for him. Haridas Giri was yet to be anointed as a saint when Subbudu met him. He had come to Moti Bagh in New Delhi at the invitation of the residents' association to perform Harikatha and sing *bhajans*. Unfortunately, his accompanist on the harmonium was unable to make it to the function, so Haridas Giri asked the organisers, if they knew of anyone who could play with him. Since by then Subbudu had become a familiar figure because of his writings in *The Statesman,* and for his own weekly *bhajan* singing, he was requested to accompany Haridas.

Subbudu did not know who Haridas was and he categorically told the organisers that he did not have time to waste. When they tried to persuade him, he asked them, "Is he really good enough?" Subbudu's arrogance was to confront him years later when at a function held to mark his 75th birthday, Swami Haridas Giri inaugurated the celebrations.

Meanwhile, when Subbudu played for Haridas, he could not believe that someone could sing so well. After the performance was over, he sought forgiveness from Haridas Giri. Though Subbudu tightened his grip on the Carnatic music and dance scene, he kept on doing reality checks to keep his ego in control. His sensitivity and fear of God saved him from getting caught in his own image.

The man who does not have ego, he goes.

— Subbudu, while responding to the accusation that he offended many artistes

Subbudu's rendezvous with Swamiji occurred a few days after he moved to Moti Bagh residence with his family. The women living in the colony had a ladies club. Every fortnight they used to meet and spend time with each other. Chandra knew of the club but never had the time or the inclination to be a part of it. Since Deepawali was round the corner, women living in Chandra's block specially requested her to take time off for a couple of hours. She reluctantly agreed.

Chandra wrapped little Ragini in a shawl and took her along. When she returned, she found that a major theft had taken place at her house. Six silver plates, along with other precious items had been stolen. Chandra immediately called Subbudu and told him about the incident. She feared the worst but his opening question put her at ease for the rest of her life. He asked her, "Are you and the children safe?" The incident became a family legend as the years elapsed because it not only indicated Subbudu's love for his family but also his lack of ambition about material comforts.

In the meantime Subbudu's trip to Madras raised eyebrows in Delhi especially of a Jewish refugee from Budapest in Hungary, Dr. Charles Fabri. In the 1950s and 60s, he was *The Statesman's* most revered dance and art critic.

Subbudu's first meeting with him was not a very pleasant experience, even though both men soon learnt to respect each other's space. This was more so since, Charles and Subbudu knew that while the former was deeply entrenched in the organisation and was an integral part of *The Statesman* in Delhi, the latter had a better idea of dance and music. However, Charles was an extremely respected figure among the dancers of the time and he was quoted extensively in order to judge a dancer's status. A look at the old brochures of veteran dancers reminds us of Fabri's golden period.

> ***Though Fabri was knowledgeable, Subbudu surpassed him. While Subbudu was passionately writing about Bharatanatyam, he also made a huge contribution to the growth of Kathak as well.***
>
> *— Kathak maestro Uma Sharma, who interacted with both Fabri and Subbudu professionally*

On March 30, 1958, the Sangeet Natak Akademi, with the help of V. Raghavan, Rukmini Devi, Hari Upal and Uday Shankar organised the first ever national dance seminar. The nine-day seminar was inaugurated by Humayun Kabir, the then Union Minister for Scientific Research and Cultural Affairs.

During the seminar, Subbudu had a chance to interview Bala for the first time. Like now, even then Subbudu was concerned about the Sringara-Bhakti controversy, which divided, defined and differentiated Bharatanatyam. Subbudu asked Bala about the future of the dance form. For an art, which had been resurrected only two decades ago, the question seemed out of sync. However, Bala's reply surprised him. She observed, "There is no future for Bharatanatyam. It will die with me." Subbudu realised much later that Bala was Bharatanatyam.

Interestingly, till a few years ago, contemporary dancer Chandralekha too thought the same. She had said, "Balasaraswati was Bharatanatyam. She is no longer there. Kalanidhi has been attempting it. The rest is fake."

In Bharatanatyam, abhinaya is a suggestion, not a statement.

— Subbudu on the relevance of abhinaya in Bharatanatyam

Bala's comments reflected her dismay and anger towards the new definitions of Sadirattam and there were moments when she was embroiled in terse exchanges with Rukmini Devi over the way abhinaya was to be presented on proscenium. Incidentally, at that seminar Rukmini Devi spoke at length about the changes that had taken place in Bharatanatyam and the factors that contributed to them.

It is believed that few months later, during a Kalakshetra demonstration in Delhi, Balasaraswati suddenly appeared and observed, "If you remove *sringara* from dance, what will people like us do?" Rukmini Devi answered, "I have no problem with sex or love, nor with portraying *sringara*, but the dance should not be sexy. Sexiness has no place in our arts."

While there is no doubt that Rukmini Devi was arguably the most influential and significant figure in shaping and preserving the dane form, Subbudu felt that her dance was dry compared to Bala's who lived each moment. He was weary of Rukmini Devi's stress on the *bhakti* element in dance which he thought, was taken too literally by her students.

A leading Kalakshetra alumni who was approached for an interview on Subbudu's life and times, refused to comment saying she did not wish to be part of any controversy because Rukmini Devi's name would be dragged in unnecessarily.

It is a pity that we never grow up to understand that human beings are not blessed with smooth ends. They become refined over a period of time. Rukmini Devi did what no one else could have. On a lighter note, the dancer, without checking the facts ended up saying, "I cannot answer any question because you are a controversial writer working on the life of a controversial man."

Subbudu was always cautious while describing the *abhinaya* content of the Kalakshetra students who, he felt, had been filled to the brim with the *bhakti bhava*. In his write-ups, he often mentioned his concerns and criticised the way certain Kalakshetra productions were choreographed.

Once, while stressing the concept of action–reaction, Subbudu criticised the way the students started peforming *jatis* at a drop of a hat. Recounting a particular incident which, he remembers vividly, he said that during a production on Sita Swayambar, King Janak continued dancing for a rather long duration, while Sita and Rama along with others maintained stoic postures seemingly unimpressed with Janak's performance. The next time Rukmini Devi saw Subbudu, she asked his uncle and father, "Who asked you to bring this crowd?" Subbudu's niece who was about to perform in the dance production walked out on hearing Rukmini Devi's remarks.

That aside, as the years passed, Subbudu's fears on the way dancers would look at *bhakti* came true. Watching them talk on spirituality and *bhakti* and upliftment, Subbudu could not help ridiculing them, often saying that he would kick any dancer who talked of *bhakti* because dance is an entertaining art and it should be treated as such.

Though, for Subbudu, Rukmini Devi was a stunningly beautiful woman, he felt Balasaraswati had the real ability to transcend on stage and this when her items were full of *sringara*. Balasaraswati had her own logic to explain the richness of *sringara* in the perfomance of any *devadasi*. She often said, "the middle class housewife could never be successful in *abhinaya* because, she was too comfortable and satisfied in her domestic security" but the *devadasi* had to remain a mystery to her lovers, to keep their interest alive in her. "Only a woman who wakes up in the morning to find her lover gone knows what *viraha* is" maintained the *abhinaya* queen

Subbudu's argument was simple—try separating *sringara* from everyday life. He further asked dancers to understand the import of the lyrics of the songs they performed.

While Subbudu was actively following the *sringara-bhakti* controversy he kept his eyes and ears open to spot latest talents-be it in music or dance. In 1959, a young *mridangist* accompanied vocalist Dwaram Venkataswami Naidu for a concert in Delhi. Subbudu covered the concert and especially praised the *mridangist*, T.V. Gopalakrishnan. One of India's best known faces of Carnatic music TVG is one of the very few artistes who are accomplished vocalists and instrumentalists. TVG who was in his mid-twenties at that time got a shot in his arm since Subbudu's review marked the beginning of a long and eventful career. However, at the beginning of the 1960s, Subbudu did a turnaround on his talent. He was accompanying M.D. Ramanathan in one of the concerts, held at the Music Academy. Mr. Ramanathan had one of the lowest pitched voices in the music fraternity at that time. TVG had to therefore alter the pitch of his *mridangam* which forced Subbudu to comment that "T.V. Gopalakrishnan jumped into the well with his *mridangam*." TVG was also a living example of the talent in the wings, because even though he had started singing quite early and had his first studio recording for the radio in 1944, it took him nearly three decades to make a debut on stage as a classical vocalist. It was not about lacking talent but the presence of stalwarts in the music arena. All through, he has valued Subbudu's support and contribution to his art.

Around the same time, Subbudu came into contact with one of the employees from his department, P. D.S. Verma. As he discovered more about him, he found that Verma was a single earning member who had great family responsibilities. Since Subbudu was looking for an assistant to do his sundry work, he asked Verma if he would be interested in earning a little extra. Verma agreed and became Subbudu's assistant.

As a music critic for *The Statesman*, Subbudu had to be alert because those days performances were reviewed on a daily basis. As soon as his office used to end, Subbudu had to rush to the performance venue to watch the recital. He used to leave for *The Statesman* from there at about 8:30 pm. By 10:30 pm he had to get his article typed and filed.

It is remarkable that even in a high-pressure environment, Subbudu did not take any notes while covering a recital. His critics regarded it as a stunt on his part. They attributed his ability to recall and remember things to his youth. However, in his career spanning nearly six decades, there was never a moment in Subbudu's life when he was caught taking notes. In fact, he stopped his assistants from even taking the programme pamphlets and often assailed them for their poor memory power. Moreover, since he had an amazing memory, he never kept a phone diary; name a person, and Subbudu remembered his or her phone number and even postal addresses. Unfortunately for Chandra, whenever he got late, she couldn't do anything but wait helplessly because she did not know who to call. However, her death also took away from Subbudu his ability to recall the timeline of events off hand.

During the course of this work, frequently, Subbudu was pressed hard to recollect the incidents in his life as they happened. Subbudu expressed his helplessness and instead offered to be anecdotal. It is rather sad that Chandra was not alive to share her thoughts on Subbudu, the woman whose presence made and unmade the man.

Interestingly, the man who is known for his cut and dry writing style didn't know how to deal with people in general. Those days, every Saturday the family used to visit Subbudu's sister Pattammal's house for a get together which included a variety of activities, from mimicry sessions to poetry sessions, concluding with *bhajan* singing led by Subbudu. He and his entire family continued visiting Pattammal's residence even after his children had become parents. However, Pattammal's husband was extremely strict about cleanliness because of which Chandra had to constantly manage Subbudu's stuff, especially when they stayed over for the night.

> ***I am clumsy. I could do all this only because of Chandra.***
>
> —*Subbudu*

Artistes and their accompanists completed his world and there was nothing more that he cherished. However, when he had to face people from the real world, Subbudu stumbled. Often at family gatherings, while Subbudu tried to enthral the people around with his puns, Chandra did the damage control exercise, often explaining what he meant even as the man chose one victim after another.

Subbudu and his older sister Pattammal on his eightieth birthday

His children too remember that Pattammal and Chandra were always with him whenever they were present at a family function. While Pattammal's role was to knock on his knuckles and chide him whenever he said something he was not supposed to, Chandra used her presence of mind to apply balm on the heart burns Subbudu caused with his tactless talk.

Even though he could be unabashedly harsh in his satire, Subbudu was very simple at heart and his family was only too aware of it. Often when his brothers and sister called him, he asked them about their health and then passed the phone to Chandra. He was too naïve to even understand that he had to demonstrate his love and concern. Subbudu never did that and fortunately for him, people understood.

His three children grew up in an atmosphere of music and drama rehearsals at home. Whenever Subbudu saw an actor not performing his role perfectly, he shouted at him, giving glimpses of a shrewd critic to his children. During the rehearsals, Chandra had to ensure that the actors were served with regular cups of coffee and snacks. While on one hand, Chandra had to play a perfect host, on the other, she had to make sure that the children studied properly and did not waste too much time watching their father run a riot in the drawing room.

And when not watching theatre recitals, Subbudu was invited to watch dance rehearsals. Once a leading Bharatanatyam Guru invited Subbudu to witness the rehearsal of his student living in his neighbourhood. After it ended, he asked Subbudu about the rehearsal. He told him that the song was in one tempo while the *jatis* were in another. Subbudu had kept his finger on the problem and till he did not force a solution from the dancers, he kept mentioning it to them. Most dancers were performing to the lyrics at linear speed whereas the *nritta* portions were choreographed at varying speeds. Subbudu felt that this gave a feeling as if *jatis* and the music were dragged to decrease and increase the tempo respectively.

But inspite of all the artistic pressures, Subbudu did not allow his work to suffer and his acting skills came in handy at his office as well. This helped him tackle any situation with a dash of humour. Thanks to this and his writing talent Subbudu became the most popular man of his office.

One fine morning, V.V. Subramaniam, a junior officer who had joined recently at Subbudu's office approached him just before lunch time and enquired if he had five minutes to spare. Subbudu asked him what the matter was and wondered if there was anything he could do for him. Subramaniam told Subbudu that he was an avid reader of his articles in both the languages and that he did not know that "the great Subbudu" was his senior colleague. Subbudu smiled, thanked Subramaniam and asked him if he was an artiste himself. Subramaniam replied in the negative but he told Subbudu that if he could be of any assistance to him, he would feel obliged. Since P. D. S. Verma had already been transferred, Subbudu decided to employ Subramaniam as his assistant. The only problem with V. V. Subramaniam was that he was not too good with time management and it was something which bothered Subbudu whenever he took him for the Madras season.

Interestingly, when Subramaniam accompanied Subbudu for the first time, he noticed that Subbudu was not carrying a pad and a pen. He thought perhaps, Subbudu had expected him to carry one for him. Before Subbudu could know what was happening, Subramaniam panicked and apologetically told him that he had forgotten to bring a notebook. Subbudu was surprised to see Subramaniam turning pale but he realised soon enough what the matter was. He told him that he did not take notes at any performance. Everything he witnessed was stored in his memory bank. Subramaniam was shocked and never recovered from it. The following day, he saw the write up in *The Statesman* and could not believe his eyes when he saw the names of the items and accompanists mentioned correctly. This is not to say that Subbudu never made any technical errors. In fact, he made a number of errors but sought forgiveness whenever artistes informed him about genuine inaccuracies in his write ups.

Even as Subbudu was getting more involved in the politics of the world of the performing arts, Chandra stretched herself to look after their children's needs. At the same time, she did not allow any communication gap to develop between her husband and their children. On their part, the children never complained about Subbudu's absence from home. They grew up watching Subbudu just the way he was — attending to his office work and busy in the world of music and dance.

However, Subbudu gave the same freedom to his children which he got from them. He never interfered in their lives and never interrogated his boys if they came home late. If not anything else, Subbudu's boys benefited from the fact that their father was on the school committee of the Madrasi school they studied in. So even if they scored lower marks in junior classes, the school teachers did not take them to task.

Though Subbudu's only daughter, Ragini was a pampered child, she never got an opportunity to hear a bedtime story from her father. Even as she carried the grudge as a kid, she forgave him when she discovered what her father was doing. But sometimes, she demanded Subbudu's attention and whenever that happened, Subbudu made sure he was around for her.

When Ragini began going to school, she made it a daily ritual to say goodbye to her Appa before she left for school. No matter how late Subbudu came home, he was always up to greet his daughter. The father and daughter became so used to the idea that during the days when Ragini stayed at home, Subbudu refused to go to work, till she woke up and said goodbye to him.

Like her brothers, Ragini attended music and dance concerts with her father and enjoyed watching him feeling ecstatic or becoming mad depending on the artiste's performance. She liked watching her father on stage and whenever possible, insisted on attending the concert where Subbudu accompanied an artiste on the harmonium. On her part, Chandra encouraged Ragini to attend music concerts because she felt her daughter had the talent to become a professional Carnatic singer. However, each time Ragini went with Subbudu, she prayed that he knew that their daughter was with him.

It is just that Subbudu sometimes forgot her. Once, he took Ragini to see a dance performance at Subroto Park in Delhi where he accompanied the dancer on the harmonium. After the performance ended, Subbudu was so engrossed in the post-mortem of the programme that he forgot Ragini had come with him. Everyone had left the auditorium and Subbudu had reached halfway home when the vocalist, who was with Subbudu, told him that he had forgotten his daughter in the auditorium. Subbudu rushed back and found his daughter, sitting calm and composed waiting for her father.

He felt genuinely sorry about the entire incident and apologised to Chandra. The couple thanked God that nothing happened to Ragini and soon both forgot about the incident. Meanwhile, Chandra decided to employ a music teacher to hone her daughter's talent. Much as Ragini wished to become a singer, she could not realise her dream. It so happened that the teacher, who was extremely conscious of Subbudu's status as a star critic, never allowed Ragini to sing alone in her father's presence. He sang along with her possibly for two reasons. One, to impress Subbudu with his own talent as a singer and two, not to allow him a chance to judge his own daughter and therefore the teacher's efforts as a Guru. Ragini yearned for an opportunity to sing alone

Ragini attending a music class

in her father's presence. But he was rarely at home. Finally when she got a chance to sing before him, Subbudu ended up scolding her as if he was witnessing a *kutcheri*. Ragini was so discouraged that she lost the will to be a professional singer. Though Subbudu pointed out her mistakes, he did not tell her how to correct them. On their part, Subbudu and Chandra thought, Ragini's guru would teach their daughter properly, but that was never to be. Morever, he was also against Ragini learning dance since he felt that it was too expensive a hobby to have. It is ironical that he got maximum fame as a dance critic.

However, when Ragini's daughter Purvaja sang before him for the first time, he made sure the critic was gagged and kept aside, as the grandfather appreciated each moment of his granddaughter's singing.

By the time Subbudu became a figure of fear and authority, his writings had left several artistes frustrated. And, even though he hurt artistes in his zealous pursuit to make them perfect, Subbudu himself could not escape being the victim of the hate campaign that the artistes launched against him. During every such incident, even though he appeared composed, cunning and courageous, he drifted into moments of extreme sadness. As a loner all his life, Subbudu fought braving the sun but always built a cocoon around him which could only be unravelled by his wife.

Subbudu with Ragini's daughter Purvaja

Once in 1962, he reviewed an annual festival organised by a bureaucrat. Incidentally, a leading shehnai player and a Kathak dancer were the regular feature on the festival and were favourites of the organiser(s).

The festival looked like a one-man affair with the general secretary of the organising committee portraying himself as an all-powerful person who could make or break the career of an artiste through his festival. Subbudu took a dig at this in his article which affected the then Union Home Minsiter of State. The minister was the patron of the festival and had little knowledge of the misgivings taking place.

Even though there were usual denials and counter charges against Subbudu, *The Statesman* stood by their man and in turn the minister had to seek forgiveness over an intense telephonic conversation with Mr. Charlton, the then editor-in-chief of the paper. Though the incident ended in good faith, Subbudu soon started receiving threatening letters in typical Bollywood style. It seemed strange that an art critic who packed his writing with pun and humour could incite someone to kill him.

Exactly nine days after Charlton spoke to the Minister, Subbudu received the first letter. It was a sunny Saturday morning, in the thick of winter, and Subbudu had just returned from his morning walk. The handwritten letter warned him of dire consequences if he continued writing. Subbudu did not bother about the letter and for him, the episode ended in one of his gossip sessions with his wife and colleagues. But, the letter became a hot topic of debate among Subbudu's sons. Ragini was too young to offer her thoughts on the matter.

The excitement turned into concern when Subbudu received another letter the following Saturday. It was more intimidating in its content. Subbudu's wife read the letter and implored him to tone down his writing for some time. Chandra had never asked Subbudu anything. She never complained to him about his lack of interest in the household duties. Their children too never sought their father's presence in the evenings. But that day, Chandra asked Subbudu to think of his family as well. She told him to lie low for the children's safety. Subbudu, while respecting her concern, told her that he could not change his style but he promised that he would not allow anyone to harm his family.

Meanwhile, Subbudu received a letter a week for three consecutive Saturdays. They were downright abusive and warned that his hands would be chopped off or that he would be killed, if he did not stop writing. Chandra lost her mental peace and begged Subbudu to never write again. But Subbudu had decided to meet the consequences head on. He met Mr. Venkataraman, private secretary to the then Home Minister, Sh. Lal Bahadur Shastri and narrated the entire incident to him. Incidentally, the last letter while containing a death threat also hinted at a safe passage. Subbudu was asked to give a written undertaking that he would not write again. He was asked to stand with the undertaking in his hand, at the entrance of Lodhi Gardens facing the Meteorological

Department building on the following Saturday at 5 pm in the evening. Mr. Venkataraman, after reading all the letters, introduced Subbudu to Mr. Sen, the then Director General of Special Police Establishment or the SPE. The SPE later became Central Bureau of Investigation or the CBI. In fact, Mr. Sen was one of the last Director Generals of the SPE because in less than a year, CBI replaced SPE.

With three days to go, Mr. Sen asked his deputy to draft a plan to apprehend the culprit. The next day, 16 policemen were sounded about the incident and they were asked to become part of the operation. The day arrived and Subbudu went about doing everything normally except that he was unable to contain his curiousity. He did not discuss it with his family since it would have created unnecessary tension at home. Subbudu reached the place on time. It was winter and the sun was yawning before going to sleep.

Sixteen policemen in plain clothes were doing the rounds of the area. For the next hour nothing happened. As Subbudu grew excited and nervous, he saw a white ambassador moving slowly towards him. The Meteorological Bhavan had a rotating spotlight etched on the top of its building, which fell on the ambassador the moment it was about to stop next to Subbudu. But the car, instead of halting next to him, raced away. The policemen rushed to the spot but since Subbudu was unable to notice the number of the car, they failed to catch the culprit red-handed. A few months later, it was discovered that the 'letter-man', as Subbudu referred to him was actually the organiser of the annual festival, which Subbudu had shred to pieces in his write ups.

Subbudu emerged stronger after the incident and resolved to be more aggressive than ever in exposing the ugly side of the world of arts. Meanwhile, as he began covering dance during the Madras season, he followed the performances of new as well as leading dancers performing in Delhi too. One such dancer was a young college student from Madras who took the capital by storm with her fine blend of cerebral and performing talent. She was Padma Subrahmanyam.

Padma gave her first performance in Delhi in 1963. She had impressed the audiences with her scintillating performance and the next day, a lecture demonstration by her was organised by famous linguist and archaeologist Dr. C. Shivaramamurthy at the National Museum for a select audience and the critics. Subbudu and Charles Fabri were among the few invited for the event. During the course of the lecture demonstration, Fabri told Padma that a dancer should depict an elephant's walk with a slight hunch which Padma had not done. Unaware of Fabri's stature, Padma caustically replied, "Perhaps you are talking about an old, unfed elephant whereas Sage Bharata talks of a well-fed wild elephant with a majestic walk."

The audience laughed uproariously at Padma's witty remark. Subbudu had a glint in his eyes the moment he heard Padma's reply and realised that the young girl had a mind of her own. As soon as the demonstration ended, Padma was told that the press was waiting for her. She quickly removed her make-up and changed into a different *saree*. As she headed for the press meet, Subbudu stopped her mid-way and told her that he wanted to speak to her for ten minutes exclusively. When Padma informed him that she was heading for a press conference, Subbudu told her, "I am from the press too but I do not want to waste my time there. You don't have to talk to anyone. Just talk to me and that will be enough. People waiting for you don't know anything." Interestingly, when Subbudu was saying this, he was aware that Charles Fabri was still the dance critic of the paper.

That was the beginning of Subbudu's friendship with Padma Subrahmanyam, who recalled that he told her that he knew that she would make a major contribution to the field. It is a coincidence that Padma's research on *Karnas* has been hailed as seminal work in the history of South Asian and South East Asian Art. To be sure that Padma was serious about her passion to research in dance, Subbudu asked her if she knew that she was diverging from the history of two hundred years? Padma assured him and said she was going to stand by her words and ambition.

Meanwhile, Subbudu's differences with Charles Fabri were fast becoming a part of public domain. The acerbic interactions had degenerated into full blown arguments. Subbudu began reacting to Fabri's complacency towards him after he acquired considerable space in *The Statesman* as well. It would have been interesting to know what Fabri thought of Subbudu but it seems that with the kind of attention and importance given to the Hungarian critic, by the Indian artistes, most Indian critics felt uncomfortable.

Subbudu had issues with Fabri's supposedly limited knowledge on one hand, and his larger than life image on the other. The dancers who interacted with Fabri rated him as a highly knowledgeable person, while the critics who witnessed the performances of the dancers in question and also saw Fabri's writings, thought differently. However, as long as Fabri was alive, Subbudu did not indulge in direct confrontation unless Fabri unnecessarily or officiously imposed his ideas on Indian music, on Subbudu.

Once, Humanyun Kabir, the then Minister for Education invited critics for tea at his residence. Subbudu, media commentator Amita Malik and Charles Fabri attended the meeting. The minister was particularly concerned about the lack of patronage provided by the All India Radio in popularising Rabindra Sangeet and therefore asked the critics to write about it. Subbudu told the minister that there was nothing like Rabindra Sangeet, there were only Rabindra lyrics. Amita Malik who shared the minister's concern was going to complete her sentence when Charles Fabri at once asked Subbudu, "What do you know about Rabindra

Sangeet?" Before Subbudu could answer him, Fabri shot another volley at him and expressed surprise, as to how he could even know anything about Rabindra Sangeet in the first place and talk about it.

Subbudu told Fabri, "When you can cover Tamil, Telugu and Marathi drama and South Indian dances without even knowing a single alphabet of the language, why can't I, who has read and sung Rabindra lyrics, and is an Indian, speak about Rabindra Sangeet?" Anticipating a showdown between the two, the Minister said, "Shanti-Shanti" before moving on to lighter issues that suited the hot tea.

While the ministers cultivated different forms of music depending on their choice and soon started influencing the policy decisions of All India Radio and much later Doordarshan, there was a growing realisation that dance had begun usurping music as a natural choice to display India's cultural heritage abroad, because of its visual impact. Many administrative and cultural changes that took place during this period indicated same. The most important being the fillip provided to Kathak in North India. On October 1, 1964, the Kathak Kendra was established. In essence, the Sangeet Natak Akademi took over the Kathak wing of the Bharatiya Kala Kendra.

Even though the Bharatiya Kala Kendra was the most presitigious institution involved in teaching Kathak, the need to develop and promote Kathak in building an image of India led to the creation of the Kendra. Since the Bharatiya Kala Kendra already had three seniormost Kathak gurus, it was felt that for two years, the Bharatiya Kala Kendra should be allowed to run the Kathak Kendra. The first Sikh male student of Kalakshetra, a dance historian and an eminent writer, Mohan Khokar became the first director in charge of the institute.

It is believed that the growing importance of Bharatanatyam in North India had accelerated the process of promoting Kathak.

It was so because the 'Nataraja' pose, so closely identified with Bharatanatyam had caught the fancy and played a major role. The most popular number expected, almost mandatory, to be performed in every programme of Bharatanatyam, was 'Natanam Aadinaar', a composition of Gopalakrishna Bharatiyar, describing the 'Aananda Taandavam' of the Lord in Chidambaram. It was felt that the growth of Bharatanatyam first by Indrani Rehman and then by Yamini Krishnamurthy in North India had eclipsed other dance forms. Indian cinema had fallen in love with this dance form. Kamala and later Vyjayanthimala were major influences behind it, both as child stars and later as professional dancers. From the Science Congress to music conferences, Bharatanatyam was making inroads in the interiors of India. Lucknow, Benaras, Patna, Allahabad among other cities had witnessed performances by leading Bharatanatyam dancers of the time even though Kathak had a strong influence on the region.

Young beautiful women had fired the national imagination. Bala, Indrani Rehman and later Sonal Man Singh became the first few female Bharatanatyam dancers to take the West by storm. It was not just dance but the captivating beauty of dancers like Indrani and Sonal which worked wonders for the dance form. In fact, Indrani introduced J.F. Kennedy to Indian classical dance through her bewitching performance. The then US President was so impressed with Indrani's recital that he sought a personal interaction with her by requesting Pt. Nehru.

Around this time, Subbudu began reviewing Hindustani music and classical dance for the *Hindustan Times* as well. Charles Fabri was the most influential dance critic of Delhi at that time and Subbudu's decision to cover dance became an easy reason for Fabri to bear a grudge against him. It was the beginning of a period of cold war between the two which ended with Fabri's death. Incidentally, Subbudu's stint with the *Hindustan Times* was short-lived and it ended abruptly because he was fired from his job. His last assignment involved reviewing a Kathakali performance. As someone who could never bring himself to appreciate the dance form, Subbudu wrote a scathing critique of the performance because he just could not relate to it at all. Within a week of writing the review, he was asked to leave the job. Subbudu hasn't been able to understand why he was told not to write again for the *Hindustan Times*.

As Subbudu's stature grew and he established a personal relationship with the artistes in Madras, he began persuading them to perform in the Capital. Subbudu was associated with Shanmukhananda Sangeetha Sabha in Delhi and he engaged artistes for the organisation occasionally. He also contributed articles to their souvenirs and made himself available for any work. Once during a concert organised by the Sabha, he discovered that even after informing the organisers, his family was made to sit in the last row of the hall. He did not ask for reservations for them but he did not expect them to be treated so shabbily. When one of his sons rushed towards him and told him, Subbudu decided to walk out of the programme immediately.

Subbudu never sought any personal favours from anyone but it's a different story that people themselves felt obliged to help him. Since he was part of the Finance Ministry, dealing with the Parliament, he got a telephone connection by virtue of his government position. However, there was some problem and his telephone was disconnected. Since he was working for *Kalki* magazine and was associated with Sadasivam and M.S. Subbulakshmi, the Kalki group offered to transfer their publication *Swarajya's* telephone connection to Subbudu. In those days *Swarajya* was billed as anti-government and his relationship with the magazine came under scrutiny. Allegations were made that Subbudu was indulging in anti-government activities but nothing could be proved because of lack of evidence. The English magazine *Swarajya* was primarily started so that Rajaji could air his views against the ruling Congress Party. The magazine was the official voice of the Swatantra Party which was founded by Rajaji when he was eighty-two years old and remained the main opposition party in the Parliament till 1969.

Meanwhile, just when Subbudu was beginning to be convinced that he wanted to move ahead and write the way he wished to, Savi met him. Savi, who was a prominent writer with the Tamil weekly *Ananda Vikatan*, had just left the magazine and joined *The Indian Express*.

Since Subbudu was not writing for *Kalki* regularly, he had also started writing for *Ananda Vikatan* off and on especially after he had been made a permanent representative of the magazine in Delhi from 1960 onwards. Savi had read Subbudu's articles in *Ananda Vikatan*.

Meanwhile, he was given the task of handling *The Indian Express'* Tamil Edition, *Dinamani Kadir*, which was a weekly paper. Savi approached Subbudu and invited him to write for *Dinamani Kadir*. Subbudu told him that he could not do so because he was loyal to the Kalki group. However, when Savi assured him that he would give him a free hand, Subbudu was tempted to accept the offer. Moreover, he informed him that to strengthen his position in the paper he had been informed to increase the sales of the paper which could happen if his paper carried lively and interesting write ups. He further added that he knew that Subbudu could help him to get an extra edge. Subbudu listened intently and after much thought agreed to write for *Dinamani Kadir* but only on one condition.

He said that he did not want his own name for his write ups. Savi understood that Subbudu did not wish to break his ties with Kalki because of Sadasivam and M.S. Subbulakshmi. And so he began writing anonymously.

Subbudu's acerbic writing style and ridiculing tone drummed the beginning of a new era of criticism. He showed little respect for the sentiments of the artistes and their fans. From his very first write up in *Dinamani Kadir*, he made it clear that he only wanted those artistes who could overawe him with their talent; else, he ripped them apart. Artistes who had survived by portraying their criticism as the violation of the sanctity of the art itself were packed off. Subbudu's refrain was, Art is sacred, not the artiste. He began pushing the artistes to imagine ambitiously.

Since he was writing incognito, there was greater curiosity to know who had dared to criticise the prima donnas. The news of the arrival of a new critic spread like wild fire and people started conjecturing about the identity of the masquerading writer. Subbudu too heard about the new writer at one of the *kutcheris* and felt amused. Copies of *Dinamani Kadir* sold like hot cakes that season and the following season, Subbudu came out of the shadows.

From the day Subbudu formally started writing for *Dinamani Kadir*, he shifted to the Express Estate. Subbudu's stay at Express Estate was going to be nothing short of a king's court in attendance. Every season he was going to receive many parents with their children in tow as well as a number of leading musicians and dancers, among them, Chandralekha too. In fact, dance critic and scholar, Dr. Sunil Kothari met Subbudu for the first time at the Express Estate during his Madras visit. The day he met her, he also bumped into a young girl, who was destined to become one of the most famous names in the history of Bharatanatyam. She was Chitra Vishweshwaran. The talented girl had come to seek Subbudu's blessings.

Most of the people came to invite me; very few came to consult me.

— Subbudu on how people valued coverage over knowledge

Subbudu's arrival at the Express Estate happened after he wrote a rather critical review of Semmangudi's performance. Interestingly, Semmangudi had also trained M.S. Subbulakshmi and was as such Sadasivam's close family friend. When Sadasivam read Subbudu's review, he subtly told him that Semmangudi was like a rose. Subbudu replied that the rose also had thorns. Even though Sadasivam and Kalki Krishnamurthy had given him his first important break, Subbudu believed that he had to write what he felt. One can speculate the face of Indian music and dance criticism if Subbudu had remained a writer in the shadow.

He informed Sadasivam about the offer he had received from *Dinamani Kadir*. Sadasivam was sensitive enough to understand that Subbudu wanted to move on. Remarkably, Subbudu's departure from *Kalki* magazine, brought him closer to Sadasivam and Subbulakshmi.

A review cannot be written on compassionate grounds.

— Subbudu

Meanwhile, artistes reacted to Subbudu in Madras as well. Subbudu attacked Guru Vazhuvoor Ramiah Pillai for his unimaginative choreography and a mistake in a *jati* and ended up questioning his credentials. This enraged his son Samraj and when he met Subbudu, he nearly beat him up. Fortunately there were people around and he was saved. Even though Subbudu was visibly shaken, he said, "What I have written is correct and I will stick to it." Later, when Guru Ramiah Pillai realised his mistake, Subbudu felt vindicated. Unlike popular impression, Subbudu was not driven by a malicious agenda of bringing down artistes, instead, he brought to their notice where they went wrong. However, he had to shout on top of his voice and stamp the ground to make his case.

Even as people began perceiving Subbudu as someone who was ruthless and cunning, the man himself went out of his way to spend more time with the artistes. He always believed that a genuine artiste can always teach a critic, because while an artiste lives his art, a critic observes his (artiste's) art.

One of the fondest memories that Subbudu still cherishes was the time when Chembai Vaidyanatha Bhagavatar, was invited to perform in Delhi and Simla. Since he was a great fan of the maestro, he decided to take care of all his needs during the entire trip. From providing him with warm clothes during his stay in Simla to managing his daily schedule, Subbudu once again relived his days as a page boy. It did not occur to him that he was a reputed critic. What excited him most was the time he got to spend with Bhagavatar and the knowledge he gained from him.

In fact, it was this thirst for knowledge that pushed Subbudu ahead. His interactions with senior *vidwans*, even if he was reviewing their performance, was marked by his desire to learn more from them, if they could afford to share, that is.

Incidentally, Subbudu learnt the ropes of dance criticism by accompanying artistes on the harmonium and the *mridangam*. From Yamini Krishnamurthy to Kanaka Srinivasan, Subbudu accompanied most of the top artistes across generations. As a rule, he never covered their recitals when he was part of their troupe. In fact, Subbudu and Padma Subrahmanyam's mother grew to respect each other because both were deft harmonium players. In music, he considered himself fortunate because he got an opportunity to accompany M.S. Subbulakshmi on one hand, and Dr. Balamurali Krishna on the other.

While Subbudu was billed as an exterminator, he increasingly found himself playing the role of a patriarch. When he was not hauling up artistes, he was taking *sabha* secretaries and their organisations to task. Whether he called the Music Academy, Agraharam (or the area where only Brahmins can enter) or he supported the Tamil Isai Movement (in the early 1940s and 50s), Subbudu always took political positions (when it came to arts) thereby forcing others to react to him. Moreover, when he was not doing that, he was fighting for the rights of the artistes themselves.

Dogs and Subbudu not allowed

— A hoarding outside the Music Academy in the mid-1980s

When Carnatic musician Papanasam Sivam was honoured with the title of Sangeet Kalanidhi, by the Music Academy, at a gala function, Subbudu noticed that as soon as the programme ended, all the organisers left the venue without checking whether the awardee had his own conveyance to go home or not. Since the musician was extremely shy, he did not ask the Academy to make arrangements. Subbudu told him, "You were the Chief Guest of the evening. They should have arranged transport for you." Next morning, in *Dinamani Kadir*, the Music Academy was retributed for its negligence.

He would walk into the sabha hall like an intoxicated elephant and go on a rampage.

— A Madras-based dancer who questioned the need to write Subbudu's biography

While Subbudu had made several enemies, he also made lifelong friendships. One of the people who has grown to be Subbudu's greatest admirers is Doordarshan Natarajan. As the name suggests, Natarajan has been one of the most powerful Directors of Madras Doordarshan. He had gone to Delhi in 1965 for a short duration to train at the All India Radio where he happened to attend a music concert at the Satyamurthy Auditorium near Birla Mandir. Two days later, Natarajan read the review of the concert by Subbudu in *The Statesman*.

Natarajan was Manna Srinivasan's friend, who was one of the earliest promoters of Indian dance and music. Manna was working with the Planning Commission and was a friend of Subbudu. Natarajan told Manna that he wanted to meet Subbudu. Manna told him that he could find Subbudu at the United News of India's (UNI) office canteen. UNI and AIR offices were at a stone's throw from each other. The following day Natarajan crossed the road and spotted Subbudu in the canteen eating *uppuma* with a spoon. He introduced himself and settled down to congratulate him for his review but not before completely interpreting Subbudu's writing style. Natarajan impressed him so much that he forgot to eat his *uppuma*! Subbudu expressed his gratitude and told Natarajan that his gesture was one of the best compliments on his writing. It was the beginning of their life long friendship.

Apart from making friends from his list of fans, Subbudu also made friendships with some fellow critics and scholars. One of them was T.S. Parthasarthy. A fellow critic, Parthasarthy spotted Subbudu for the first time at the annual Arunagiri Nada Festival. He had gone to attend the festival because Guru A.S. Raghavan was singing *bhajans* before a crowd of over a thousand people. Subbudu was accompanying Guruji on the harmonium and his command on the instrument surpised Parthasarthy especially because the notes of certain *ragas* cannot be played on the harmonium since it is a tempered instrument. The programme lasted for nearly four hours and after it ended, Pathasarthy introduced himself to Subbudu and admired his style of handling the harmonium. The following year, Guru A.S. Raghavan performed at Parthasarthy's home where Subbudu again accompanied Guruji on the harmonium. Parthasarthy had a keen interest in classical dance and after retirement he became a full-fledged dance critic and researcher.

In fact, Parthasarthy along with Subbudu and the critic of *The Times of India*, K.S. Srinivasan, used to spend time while discussing the artistes and art forms. Right from arguing over the choice of *raga* to the quality of sound, the critics had confrontation sessions dedicated to themselves each time they met. At that time, there was an impression that K.S. Srinivasan gave Subbudu a tough time because of the lucidity of his style but while he was diplomatic, Subbudu was upfront. In fact it was this honesty, which made artistes shudder. Subbudu's fellow critics, then and now feel that if he likes an artiste, he can go out of his way to help and if he does not like someone, he can be hostile. A view that started gaining ground among other critics was that Subbudu was abrasive and offensive. His criticism, they felt was too harsh to leave an artiste with any enthusiasm to perform. He razed the artiste to the ground. Subbudu reasoned with his friends by joking that he had to balance what they wrote.

I wrote a book on Bharatanatyam, but a fellow critic tore it apart. I did not know how to promote it.

— Subbudu, rueing the fact that his book, entitled Bharatanatyam, was not taken too well by his own colleagues

At the peak of his career, Subbudu appeared to be inaccessible and fearful. Artistes were afraid of him. He initially commanded respect out of fear and it was only when artistes discovered the man behind the critic, that they began respecting him out of love.

But, Subbudu could be extremely uncharitable. The difficulty was not in his caustic remarks but as artistes pointed out in his inability to see the side of an artiste, even at a time when he was himself an accomplished harmonium player. To impress Subbudu, one had to follow a simple diktat, 'Be a complete entertainer. Once on stage, you should be just concerned with the stage, the art and the audience. Everything else should become secondary.' To be fair to Subbudu, he did not ever question the wisdom of the audience because he was conscious of the fact that he was popular, thanks to his readers.

I hear you, I comment.

— Subbudu, responding to an artiste who asked him why he was targeted each time

Meanwhile, Carnatic music and classical dance had not only become a national rage but were also getting highest recognition abroad. On October 23, 1966, M.S. Subbulakshmi performed at the United Nations and created history. She achieved the feat with the help of C.V. Narasimhan who was responsible for popularising Carnatic music in the West. He was an ICS and played a crucial role in inviting MS to the UN.

For a long time the West believed that Indian classical music meant Hindustani music. But C. V. Narasimhan took it upon himself to pursuade US organisations to invite South Indian musicians. Though Subbudu had high regards for CVN, he thought of him differently as an artiste. At one of his performances attended by Subbudu, Narasimhan rendered Amritavarshini *raga* which is known to bring rain. He claimed that he sang the same *raga* in Bangkok and it rained heavily.

Next morning Subbudu wrote in his review, "I come from Burma where in the South East rains lash out for almost nine months in a year. Therefore I would have appreciated if he could invoke rain by rendering this *raga* in the dry belt of South India."

A few weeks later, the Minister in charge for Information and Broadcasting telephoned Subbudu's brother and told him to record Narasimhan. Since he was not an auditioned artiste and also did not get a favourable review, Subbudu's brother was at his wit's end. However, he told his predicament to the minister who refused to move, so later P. V. Krishnamoorthy just recorded Narasimhan but did not telecast it.

Though Subbudu was frank and brutal, he was writing at a time when some artistes were mature enough to see through his attacks and learn from them. Once while giving a performance in Delhi, M.S. Subbulakshmi gave a slight Hindustani touch to her rendering of Shudha Saveri *raga*. Since she was an extremely popular singer and an entire generation of Carnatic singers looked up to her, Subbudu feared that if the singer continued to sing like this, the entire structure would slowly be lost. This is because, a number of up and coming musicians of the next generation, saw MS as their role model. For them, what she sang was a divine gift. Whenever MS touched the wrong note, Subbudu cautioned her.

Returning to the performance, after it ended, Subbudu expressed his discomfort with her rendering of the *raga*. To correct this, the very next day, MS and Sadasivam visited him at his residence and MS sang the same song again requesting Subbudu to correct her immediately, so that she did not commit the error again.

They paint while we plough.

— Subbudu, explaining the difference between Hindustani and Carnatic singing to a Hindustani vocalist

Meanwhile, Subbudu's trip to Madras had become an annual pilgrimage. Before *sabhas* became a common feature in every nook and corner of the city, Subbudu used to select one *sabha* of a particular area every day during his Madras season. He used to start his day at 2 pm and would wrap up at 10 pm at night. Moreover, from the mid-1960s onwards, the *sabhas* began looking for fresh dancers. Though the demand for younger dancers was always there, it gained ground after the *sabhas* realised that Kalakshetra was not open to the idea of having solo dance productions outside its premises. Even otherwise, Kalakshetra stressed on group productions. The trend to spot new talent gave a tremendous boost to non-

Kalakshetra trained dancers. Celebrated Bharatanayam dancer Alarmel Valli, who had her *arangetrum* in the late 1960s, was spotted by a couple of *sabha* secretaries who witnessed her maiden solo performance and gave her a platform to perform soon after.

Valli was around ten years old when she had her first performance at the India International Centre in Delhi. Her uncle, S. Gurudev knew Subbudu and he invited him to her recital. Subbudu was associated with Valli from the start. After reading Subbudu's review, there was considerable jubilation among the family members. She infused tremendous energy into the Pandanallur style of Bharatanatyam, to the extent that Subbudu called it Valli Natyam.

Meanwhile, *The Indian Express* invited Subbudu to start writing for them from 1968 onwards. The Express editors had noticed the stupendous growth of their Tamil edition, *Dinamani Kadir*. The common people flocked to the paper. For the first time, the classical arts had a readership which included barbers on one hand, and autorickshaw drivers on the other. Everyone lapped up his puns because he did the unthinkable by capturing the mood of the music and dance concerts and using the common lingo to describe it. The prosaic, dull language had given way to a conversational style. Moreover, for the common folk, Subbudu became their representative who could strip any artiste of his/her halo and make them appear more human, more vulnerable than ever.

Artistes on their part, corroborated the fact that they had a thin skin when they reacted sharply to Subbudu's criticism. With the language which addressed the middle and the lower middle class and the intellect which confronted the accepted beliefs of the upper middle class, Subbudu had something to offer to everyone. But most significantly, it was his way of talking from the point of view of the common man which did the trick. He made his readers believe that artistes were not God send, that they could and infact they did, commit errors. He sent the message across to the artistes that just as the common man had to work to make his ends meet, they too had to stretch their limits to impress him. Once the artistes responded, he took them to dizzying heights.

> ***During December in Madras, his comments became the starting point of conversation even between strangers.***
>
> — *N. Vijay Shiva, Carnatic vocalist*

In 1969, Subbudu's father Venkataraman died. The same year, M.S. Subbulakshmi became the first woman to be honoured by the title of Sangita Kalanidhi. She stormed the male bastion and later conquered it. In 1969 itself Padma created history by introducing Pushpanjali to the Bharatanatyam repertoire.

Once she presented a Jatiswaram in Raga Kiravani, at one of her performances in Delhi. Subbudu was so impressed with the

Saraswati and Venkataraman

People begged, cried, suffered and attacked him but could not ignore him.

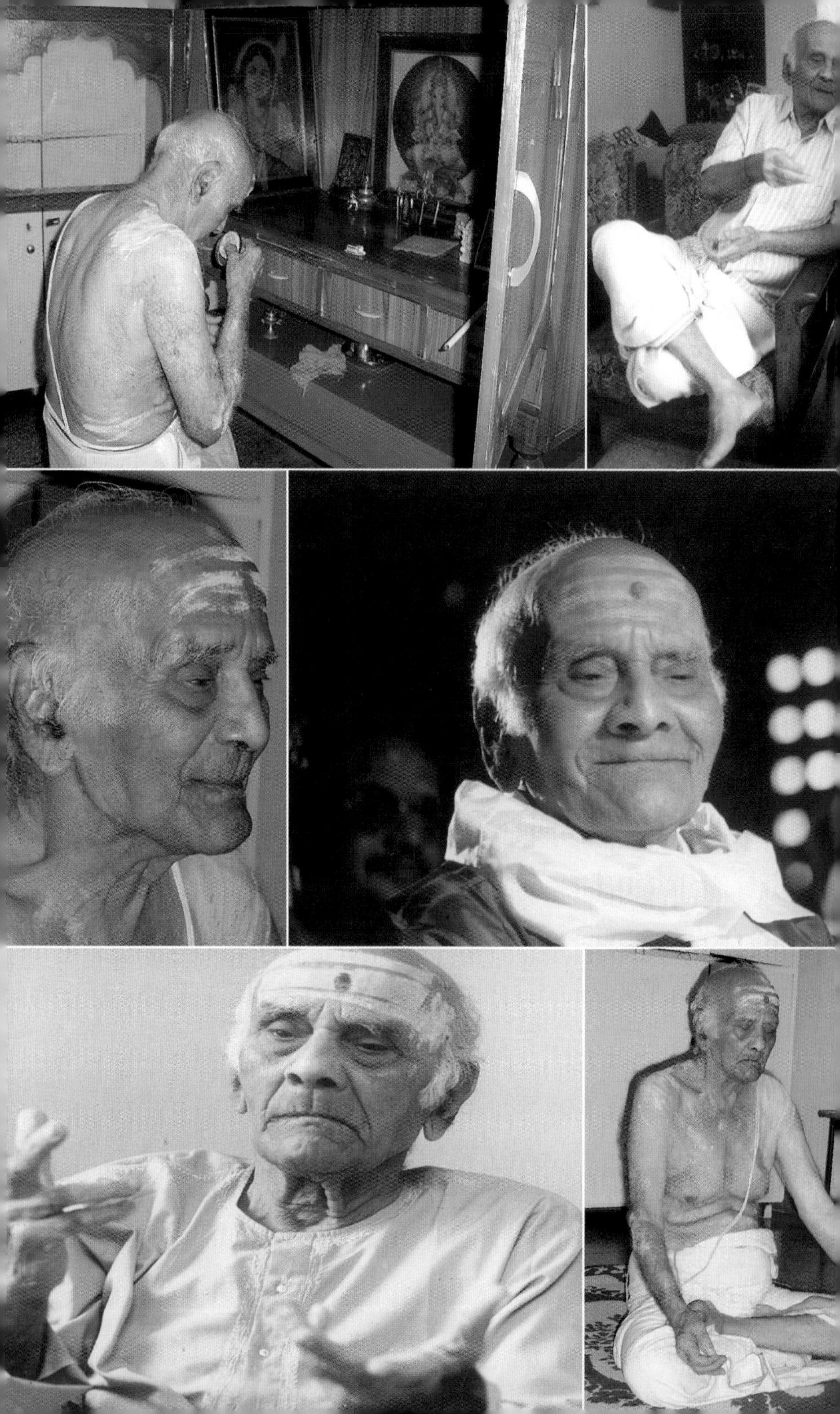

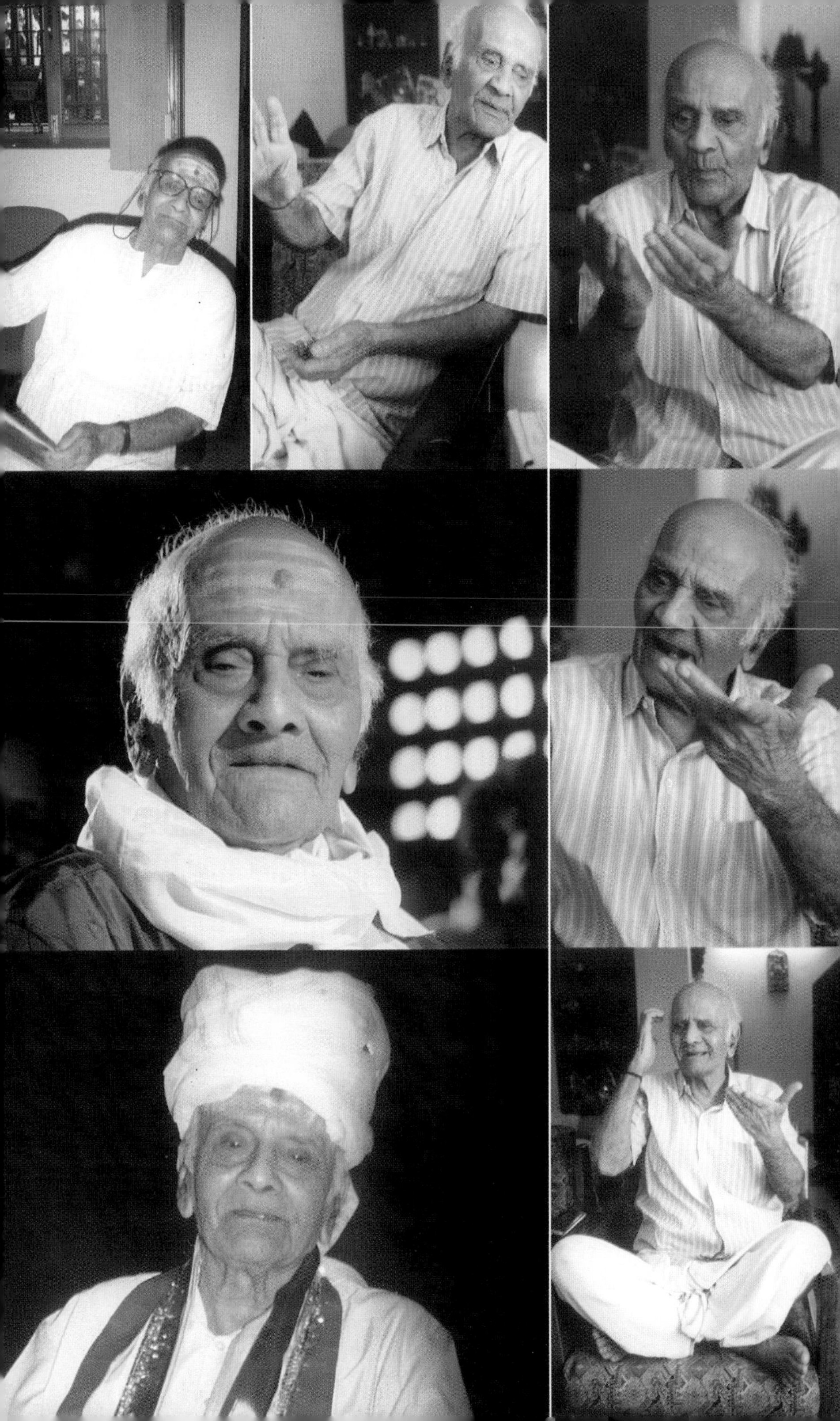

Subbudu lived!

Subbudu's Saraswati's Kanakabhishekam.
Subbudu is standing on her extreme right

item that he came back stage and congratulated the dancer on her feat. He felt that Padma's special choreography should be documented by the Sangeet Natak Akademi and told her, "This is something, I will never forget in my entire life." Subbudu proved this when two decades later, at a function, they bumped into each other and he sang the same rendering of the Jatiswaram. Padma was surprised beyond belief and felt that she was blessed to have encountered Subbudu.

On July 20, 1969, Neil Armstrong landed on the moon and the following day Yamini gave a recital at the Ashoka Hall. Incidentally, that day Yamini presented a Dikshitar composition "Chandram baje". While introducing the item, Yamini's father Prof. Krishnamurthy, who had the gift of the gab, said that Yamini had composed a special song to celebrate the landing on the moon. Fabri covered the recital and he wrote the review verbatim. When Subbudu read the article, he wrote a letter to the editor in which he explained the matter. He criticised Fabri and also mentioned that Yamini's father should not have given the credit of Dikshitar's composition to his daughter. According to Subbudu, Prof. Krishnamurthy was speaking to a foreign audience and perhaps, he therefore decided to pass the buck. If one were to attempt an objective scrutiny of the episode, it is quite plausible that Yamini chose to dance to a Dikshitar composition because her performance was to coincide with man's landing on the moon. Whatever it was, Subbudu's knack for sniffing any smart talk often landed him in trouble but that did not stop him from his pursuit to separate talent from archness.

In another instance, Prof. Krishnamurthy while discussing the new *varnam* composed by his daughter maintained that the said item was composed in *Chatushra Jati Triputa Talam*, meaning *Adi Talam*. Fabri who covered her recital wrote that Yamini had composed a new *varnam* in a new *talam*. After reading the article, Subbudu wrote another letter to the editor of *The Statesman* and pointed out the silly mistake made by the critic.

> ***Thank God, he did not come to political writing, else we would have been out of a profession.***
>
> — *Cho. Ramaswamy, journalist and former MP, Rajya Sabha, referring to the sting and satire in Subbudu's writing*

Subbudu's rise was also attributed to artistes seeking publicity and critics provided them with that element. As the number of artistes increased the demand for having critics review their performances also increased because the government patronage could not be extended to everyone and, as a result, critics gained importance. Manna, who was involved in arranging the concerts for artistes from down South found that each time the artistes landed, they wished to speak to Subbudu. He also recalled that, "The Supper Club at the Ashok Hotel was presenting dance 'shows' regularly, providing many opportunities to both established and up and coming artists; Bharatanatyam was featured often. The Trade Fair Authority of India (now known as ITPO), has been featuring many dance programmes during their annual Fairs." And for every such occasion Subbudu was a must have.

Hobnobbing with the leaders

With Pt. Jawaharlal Nehru, then Prime Minister of India

With Sh. R. Venkataraman, former President of India

With Congress leader Dr. Karan Singh

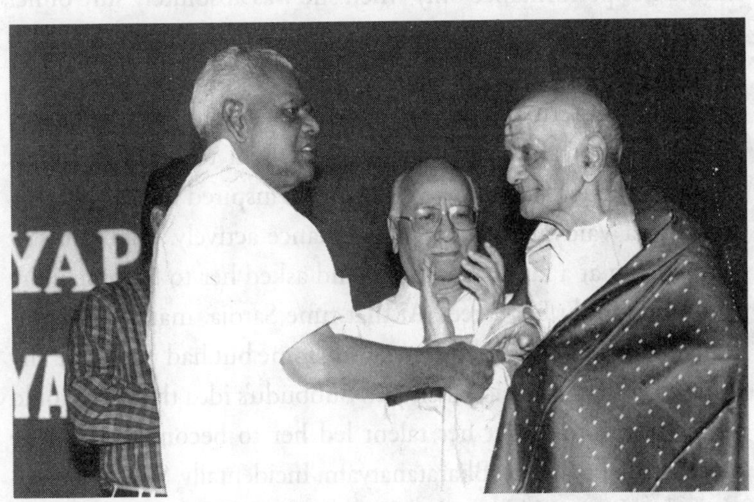

With Congress leader Late G.K. Moopanar

Riding the Chariot

Ironically, Yamini got some of her best reviews from Subbudu and other critics before he and the dancer fell out in the late 1980s. In fact such was Yamini's craze that popular Bharatanatyam dancer Rama Vaidyanathan's mother who was expecting her, stood on chair to watch one of her performances because people around had blocked her view. She was in full term pregnancy. As luck would have it, Rama became Yamini's first student. One of the things about Subbudu that Yamini told Rama was that she should invite him to her performance only when she was absolutely sure of her dance. She believed he "just needed to spot a minor fault to go ballistic".

Unlike the critics who kept safe distance from amateur artistes Subbudu went ahead and encouraged them to become serious about their talent. In fact, that is how he inspired his distant relative Saroja Vaidyanathan to pursue dance actively. Subbudu saw her dancing at a family gathering and asked her to become more ambitious about her career. At that time Saroja, married to a bureaucrat, was teaching children at her home but had not made any impact on the professional circuit. Subbudu's idea that she should be more serious about her talent led her to become one of the most familiar names in Bharatanatyam. Incidentally, Saroja's daughter-in-law Rama Vaidyanathan became one of Subbudu's favourite dancers of the 1990s.

While the Yamini wave was sweeping North India in late 1960s and early 70s, a young intelligent dancer, tutored by Martha Graham in contemporary dance who later introduced the concept of group choreography, had become the most popular non-Kalakshetra face of Bharatanatyam in Madras. She was Sudharani. Savi introduced Subbudu to Sudharani in 1970. Among her generation of dancers, Sudharani was Subbudu's favourite. Present-day dancers like Anita Ratnam grew up dreaming of getting the kind of reviews Sudharani got in her prime. In the fifty-seven years of her dance career, Sudharani never came across a critic who spotted her weaknesses and her strengths as an artiste like Subbudu did. When Subbudu saw Sudharani perform for the first time, he was so ecstatic that he told her that she was as perfect as a white bed sheet which just needs the presence of a mosquito to break the symmetry of its beauty. Just like the mosquito dispells the spell of the bed sheet's whiteness, similarly strands of hair hanging loosely around her forehead take the mind off her dance because everything else is just so perfect. Sudharani was so taken by his praise that she did not know whether to believe the man or to accept him as one of the many admirers of her dance whose praise bordered on sycophancy.

He made me work through absolute perfection because I listened to him.

— Sudharani Raghupathy on Subbudu's impact on her dance

Sudharani, Padma and Chitra ushered in a new era of dancer-scholars who introduced the concept of research in dance. Two years before Subbudu met Sudharani, a young dancing couple decided to move out of Kalakshetra. They were V.P. Dhananjayan and Shanta Dhananjayan. The couple took Bharatanatyam out of the proscenium set up arguing that if Carnatic singers like M.S. Subbulakshmi could sing at marriages, why can they not dance on such occasions? Driven by a sense of carving their identity and running their home, Dhananjayans became a sought after name for those seeking to package the spirit of India through dance capsules. To an extent, they played a significant role as one of the main promoters of India as a land of cultural richness for the Department of Tourism.

Meanwhile, the death of Indologist and art critic Charles Fabri in 1970 became the turning point in Subbudu's life since he also became the dance critic of *The Statesman.* Charles was respected for his knowledge by the artistes hailing from the world of art, theatre and dance. However, those who had a chance to interact with him and knew of him believed that the critic was in a mutually beneficial relationship with some of the artistes — dancers included.

Incidentally, the same year when Subbudu became the dance critic, veteran culture commentator, Shanta Serbjeet Singh began writing on the arts for *The Economic Times.* Four decades later, when we know for sure that the amount of research conducted in the West on Indian dance can easily dwarf our body of work, it is tough to speculate how much the Western critics, who dominated the art scene in the 1950s and 60s know of Indian art. Shanta who also took over from a foreign critic in *The Hindustan Times*, said that even though she didn't know the language at that time, the then editor of the paper, B.G. Verghese told her, "When the foreigners can cover Indian dance, why can't an Indian art lover and observer like you do that?"

The news of Subbudu's appointment as a dance critic created a flutter among many leading dancers of the time. In fact, a very popular dancer of the 1950s and 60s, who was later affected by Fabri's death, invited Subbudu for a lunch-meeting which turned out to be more than just that. She sent a message to him saying that she wanted to felicitate his appointment as a critic by hosting a lunch for him. Subbudu had some idea what the dancer was trying to hint at but since he was not too sure, he accepted the invitation.

The day of the meeting coincided with Subbudu's duty as an invigilator for a government examination. Fortunately, the examination centre was four blocks away from the dancer's residence. So, he decided to visit her during the interval. It was a beautiful house with a lawn leading to the entrance. The drawing room was aesthetically decorated and in keeping with the dancer's image as a woman of rare beauty and refined taste. Unusually warm in her demeanour, the dancer welcomed Subbudu by almost touching his feet. The two were meeting outside the proscenium set up for the first time. After the usual gossip on the recent performances witnessed by Subbudu, the two sat down for lunch. While serving the food, she casually remarked on how she wished to be the best she was. With Subbudu eating rather indulgingly, she paused and looked at him. There was no word from him. Not able to guess what he was thinking, she observed that Charles Fabri was as gifted a critic as Subbudu but his work never left him with much money. Subbudu was still silent and had already finished his lunch. He was now admiring an oil painting, with his back towards the dancer. There was complete silence as the clock ticked. Suddenly, Subbudu decided to leave. He was left with minimal time before the examination was to begin. As he turned around, the dancer bluntly offered to sponsor Subbudu and that too unconditionally. She hastened to add that she was doing so because she did not wish critics to be poor.

She said, "You are doing great service to the arts in India."

Subbudu told her that had he not eaten the food cooked by her, he would have sworn not to see any of her performances. Saying that, he left the dancer's spacious drawing room, her manicured lawn and her ambition to purchase his pen.

Unlike now, as a dance critic, Subbudu was particularly allergic to lecture-demonstrations especially because he did not wish to put the dancers in a tight spot. He maintained that most dancers, did not know what they danced or taught and the lecture-demonstrations exposed their lack of knowledge. In 1973, the same dancer who tried to bribe Subbudu and was a considerate patron of Charles Fabri, invited him to one of her lecture demonstrations. Subbudu told her clearly that she should not expose herself by calling him because if he spotted a mistake, he would be tempted to criticise her.

Perhaps, the dancer was confident of her hold on her subject and she prevailed upon Subbudu only on condition that she would not ask him to ask any questions in public. Subbudu wanted to be a silent spectator "to a morning of circus". The lecture-demonstration ended and Subbudu knew where the dancer had made an error. While critics from other newspapers and students of dance emptied their bag of questions, one man sat silent with his fingers playing a *jati* on his forehead. Subbudu's eyes were closed and Kuldip Nayar, the then Editor of *The Statesman*, was observing him. Suddenly, the dancer asked Subbudu if he was curious to know something.

Subbudu tried maintaining his side of the promise but the dancer's repeated requests and prodding by Kuldip Nayar, forced him to lay the trap for the dancer. He asked her to put the Second Tirimanam of her *varnam* on *Taala* and asked her to explain the *sancharis* of her *varnam*. The dancer was unable to do both and walked out in protest. Later, when other critics, petrified by the reaction of the country's leading dancer went backstage, they were confronted with the most melodramatic scene. The dancer was crying her heart out and accusing Subbudu of making a mess of her lecture-demonstration.

Fellow critics rushed to Subbudu and asked him to see her backstage. Though, Subbudu always maintained his distance with a dancer in public regardless of her talent, he relented and met her. In the presence of other critics, she asked him why he wanted to destroy her. Unable to stand a false accusation, Subbudu spilled the beans and told her not to dream of inviting him to her lecture-demonstration. As Subbudu walked out, he felt triumphant. The dancer and her image had become one and other critics realised her shadow could be measured after all.

Interestingly, decades later, Subbudu attended another lecture-demonstration, which he felt, could put even a cabaret dancer to shame except that the dance movement was full of grace. Orissi dancer Madhavi Mudgal successfully demonstrated hip movements that are incidentally part of the dance structure. After witnessing her recital, Subbudu felt Madhavi taught him something he had not known about Orissi and he remained grateful to her. Incidentally, down South, when Padma Subrahmaniam presented hip movements, a critic had labelled it 'cabaret' dance. Padma had then quoted a verse from the *Natya Shastra* which established that hip movements are justified as long as they are not provocative in nature.

Till date, I never called him up to invite him to my performances.

— Madhavi Mudgal on how Subbudu does not make it an issue if the dancer does not invite him formally

By the late 1960s and early 70s, Subbudu started sharing his concerns on the lack of ambition among the rising Carnatic singers to experiment with unused *ragas.* If at all, he also noticed a disturbing trend where the new czars of Carnatic music sang their own compositions more frequently than those of the trinity and other composers of yore. When Dr. Balamurali Krishna was a rising star, Subbudu criticised him on the same account and advised him to sing the trinity's compositions in three-fourths of the programme and his own in the remaining one fourth. In fact, Balamurali was so alienated with Subbudu's continuous hammering that he once asked the organisers to point at Subbudu when he performed, so that he could know who he was. It is a different story that now Subbudu and Balamurali choose to downplay their arguments because of the admiration they have for each other.

Unless you ask him to leave, I will not perform.

— A leading Carnatic vocalist reacting to Subbudu's presence in the audience

Not only critics, eminent musicians too rued the fact that young Carnatic musicians were not too serious in experimenting with hitherto unexplored ragas. Leading Veena player S. Balachander expressed similar fears and wrote that *ragas* like Hemavathi, Bhavapriya, Gama-nasrama, Dharmavathi, Vakulaabharanam, Kokilapriya, Nata-bhairavi, Shadvidamaargini, Sarasangi were not popular enough. A reputed musician himself, Veena S. Balachander was one of the few musicians who mastered the tabla, harmonium, bul-bul-thara, mridangam, thar-shenai, dilruba, tabla-tarang and sitar before he discovered the veena. In fact, Veena Balachander's love for the veena and Subbudu's hatred for the instrument was one of the reasons that created a wedge between the two with the passage of time.

If you put a veena in a box, it looks like a coffin.

— Subbudu leaving little to the imagination on what he thinks of the instrument

While young musicians' lack of seriousness worried Subbudu a growing number of young dancers became his new protégés. In

1971, young Bharatanatyam dancer Anita Ratnam created history of sorts by inaugurating the Madras season of the Music Academy. She had been recommended by M.S. Subbulakshmi to open the festival. A strikingly beautiful upper class Brahmin teenager, Anita could have been smug about her social standing and talent but for Subbudu. He created a rupture for her when two days after her performance, he went over to her residence and asked her to put *talam* to a *trikala jati teeramanam.* Anita could not do it and realised that her Guru Adyar Lakshman was not teaching her enough.

Alarmel Valli who was and is Anita's contemporary, was training in Carnatic music as well. Subbudu told Anita that if she was serious about her dance, she should look at the way Valli pursued it. As teenagers, Anita and her sister found it highly improbable to believe that Valli with a rather small frame could possibly be one day the most sought after dancer but Subbudu's criticism forced Anita to give up her complacency about her beauty and look beyond herself. He exposed her to Valli's dedication and her commitment to dance.

After Subbudu left, Anita could not believe that he had actually come to her place. However for Subbudu, his work did not end with the few hundred words he wrote in the article. It went beyond him. He was completely involved in shaking and shaping an entire generation of young dancers who were coming up and perhaps creating jealousies among them too. Anita remembers growing up feeling envious of Valli for the praise she got from Subbudu.

Around the same time, Adyar Laxmanan, Madurai Krishnan, Madurai Sethuraman and Trichur Ramanathan left Vyjayanatimala Bali's institution. Anita Ratnam's mother employed the entire entourage and so the young dancer inherited a composer, a musician, a guru and a *mridangist.* Anita and her sister, became the channel for the entire group to experiment and execute their new works. Moreover, with dance gaining popularity, a number of concert musicians, began flirting with dance professionally. The reason for this was the lack of performance space available to second level musicians since the likes of M.S. Subbulakshmi and Semmangudi dominated the music scene. The students of leading musicians therefore shifted their preferences. Madurai Krishnan, a disciple of Ariyakudi Ramanuja Ayengar, was one such artiste and he left a deep impact on the dance scene.

> ***I would much rather receive a passionate negative review from Subbudu than a lukewarm carbon copy of my press release.***
>
> *—Anita Ratnam, affirming that Subbudu never gave her a flattering review*

In 1971 itself, Subbudu's eldest son decided to join the Army and got himself admitted to the Indian Military Academy, Dehradun. Sriram's grandmother Saraswati was concerned about his well being and did not want him to join the army, but she did not force her fears on her grandson. When Sriram graduated from the academy, he was asked to report at Devlali. He had come home for a very short duration. The day his mother and uncle dropped him at the railway station, Subbudu left for Madras yet again.

In 1972, Subbudu was honoured with the title of "Kalai Mamani" for his contribution to the fine arts. Actor Hema Malini too received the title the same year. However, that did not stop Subbudu from criticising her dance recital a few years later. He wrote that her dance was influenced by film choreography and that she changed her costumes too often. The article had a cutting heading. After reading Subbudu's article, the actor's father complained to Ramnath Goenka, who demanded to meet Subbudu. Subbudu felt that he might be sacked and just as he was preparing to go and face the consequences for what he had written, the news editor came to Subbudu and told him that he should take Lord Balaji's prasad to appease Goenka. Goenka was a devout devotee of Lord Balaji.

The trick worked and Goenka asked Subbudu if he had given the controversial heading to the article and he answered saying it was not his job. The matter ended with Goenka telling Subbudu that he should not bother so much about film celebrities.

Meanwhile, Subbudu wrote an extremely satirical article in *Dinamani Kadir*, again in 1972, where he reflected on the changes in the Tanjore region. He questioned the accepted belief that only artistes from the Tanjore region were truly gifted and that only they could reach the top. Subbudu substantiated his claims by referring to artistes who had become popular despite belonging to other districts; people like M.S. Subulaskhmi from Madurai, Ariyakudi Ramanuja Ayengar from Ramnad District, Muthiaya Bhagavatar and S.G. Kittapa Pillai from Tirunelveli. The late John Higgins, an American, learnt Carnatic music in just three years and could render a full concert. All this betrayed the belief that artistic greatness had anything to do with a person's regional background. Though Tanjore's greatness as the nerve centre for music and dance died with the passage of time, the people refused to believe that their region no longer represented the greatness of the South Indian art forms.

So he wrote that Tanjore's musicial superiority was just a myth. That year Subbudu was also asked to cover the Tyagaraja Aradhana festival at Thiruvaiyaru. When Subbudu arrived at the station he was greeted by a poster reading "Subbudu Go Back". "A poster for an impostor" Subbudu exclaimed. Fearing an attack on him the organisers whisked him to the site of the festival.He entered the pandal and the late Congress leader G.K. Moopanar noticed him. He was the President of the Aradhana Committee and he asked Subbudu to come next to him.

When the concert was on, Subbudu noticed two men standing at the wicket gate. They implored him to come and listen to them for only two minutes. Subbudu thought he was going to hear some praise but to his surprise, those two men held Subbudu by his collar and started abusing him in choice Tanjore expletives.

They thundered, "How dare you criticise Tanjore? We are going to tear you into pieces. We have had enough of you." They started beating Subbudu and as he tried to run away, they tore his shirt. In desperation, Subbudu cried for help and Moopanar immediately came to his rescue. He decided to take action against them but Subbudu prevented him by saying they did not know what they were doing because of their intense love for the Tanjore heritage. Meanwhile, Moopanar told his PA to immediately take Subbudu to the market and get him a new shirt.

The incident did not affect Subbudu one bit and he continued ploughing the field. In fact, the same year, Subbudu also discovered another talent who is today one of the most respected gurus on the dance circuit. Her name — Kanaka Srinivasan. Kanaka's husband, V.B. Srinivasan and Subbudu shared the same office at the Finance Minsitry. At that time, a bachelor, Srinivasan's demeanour and presence of mind had greatly impressed Subbudu. At the same time, Yamini Krishnamurthy's make up man, Setumahadevan told Subbudu that a young dancer called Kanaka had considerable potential to make it big in the dance circuit. Subbudu was so engrossed in Yamini's dance that he did not pay attention to what Setu said. Meanwhile, Kanaka came to Delhi to present a recital at Pragati Maidan and won the hearts of the audience. Keshav Kothari, then Assistant Secretary of the Sangeet Natak Akademi happened to witness Kanaka's recital. He was so bewitched by her performance that he went backstage to congratulate the teenage dancer. The same night he telephoned Subbudu and told him about Kanaka.

On his visit to Madras for the season, Subbudu telephoned Kanaka and her mother answered the call. Oblivious of the 'protocol' with Subbudu, Kanaka expressed her reluctance to come on the phone. It was only when Kanaka's mother was able to convince her that she agreed to talk to Subbudu on the phone. He asked her, if she knew the meaning of her name. Kanaka told him that it meant gold. Subbudu asked if he could come and see her perform at her class to which the young dancer agreed.

The same evening, Subbudu met Kanaka's Guru Raja Ratnam Pillai and told him that the following day, he would come to see Kanaka. Interestingly, he told her Guru that he would see her performance only if he also sang. Subbudu thought highly of Guru Rajaratnam's singing. Next day, he met Kanaka for the first time. After watching her performance, he told her that he had not come across an artiste as consummate as her. Subbudu was so excited at having found another great dancer that he immediately asked her to perform on a *sloka* composed by him. As Kanaka performed with grace and understanding, she also sealed her fate. Subbudu told her that he was looking forward to seeing her performance in the near future.

Indrani Rehman, also came to know about Kanaka and organised a number of performances for her in Delhi early next year. Subbudu saw one of them and he was so impressed with her stage presence that he gave her a four column review. For a newcomer, getting that kind of attention from him was no mean achievement and he knew that himself. In fact, he was so conscious of this fact that he used to wait for the artistes to call him and thank him for writing a rave review for them. But then, he expected an artiste to call even when he tore her to pieces and shower him with abuses.

Subbudu used to feel artistes abused him when he punctured their ego and the very fact that they took him to task, was evidence of their attempt to protect their ego. He felt that they acted so only when they could better themselves. He believed that even if they did so to silence him, it was worth it. At least, he could wake them from their slumber.

However, from Kanaka, who was his favourite dancer, he expected a telephone call filled with gratitude. Two days had passed and Subbudu did not receive any call from her. He kept checking the phone for two days. In fact, Srinivasan asked Subbudu if he was all right because he showed signs of extreme impatience. Finally on the third day, Subbudu could not contain himself and called up Kanaka on his own. He told her that he had not come across a more headstrong person than her.

"I have been expecting a call from you. Why didn't you call?" Kanaka, confused and astonished, did not know how to react and instead told him that she had no idea that she was expected to call him. Subbudu told her, "I do not know, why I tolerate you because no one has spoken to me in this manner."

Incidentally, by then Subbudu had become used to artistes bowing before him. Wherever he went, he was surrounded by dancers and musicians, each asking him how he was. Subbudu too enjoyed the attention he got from the artistes but then he confined himself to only those kind of favours. He expected people to be polite to him, at least those who were not attacked yet.

Meanwhile, on her second visit to Delhi the same year, Kanaka again proved that she was one of the best upcoming talents in dance. However, on her way back to Madras, her mother who was a strong influence on her suffered a heart attack and collapsed. By then, Subbudu had become like a family elder to Kanaka and her relatives. Her brother called Subbudu after a few days and told him about his mother's death. He also informed him that he wanted to get Kanaka married off to a decent man and requested Subbudu to also look for an eligible man. Subbudu had just disconnected

Subbudu with the newly weds, Kanaka and Srinivasan

the phone and he hit upon an idea. Srinivasan's elder sister had come to meet him in the office. Subbudu was sitting across the table and he told Srinivasan and his sister about Kanaka. Before they could firmly make up their minds, Subbudu got a ticket arranged for Srinivasan and sent him to Madras. A few days later, Kanaka became Kanaka Srinivasan and Subbudu became a critic turned match-maker.

> ***He would come home for lunch and just talk about dance and leave without eating, arguing that he had his fill.***
>
> *— Kanaka on Subbudu's passion for the arts*

As time was passing by, Subbudu's children had also grown up. In 1973, his daughter Ragini completed her higher secondary. When he advised her to pursue some professional course, which could guarantee a job, Chandra put her foot down. She categorically told Subbudu that till Ragini completed her graduation, she would not pursue any professional course. Chandra valued education above everything else and her decisions on the career choices made by their children were final. On his part, Subbudu was only concerned with their happiness and came forward to help only when he was asked to. However, whenever he saw that his children were not following their dharma as human beings, he scolded them.

Having survived without food and after witnessing deaths due to hunger, Subbudu vowed never to allow anyone to leave with an empty stomach from his home. He made sure that he taught his children to never turn away any beggar who knocked on their door, regardless of whether he was genuine or not. Once Ragini refused a beggar within Subbudu's hearing. He rushed from his room and began shouting at her. After he stopped the beggar, he warned her not to do so in future and immediatelty went to the kitchen and came out with a plate of curd rice and placed it before the beggar. Subbudu did not allow the beggar to leave their home till he completely finished the entire food. Later he told her, "If you are not sure whether the beggar is telling the truth or lying, make him or her eat before you, so that the food goes to his stomach and is not wasted."

Such instances were rare but they left a deep impact on his children. But sometimes, Subbudu also amazed himself with his ignorance. He did not know till very late that Ragini had bolted her room's door and had cried her heart out on the day of her Tamil paper for her secondary examination. While Subbudu got up and left for office, Chandra had to call Ragini's friend's father and seek his help. He came home, convinced her to open the door, consoled her and took her to her examination centre. In present-day circumstances, it would be impossible not to criticise a father for being so uninvolved but Subbudu never pretended to be different from the very beginning and it seems, Chandra was fully aware of that.

Meanwhile, the young musicians Subbudu had reviewed in 1950s had become the Gurus of the 70s. In 1974, T.V. Gopalakrishnan took Subbudu to the concert of one of his favourite students, saxophone player Kadiri Gopalnath saying that he had trained the boy for a decade. The young disciple found favour with Subbudu's pen. After reading Subbudu's review, many organisers invited Kadiri. However, a few years later, attending one of Kadiri's performances, Subbudu got so annoyed that he ripped him apart. Not only that, after listening to him, he shouted at T.V. Gopalakrishnan and asked him where his student was heading and the same day Kadiri came to Gopalakrishnan's house and howled. When Gopalakrishnan tried to console him, Kadiri said, "I am finished."

> ***People often ask themselves the question, "Why do artistes take all that Subbudu dishes out?" Simple, because they know that he knows and nobody can browbeat him into acceptance of anything he is not fully convinced about.***
>
> *From a citation awarded by the Madras Telugu Academy*

As if critcising Kadri was not enough, Subbudu achieved another feat by ridiculing Gopalkrishnan's Guru Chembai Vaidyanatha Bhagavatar. After watching his performance, Subbudu wrote in his article, "In 1969 he came to the concert platform fully attired with a *zari dhoti, banian,* a *silk kurta* and an *angavastaram* to match. In 1970 he discarded the *angavastaram*; in 1971, the *silk kurta* and in 1972, the *banian* also." Subbudu commented on the changing attire of the doyen and wrote that he would not risk attending his performance and watch his strip tease affair. Gopalakrishnan drew Subbudu's sarcastic article to Bhagavatar's attention. He was so furious with Subbudu that he took his walking stick and dashed to his brother P.V. Krishnamoorthy's office in Madras and shouted, "Has your brother gone mad? Does he come to listen to my music or write about my dress? Who is he to question me on what I should wear or not? If I want I will sing with my *kaupeenam* (under cloth)."

Subbudu's brother was struck speechless by this outburst but regained his diplomacy to pacify Guru Bhagavatar. Finally he calmed down and said, "I had taken a vow to sing bare-bodied before Lord Krishna in Guruvayoor if he cured me of my voice failure. He kept his word and I am fulfilling my part of the contract. And there is one thing I want to tell you, I always read his reviews, which reveal his knowledge of music and sense of humour but tell him to ascertain facts before putting pen to paper."

Subbudu did not mean to hurt Guru Bhagavatar's sentiments and he converyed this while maintaining that an artiste on stage should conduct himself like an artiste at all costs.

Apart from Kadiri, there was another promising youngster who was torn apart by Subbudu. Violinist Kunnakudi Vaidyanathan was a rage and was playing to a capcity crowd the day Subbudu saw him. But he failed to impress him and ended up receiving a scathing write up. When Kunnakudi saw the article, he tried to assault Subbudu who decided to never cover his recital again.

On the day of Kunnakudi's performance, Subbudu was approached by a young man who had been following his writings in Tamil since his teens. He was A. Kandaswamy. Kandaswamy was afraid of Subbudu because of the reputation he enjoyed but when he saw him regaling the people around him with his jokes, he felt encouraged. Kandaswamy told him that he admired his writing style and that he thought, he was the best writer. Subbudu acknowledged his greetings.

Nearly fifteen years later, by which period, Kandaswamy had become Subbudu's assistant, Kunnakudi approached Kandaswamy who was sitting in the canteen outside Narada Gana Sabha and asked him if he was Subbudu's secretary. Kunnakudi requested him to bring Subbudu to his concert. In the last fifteen years or so, Kunnakudi had struggled hard to establish himself. He had dabbled with film music as well, during this period, but there was no acknowledgement from Subbudu for his work. Kunnakudi felt that had affected his efforts to break into the league of A grade artistes. Kandaswamy was Kunnakudi's fan but he never let Subbudu know about it. The only thing that mattered to him was Subbudu's pronounced likes and dislikes.

Two days later when Kunnakudi bumped into Kandaswamy, he again requested him to bring Subbudu to his concert. Kandaswamy told him to meet Subbudu and convince him. Kunnakudi gathered courage to meet Subbudu who told him that he was a pure vegetarian and he could not stand the sight of non-vegetarian food.

Kunnakudi understood what Subbudu meant. He promised that he would only play Carnatic music. Subbudu had his reservations but he decided to give the artiste another chance and finally attended his concert at Bramha Gana Sabha. The moment he entered the *sabha* hall, Kunnakudi stopped for a minute and informed his accompanists that Subbudu had arrived. They tuned their instruments and Kunnakudi decided to play Subbudu's favourite *ragas*. Artistes could know if Subbudu enjoyed their music or not by the way he shook his head and ate *supari*. Subbudu asked for *supari* from Kandaswamy only when he enjoyed a concert. It was well known that no matter how much you hurt Subbudu, if you played great music and his favourite *ragas*, the man could be floored.

Former President R. Venkataraman honouring Subbudu at a fuction organised by Kunnakudi Vaidyanathan who is seen standing on extreme left.

Two days after the performance, Subbudu extolled Kunnakudi's talent through a grand review. The artiste was so touched by Subbudu's write up that he went to Subbudu's hotel room with a pail full of roses. Kandaswamy opened the door and was greeted with a dazzling smile by Kunnakudi. He rushed to touch Subbudu's feet and then showered him with petals of roses. Kunnakudi, the star was born again and Subbudu, embarrassed but moved by his gesture, told him not to thank him but to further build on his talent.

Back in Delhi, Padma's performance at Mavlankar Hall drew protests from Subbudu's friends. In her pursuit to popularise 'Sukhalasya' and in her quest to make Subbudu agree to what she felt, she invited him to come on stage and sing a composition for her to perform. She announced that she wanted to experiment with her newly evolved dance style. Always excited at the prospect of having a public dialogue with an intelligent artiste, Subbudu readily agreed. But the danseuse got so engrossed in her performance that Subbudu thought she had forgotten to invite him. Subbudu left the auditorium when he did not receive an invitation even after the interval.

Later when Padma called for him, someone from the audience shouted that he had left. Hearing this, Subbudu's supporters protested and the situation nearly got out of hand, till it was made clear that Subbudu left because there was a delay in inviting him. Soon afterwards, Padma wrote a letter to the Editor of *The Statesman*, to clarify her position.

However, Subbudu proved his detractors wrong next time when at yet another public invitation by Padma during her recital at the India International Centre in Delhi, he sang an *alaap* on stage while she performed Bharata Nrityam on that. Subbudu's running argument with Padma was on two grounds. One, she was not doing Bharatanatyam but Bharata Nrityam (the term was not coined by Padma at that time), since Bharatanatyam was a codified dance form and it did not have balletic movements and two, if Padma agreed that it was not Bharatanatyam then why did she not codify it?

Incidentally, a decade earlier, Padma had informed Subbudu that she had composed a new dance form 'Sukhalasya' and that she wanted him to share his views on that. Unimpressed with the performance, Subbudu observed that it was not Bharatanatyam but Padmanatyam.

More than three decades later, Padma recalled reading that article with a sense of astonishment and surprise but unlike other artistes who chose to hit back at Subbudu, she did not react to it. In fact she was so unperturbed that Subbudu wondered if she was annoyed with him.

Now, not only has Padma tutored a number of good Bharata Nrityam dancers but she has gone and codified the dance form too. The fact that Subbudu kept pestering Padma for this amuses him now and he chuckles, with one hand on his stomach because of the severe pain he experiences each time he talks and the other hand running on his monkey cap, indicating that his mind is at work.

> ***That is what makes him spicy even at this age. The man is full of spice.***
>
> *— Rama Vaidyanathan reacting to accusations that Subbudu's style of writing was harsh and offensive*

By mid-1970s female Carnatic vocalists had created for themselves a distinct constituency of fans that preferred them over their male counterparts. ML Vasanthakumari was one such female vocalist. During one of her concerts in Madras around 1975, she sang a Pallavi specially composed by Ghatam player K.M. Vaidyanathan. The Pallavi contained all the *jatis* and for once, Subbudu, could not keep track of the rhythmic patterns. To his surprise, he saw five college girls, with *vibhutis* on their foreheads arguing, putting correct *jatis* and keeping pace with Vasanthakumari's singing. He met the girls in the canteen and offered them free cups of coffee provided they shared the trick of keeping the pace with the changing pattern of Vasanthakumari's singing. Embarrassed, the girls spilled the beans and were treated to coffee with their favourite critic. That evening, Subbudu learnt that formula was simple but execution was different. So long as he got to learn, it did not matter to him who was his teacher.

1975-76 were crucial years in the history of the development and encouragement of the performing arts. That year, in an unprecedented move, the Department of Culture set up maintenance grants. It was one of the most important single financial assistance to important performing arts institutions and individuals. The intention was to enable these places to sustain themselves and a group of 50 to 100 people. After maintenance grants were offered, an idea was mooted that production grants must be accorded to the institutions as well, so that after they were able to sustain themselves they could also produce something worthwhile. The only condition was that the productions should be staged in two or three neighbouring states. This way the government could afford greater regional cultural interaction. While the idea had great potential, over the years, it also became one of the breeding grounds for mediocre artistes with deft PR. The main problem was the identitification of genuine institutions devoted to culture because many of the good and leading artistes, performers and other eminent personalities were allergic to bureaucracy and did not wish to go through the procedural requirements of the government. Moreover the government grants were not substantive at all.

In 1975 itself, the Khajuraho Festival was started with a view to showcase India's rich culture and heritage. Though festivals such as Khajuraho invited artistes across the board, they acted as vantage points for scholars too. However, with aggressive billing to portray India as the land of exotica, the culture bit was lost. It soon boiled down to getting the maximum people to the heritage sites, in order to not only popularise India but to also earn revenue. Heritage tourism therefore became visiting tourism in a matter of a few years. Subbudu went to cover the Khajuraho Festival a couple of times before he decided to call it quits.

Meanwhile, on June 1, 1975, he retired as an Under Secretary from the Revenue Department of the Ministry of Finance. The only change in his routine after retirement was that instead of leaving home at 9 am in the morning, he used to leave in the afternoon around three o'clock. And retirement didn't mean that Subbudu came home early. His late arrivals were often greeted with Chandra standing outside her home, waiting for her husband to arrive.

Once Subbudu's friend Manna Srinivasan took him to meet artiste Sidheshwari Devi. Subbudu got so busy talking that he forgot he had to go back home. Meanwhile, Chandra got worried at home because Subbudu had never stayed outside past-midnight. She and Sriram decided to meet her brother who lived near by. Sriram's uncle feared that Subbudu may have met with an accident and just when all the three were planning to visit the city's hospitals, they found Subbudu and Srinavasan coming towards them, gossiping loudly. When Subbudu saw all the three standing on the road, he advised Manna to run away. The fast paced walk turned into a cautious gait with Subbudu smiling sheepishly. When Chandra asked him where he had been, he said he had forgotten about time. It is tough to imagine, if somebody other than Chandra could have coped with Subbudu's incorrigible behaviour. But then as Sriram said, Chandra loved Subbudu deeply.

In 1976 at the age of twenty-six, Sriram informed Subbudu and Chandra of his decision to get married. Soon, Chandra and

Sriram and Jayshree at their wedding reception in 1976

Subbudu with his first grandchild, Swetha

her brother started looking out for a match for him. One fine day, Sriram got a call from his uncle informing him that there was a suitable match for him in Bombay. He asked him to go to Bombay and see the girl. Subbudu was busy with the Chennai season, so he could not accompany his son. Interestingly, Sriram was accompanied by his uncle and aunt and the girl's parents were also represented by her uncle and aunt. Sriram and Jayshree liked each other and in 1976, they were married.

When Subbudu and Chandra met their daughter-in-law Jayashree's parents before marriage, Subbudu told them, that he expected them to send their daughter only in her marriage attire. It so happened that Jayshree's grandfather wrote a letter to Subbudu listing the things he had saved and purchased for his granddaughter for her marriage. Subbudu replied in one line saying, "We have not come to buy cattle." His gesture and magnanimity touched Jayshree's heart and over a period of time, from being a daughter-in-law, she became the daughter of the household.

The following year, Subbudu and Chandra became grandparents. Their granddaughter was named Swetha. Subbudu thought, she was lucky for him, because her birth brought an end to a series of accidents with his Vespa scooter which were happening since 1972. Much as Subbudu's children and his wife, used to ask him to drive carefully, Subbudu met with one serious accident every year for five consecutive years. Despite that, he held on to his Vespa scooter till the early 80s after which his family forced him to stop driving because he showed no signs of improvement. In one of the most hilarious accidents of his life, Subbudu ran into a herd of buffaloes near Shantipath and fell unconscious. Later when he regained consciousness, he could only recall that none of the buffaloes turned around to look at him even once. Subbudu demanded attention from unexpected quarters sometimes!

However, the most horrifying accident took place when Subbudu and his secretary Subramaniam were travelling in an auto rickshaw, which got trapped between two trucks trying to overtake each other. The rear side of the truck hit the front side of the autorickshaw, which turned in the opposite direction and was hit by another truck. The autorickshaw driver, Subbudu and Subramaniam were thrown out of the vehicle. Though Subbudu did not suffer major injuries, the autorickshaw driver was badly bruised and Subamaniam received multiple arm and leg fractures. The accident left Subramaniam incapable of climbing the stairs properly. The man who had promised himself to be with Subbudu as he grew old, found his situation frustrating. Meanwhile, Subbudu ensured that he got him ground floor accommodation so that he didn't have too much of a problem moving about.

Coming back to Subbudu's first grand child, Swetha'a arrival was preceeded by another joyous moment. He completed sixty years on March 27, 1977 and to celebrate the occasion, his children, close friends and members of the extended family gathered to greet him. It was going to be a memorable year for him, since in December that year he attacked Semmangudi and virtually brought the Madras season to a grinding halt.

Even in the 1960s when Subbudu criticised Semmangudi, he appreciated his double reed voice which rang like a church bell. However, through the 70s, he noticed that Semmangudi had developed a knack of starting his performance with an apology. He would complain about a sore throat and his poor health. It is

JAI SRI RAM, RAVI & RAGINI
Call on friends and foes
to
a rejuvenation ceremony
in which
the youthful candidate/parent

'SUBBUDU'

after successfully completing a tenure
of
Sixty eventful years, is to be
re-elected unanimously and unopposed
to another long term
of
witticism and criticism !

Come one ! Come all !!
Reserve your vote without Reservation
for the symbol of happiness and laughter

The Symbol of
PEN & INK
Remember

Some laughter a day — Keeps your troubles away !

Polling Details ;
Saturday, 26th March 1977 11.00 a.m. to 12.00 Noon Ten Sixer

Polling Booth :
DII/A-1, South Moti Bagh, New Delhi-110021

An invitation card prepared by Pattamal's daughter-in-law Malathi Jaikumar believed that M.S. Subbulakshmi and Semmangudi Srinivas Iyer were affected by tonsillitis and they had to consult a surgeon, who refused to remove M.S. Subbulakshmi's tonsils arguing her voice was a national treasure. However, Semmangudi's tonsils were removed as a result of which, his voice was impaired and he got a nasal infliction due to sniffing as well.

After the operation, Subbudu felt, Semmangudi had lost his magical touch and started giving nasal recitals and over a period of time, his recitals developed a high element of theatre as well. And while Semmangudi indulged in theatricals, Subbudu believed that Semmangudi liked to sing in chorus because it gave him a chance to conceal the limitations of his voice. He believed, Semmangudi was cheating the *rasikas*. Incidentally, the *rasikas* did not have any problem with Semmangudi's style. The reason, Subbudu thought, was that South Indian *rasikas* were not bothered about the quality of the voice which is also the reason why most Carnatic singers have failed to make an impression in North India, where the stress is on the purity of *sruti*.

During his performance at the Tamil Isai Sangam in 1977, Semmangudi said, "I have a very bad throat. Instead of musical phrasing only phlegm is visible. I hope you will bear with me." He had T.N. Krishnan on the violin and Ramabhadran on the *mridangam*. As Subbudu recalled, "The very opening song saw him in bad shape. Next he tried an *aalapana*, the result was ditto. But Krishnan had thunderous applause for his interpretation of the *aalapana*. Next, Semmangudi picked up his very favourite *raga* Karaharapriya but his voice did not cooperate with him whereas Krishnan brought the house down."

Halfway through the recital, the crowd started reacting to Krishnan's superb rendition and by the time *Thani Avarthanam* arrived, there was thunderous applause. It seems, this upset Semmangudi who could not help saying, "It looks bad when the audience only applaud the violinist. You must also applaud the vocalist." Subbudu found Semmangudi's demand ridiculous and arrogant and decided to sting his arrogance.

Two days later, *The Indian Express* and *Dinamani Kadir* carried Subbudu's article which sent shock waves through the city. For Subbudu, it had become extremely important to end Semmangudi's style of singing because he thought the maestro was setting a bad precedent for the next generation of Carnatic singers. His argument was simple, "If Semmangudi has trouble singing why must he sing?"

Already in 1965, Subbudu had upset Semmangudi when he reviewed his performance in Delhi. Even then Semmangudi had begun his concert by saying that he had been unwell and that his voice was playing hide-and-seek with him. Subbudu summed up the performance with a two-line review. It was the shortest review written by him and he took pride in his own sense of humour. Subbudu recollected he wrote something akin to — "Semmangudi complained of poor health and a poor voice quality and asked members of the audience to coopearate with him. I wish him all luck with a better performance and better health." Semmangudi was furious after reading the review and complained to T.T. Krishnamachari, who was the then Union Finance Minister and a close friend of Semmangudi.

Upset at the way his junior behaved with a senior artiste like Semmangudi, Krishnamachari asked his Secretary to order Subbudu to come to the office immediately. Before Subbudu met Krishnamachari, he was informed by his Secretary to beware of the boss since he was seething with anger.

Subbudu, with his typical unassuming behaviour remarked, "If they want to transfer me for what I have written, let them. I have not written anything wrong."

He met Krishnamachari who warned him to mend his ways. Subbudu, fully aware of the close relationship between legendary singer Veena Dhanammal's family and T.T. Krishnamachari, humbly explained the situation to his boss and at the end of it, taking a dig at Semmangudi's *Javalis*, requested Krishnamachari to inform Semmangudi to learn them from Veena Dhanammal's family. It is believed Semmangudi and Dhanammal's family were never on cordial terms and exploiting the close contacts between his boss and Dhanammal's family, Subbudu scored a point again.

This time around however, Subbudu decided to be tactless in attacking Semmangudi and the article became the sharpest critique of the artiste by any critic ever. Subbudu wrote, "Even the dreaded Emergency has come to an end but there seems to be no end to Semmangudi." He advised, "Semmangudi would do a great service if he stopped singing and retired forthwith." On top of it, Subbudu deliberately selected the ugliest snap of Semmangudi and filed his article. *The Indian Express* and *Dinamani Kadir* did brisk business that day and by afternoon, they had sold all the copies.

> ***You may have an audience of a thousand rasikas, I have a readership of one lakh.***
>
> *— Subbudu during a heated exchange with an artiste*

A reason for having Subbudu on the rolls was that he ensured a definite readership. In that sense, his impact and power was much like that of Mayawati, the Bahujan Samaj Party President, who has a sweeping effect on her voters and can transfer them entirely to any party she allies with.

Meanwhile, an emergency meeting was called at the Music Academy and the lecture demonstration in progress in the auditorium was cut short.

Incidentally, Semmangudi was performing the same evening at the Academy and perhaps wanted public approval to help him tide over Subbudu's shocking critique. By the time the meeting began, a huge number of protestors had gathered outside the venue. The crossing adjacent to the Music Academy was jammed and affected the vehicular traffic. As eminent people from the world of music, media and industry rallied behind their revered musician, there was little doubt that the day belonged to Semmangudi. But heroes were made and unmade within a span of twenty-four hours.

Prominent among those who attended the meeting were, S. Parthasarthy, former Editor-in-Chief of *The Hindu*, Dr. V. Raghavan and Dr. Balamurali Krishna. T.N. Krishnan, it is believed said that he existed because of Semmangudi.

A resolution denouncing Subbudu and reaffirming the greatness of Semmangudi was passed. An idea was floated that the resolution be carried in all major dailies and Ramnath Goenka of *The Indian Express* be informed of the development so that he could fasten the incorrigible critic with straps. The Secretaries of the Madras Academy were also asked to ban Subbudu from entering the premises.

If Subbudu had been around, the mamas and mamis of Madras would have muzzled him. However, in their wisdom, none of the papers and magazines decided to give much coverage to the episode. Semmangudi had his share of critics in the city. The kingmaker, as he was known among the Carnatic musicians had a notorious image of not allowing his students to flourish on his own soil. Whether the accusations were true or false is a matter of debate and a page of history best left untouched.

In the early 1980s, Subbudu again attacked Semmangudi saying that there was only video and no audio in his performance. He wrote categorically, "you are not good and you should accept that." Semmangudi responded by saying, "You are very harsh in your criticism and your words tarnish the ears of my listeners." Later Semmangudi asked Subbudu not to cover his programme. On an emotional note, he said, "If I am old, let me be alone." But Subbudu countered Semmangudi reiterating, "You are a public figure and therefore accountable to the public." Subbudu's line of defence was unimpeachable because an artiste had to be best when he performed. He rued the fact that leading artistes never became great gurus and wondered why they did not give back what they learnt from the world. At his own level, Subbudu was becoming concerned about his old age and his need to train someone who could succeed him and take care of his legacy.

However on January 19, 1990, Semmangudi presided over a function held to honour Subbudu for his contribution to the performing arts. The event was organised by Karthik Fine Arts along with the cooperation of all the *sabhas*. Mandolin Srinivas and Namagiripettai Krishnan gave short recitals as a token of appreciation on the occasion. At the end of the function Semmangudi said, "You are all under the impression that I am going to lambast

Semmangudi and Subbudu in an intimate dialogue at Karthik Fine Arts Society

Semmangudi honouring Subbudu for the first time at a public function

A section of the audience at the same function
Seated from left to right: M.S. Subbulakshmi, Sadasivam, T.T. Vasu from the Music Academy, Semmangudi, writer Savi and Subbudu

Nadaswaram Maestro Namgiri Pettai Krishnan giving a recital at the same function

Subbudu. You are mistaken. I have to praise him for his musical erudition and outspoken nature. He is a very good harmonium player and knows the *Natya Shastra* backwards. I wish him a full century of health, wealth and prosperity.

Semmangudi is dead but his gesture touched Subbudu and he took a bow before him.

The decade of 1970s had Subbudu written all over and therefore taking on someone like Semmangudi did not affect his might. However, his name was feared not loved. While he was a familiar face by virtue of his personal relationships with artistes, veteran dance critics like N.M. Narayanan of *The Hindu* were largely known as bespectacled entities who sat in the third or fourth row, took notes and left after the third or fourth item. While other critics were known as purists, Subbudu had established himself as a highly opinionated, knowledgeable man. The crux of his fame lay in his unique style with which he could reconnect with the masses. Be it every day instances or current events, He linked everything with the arts and still made sense. But Subbudu's persona betrayed his physical presence. He was known to the artistes not to their followers. And sometimes, it proved to be fortunate. During the controversy with Semmangudi, Subbudu and Kandaswamy were stopped by a rather heavily-built man as they were walking back to the Woodlands Hotel. He asked Subbudu "*Mama*, Subbudu Teriuma?" Before Subbudu could answer the man, the enquirer made his intentions clear by saying that, "If I get hold of Subbudu, I will beat him with my slippers!" Luckily, Subbudu was saved that day.

Though the Subbudu-Semmangudi brawl hogged much of the limelight in 1977, the same year Subbudu also discovered that M.L. Vasanthakumari's disciples were truly gifted artistes. For her concert at the Music Academy, Vasanthakumari decided to present Panch Nada Pallavi and also asked one of her favourite disciples Charumati Ramachandran to accompany her. Midway through the Pallavi, everything stopped: Vasanthakumari, Charumati, the violinst and the *mridangist*. After that 15 second pregnant pause, which seemed like an entire lifetime to Charumati, the talented disciple picked up from where her guru had stopped and started singing. Immediately the accompanists followed. Vasanthakumari looked at Charumati and smiled. After the performance ended, Subbudu, who had been observing this came and blessed Charumati for saving her guru's recital.

Apart from the female trinity — M.S. Subbulakshmi, D. K. Pattamal and M.L. Vasanthakumari — there was another female singer, who was admired and feared by her male counterparts. She belonged to the lineage of Veena Dhanammal. Her talent was as spontaneous as her wit and she used both to charm Subbudu. She was arguably the only musician who had the courage to mock him by saying, "I am sure you have already written the review" when she found him attending M.S. Subbulakshmi's concert. But that did not take away the fact that she admired Subbudu's writing style. Apart from their wit, Subbudu and Brinda had another interest in common, their love for *supari*. However, he never got a chance to review T. Brinda. In 1977, T. Brinda became the recipient of the Sangeet Kala Nidhi award of the Music Academy.

You are a time bomb.

— T. Brinda while addressing Subbudu

While Subbudu set Madras on fire in 1977, Shanta Serbjeet Singh's head on collision with a powerful dancer became the hot topic of debate next year. Incidentally, she had a face off with the same dancer who also tried her level best to oust Subbudu from *The Statesman* few years later. The annual ITC festival series, which began in the early 1970s, used to present a dance performance by a leading dancer as its grand finale. That year, an unknown face gave a mediocre performance. Shanta, who discovered the dancer's antecedents before filing her article criticised the organisers of the festival and the dancer in question. She felt the organisers had set a bad precedent.

Shocked and livid, the dancer took Shanta and *The Economic Times* to the Press Council and battled it out with them for two years before a compromise was reached. Soon after, Shanta also discovered that the FERA and the Income Tax raid at her residence had the blessings of the same dancer. In the mid-80s, Subbudu attacked the same dancer and invited her rage. By now she had earned a reputation of being an arrogant artiste. The danseuse used her contacts and presented a one-sided story to the then Editor-in-Chief of *The Statesman*, M.L. Kotru. Kotru, who followed high principles of journalism was upset and demanded an explanation from his News Editor who was responsible for Subbudu's article in the first place. Immediately an unqualified apology was demanded from him. Terribly hurt and upset,

Subbudu asked Shanta to bail him out in the matter. Subbudu was under tremendous pressure. Since Shanta knew Kotru personally, she told the Editor that his critic was true in his opinion about the dancer and so the matter was resolved.

In the late 1970s, Subbudu got involved in another controversy when he got a chance to witness Balasaraswati's daughter Lakshmi Knight's performance. He felt that because Lakshmi started learning rather late in her life, she had trouble moulding herself as a dancer. Since he was particular about the physical appearance of a dancer, Subbudu was unable to appreciate Lakshmi's dance because she was hefty and her sense of rhythm was problematic. Moreover, Bala's halo weighed heavily on her. Subbudu's write up created a wedge in his relationship with Bala's family because of his scathing criticism and satire. He began the article by referring to Bala's statement, "Let Bharatanatyam die with me" and later wrote, "After seeing Laskhmi's performance, Bala could not have been more prophetic." It is a different story that Subbudu genuinely felt that there was never going to be another Bala. However, Lakshmi's mother and her family were offended by the entire episode.

First, Bala's brother called him and abused him in chaste Tamil and then Bala herself made a jibe at him. However, before that, Subbudu's telephonic conversation with Bala's brother must be mentioned here. He was leaving for his office when he picked up the telephone to answer a gruff voice on the other side. Bala's brother said that he would beat him to death to which Subbudu replied that he should not forget that he was in Delhi and not in Madras and here, he called the shots. "If you are a man, then come out today and I will show you that I can do anything to you anywhere," Bala's brother retorted. Subbudu shot back saying, "I am coming to see Indrani Rehman's performance at the AIFACS in the evening and I will be there half an hour before you arrive."

Subbudu further challenged him saying, "Do not forget that I am extremely popular here, and there are people who can do anything, so before you decide to come and beat me, count the men who will stand by you."

As if this was not enough, Subbudu added, "If I am beaten, everyone would know. If you are, no one will know. So see you then."

In the evening, he reached the venue half an hour earlier but there was no trace of Bala's brother and so he was relieved of a show of strength.

A few months later, when Subbudu bumped into eminent scholar Dr. Kapila Vatsyayan and Bala, in the foyer of the Music Academy, Dr. Vatsyayan introduced him to Bala, who said, "I know this fellow. He is a donkey." Amused at her comment, Subbudu smiled saying, "Thank you Akka." and walked away.

Meanwhile Subbudu's brother Krishnamoorthy retired in 1979 as Director General of Doordarshan, after a long stint with AIR and Doordarshan. Right through his life, he was repeatedly asked, how he and his brother could coexist in the cultural world. Krishnamoorthy always had a ready answer, "My job is to enlist the cooperation of artists by holding on to their feet while Subbudu's job was to pull their feet."

Meanwhile, his brother Krishnamoorthy too came under Subbudu's line of fire. "As a youngster, I knew I could not compare with him in the field of Carnatic music. So I chose to experiment with light music based on folk, traditional and semi-classical airs but even here I was not spared by my illustrious brother." A National Programme called Bharat Teerth composed and conducted by Krishnamoorthy got him rave reviews but Subbudu thought the attempt was half-baked.

It had been two years since Subbudu's earth shattering duel with Semmangudi which had rocked the city, when the found himself ushering in the tabloidisation of the media. With Subbudu ensuring spicy write ups and pinning artistes to the ground, it was an accepted fact that he had become larger than the art itself.

The Madras season of 1979 was marked by an infamous incident which yet again involved Subbudu. VS Manian, the de facto editor of *Ananda Vikatan* had differences of opinion with the owner of the magazine and decided to start his own weekly. He named it *Idayam Pesukirathu* or the Heart Speaks. Since he was on cordial terms with Subbudu and loved his style of writing, he invited him to join his magazine.

For his inaugural issue, Manian put a massive poster depicting an artiste in the form of a *ghatam* and Subbudu as the *ghatam* player beating the guts out of the musician. The accompanying caption read, "Artistes Beware, Subbudu is in town". The poster was hung opposite the Music Academy and created such a flutter in the city that the Academy thought of calling the police to remove it.

From accusations that he accepted the taxi fare to drive to the venue and hence he wrote rave reviews for certain people to the claims that he moved in the power circle only, Subbudu and those cashing in on his pen remained unfazed. It is strange that a few could realise that a mere dance and music critic had become so powerful that the entire marketing policy of the magazine depended on him.

> ***I convey my heartfelt gratitude to you, the one who is outstandingly the best critic in the fields of Carnatic music, Hindustani music, Bharatanatyam, Kuchipudi, etc., for sending me, your wishes in your own way...***
>
> *— J. Jayalalitha, Chief Minister of Tamil Nadu, in her letter written to Subbudu recently*

Much as one tries to analyse the past, there is no instance of any other critic covering any genre of the performing or visual arts, who wielded such influence. Few parents of leading musicians recollected that they stood in the queue to meet Subbudu at Express Estate for their children and later found their children doing the same at Maris and Woodlands Hotels for themselves. Subbudu had tremendous clout because he did not ask for any favours from anyone. If at all, he only referred the names of young and upcoming musicians and dancers, to the *sabha* secretaries, with the request that they judge the talent on their own.

I have waited to meet him at Woodlands Hotel at 6 am in the morning too.

— Critic K.S. Mahadevan, confessing that he was a ringside critic while Subbudu was the ring master.

It is true that Subbudu cultivated strong friendships with influential people but it would be little naive to conclude that he did that at the cost of selling his integrity since he did not seek any favours. A simple instance could be the rebuttal he gave to Padma Subrahmanyam. He had watched a dancer's performance and was about to leave when Padma arrived and requested him to stay for her performance as well. When Subbudu told her that he had to go, she told him that he need not cover the performance but could just stay and see it, Subbudu shot back, "Who are you to tell me what I should do? It is my business and my concern if I write or skip it. Just like I do not interfere with your dance, you cannot interefere with my writing. It is sacred to me." It seems, for no fault of hers, Padma enraged Subbudu but then inconsequential things upset him most. However, the larger point here is the word he used to describe what writing meant to him — sacred. The word falls into the family of words, defining prayer and faith.

It seems unlikely then that Subbudu could have set a price for that.

Moreover, he was always involved himself in the personal affairs of the artistes as a family elder. In 1979, Padma got a PhD degree for her extensive research on "Karanas in Indian Dance and Sculpture". It was a matter of great jubilation for her. However, there were some fundamentalists who were upset with the danseuse and decided to challenge her PhD in the court. Subbudu happened to overhear one such conversation and he got paranoid. Same night at 11 o' clock, he telephoned Padma's brother Balakrishnan recounting the entire episode and asked him to consult a lawyer. The next day, Padma spoke to her lawyer who told her not to worry because no one could challenge her degree. A month later, a group of people filed a PIL but the court dismissed it. To this day, Padma feels indebted to Subbudu and confesses that she still does not know how and why he carries everyone's burden on his frail shoulders.

> ***What Padma does not know in dance is not worth knowing.***
>
> — *Subbudu on Padma's contribution to Indian dance*

Meanwhile, the same year, Sudharani was honoured with the title of Nritya Choodamani. While covering her performance at the Krishan Gana Sabha in 1979, Subbudu felt that the dancer was not in her element and after the performance ended, he asked her why she was looking so sad.

"Dance should be a thing of joy," Subbudu told her and kept asking her what the matter was. At that time, Sudharani was passing through a difficult phase in her personal life and she was astonished to find that her face reflected it all. Their friendship had grown to such a point that they could confess anything to each other. Subbudu had often admitted to Sudharani that he indulged in hyperbole and chose exaggerated expression deliberately.

He told her that he throve on the idea of pushing an artiste to a pinnacle and then waited for him/her to tumble down. Many men and women, dancers and musicians collapsed but Subbudu continued with his experiment. Sudharani who has a passion for yoga still recalls that he told her to stop dancing when her body began to sag.

With very few dancers dancing on the professional circuit in those days, the performing opportunities between leading dancers were almost evenly divided. This also meant that there was less acrimony among them. With more time on hand, since the dancers knew that they had their individual spaces in the professional circuit, there was a greater interaction between them and Subbudu.

They were willing to discuss their mistakes since there was no danger of other dancers highlighting their weaknesses. But even then, Subbudu's comments were hard to digest because apart from the innate talent he also stressed on the physical beauty of an artiste. He often told his favourite dancers, "Before the dancer starts performing, his/her physical presence catches the eye. An image is formed immediately and it is only later that one gets to see the talent beneath the body. A bad dancer fails to live up to that image, a good dancer embellishes that image and a great dancer outgrows that image."

Right through his career, Subbudu was careful to point out that very few dancers like Balasaraswati actually inverted the concept of physical beauty because they were dance, not just dancers.

While Subbudu was lenient during the exchange of ideas with the artistes, he was acidic sharing the same through his pen. Those who grew reading his articles remember that his writing was deliberate sometimes. He fed on the idea of serving the arts, full of spice. If members of his family or those around him felt uncomfortable about his style of writing, he told them, that he adopted such a style because that is what his readers sought.

He was clear in his head that he wanted to inform but not without entertaining the readers and making a public display of an artiste's lack of capacity. Be it his/her physical presence or a technical hitch, Subbudu knew that he had to write each article in such a way that it became a rage.

He therefore made caricatures out of artistes and allowed the common man to laugh at their expense. Even if one were to negate everything Subbudu has stood for, one can still apply the same logic which has become a mantra for any successful marketing blitzkrieg, "Know your consumers well."

But sometimes for him, matters went out of control. Subbudu had a bitter experience when a famous Kathakali troupe from Kerala presented a number of dance dramas at the YMCA lawns. While the dancing was of a high standard, the stage management was pathetic. When an episode from the Mahabharata was being enacted on the stage, an attendant with only a *mundu*, entered the stage with a Dalda tin containing oil for the brass lamp placed at the centre on the stage. In fact, when a character hiding behind Terai Cheelai or the curtain was brought on stage by two people wearing full pants, terylene shirts and watches, Subbudu could not control his annoyance. "The man who sang along sported a harmonium sruti box. In the middle of the performance, he spoke in sign language to somebody in the wings showing his forefingers. As the person was not able to comprehend what his *mudra* meant, he asked back in sign language, again what he wanted. The singer, not aware of the mike blurted out, "I want to urinate." Subbudu reported that serious lapses in the stage management killed the performance.

The next day when he attended another performance, the escort at the gate after seeing his identity card enquired if he was actually Subbudu. Subbudu excitedly said yes and "was expecting a garland" but instead the man held him by his collar. He asked him, what he knew about Kathakali and labelled him *Nayeenda*

Mahane (son of a bitch). While on one hand, the man abused Subbudu, on the other, he offered an explanation.

He told him, "The artistes could not bring their whole troupe owing to financial difficulties and therefore they had to depend on the local help and that is why the two Terai Cheelai holders appeared unwittingly wearing pants." He wondered if he expected a silver vessel instead of a Dalda tin.

Fortunately another invitee to the programme recognised Subbudu and saved him. Now, Subbudu had reason to hate Kathakali even more. And while he continued despicing the dance form, his job of spotting young talent in Bharatanatyam kept him busy as ever.

In fact he discovered a child prodigy and ensured that he promoted her unabashedly because he was convinced about her talent. As it turned out young Srinidhi Rangarajan, indeed remained crowd favourite for many Madras seasons!

Subbudu had spotted her for the first time when he witnessed Kamala's dance drama, "Sita Kalyanam". Srinidhi was just six years old and played the role of Baby Sita. Subbudu liked the young girl instantly and later discovered that Srinidhi's father, Dr. Rangarajan was the son of Subbudu's close friend from his days in Burma. Thus, the old friendship was revived.

From then onwards, Srinidhi became his protégé and that continued through the 1980s and 90s. Soon after leading Bharatanatyam dancer and filmstar Kamala left for the USA in 1980, Subbudu asked Srinidhi to shift to Guru S.K. Rajaratnam. Though he bemoans the fact that she did not pursue it aggressively and is now pursuing a career in medicine. However, that did not stop other dancers for suspecting the authenticity of Subbudu's praise for Srinidhi's dance.

The Protective Vulture

In the 1980s, the Indian government hit upon a novel idea of building friendships by promoting its culture abroad. While over the years "The Festival of India Series" became a breeding ground of controversy with a number of artistes using political clout to get invited, the series was a sure fire success in its early years. Prime Ministers Margaret Thatcher and Indira Gandhi inaugurated the "The Festival of India Series" in the UK.

Though projection of India's culture abroad was the prerogative of the Ministry of External Affairs, the Ministry of Education took the lead in organising the Festival of India Series along with ICCR.

Meanwhile in 1980, Subbudu's daughter Ragini married Krishna Kumar. Few people could have imagined that Subbudu would grow to trust his son-in-law more than anyone else in the family. The relationship between him and Kumar was based on mutual respect. Unlike his children, Kumar could view Subbudu and his ideas dispassionately and counter him with his own. That he was a lawyer by profession was only incidental. However as the years went by and controversies dogged him, Kumar became Subbudu's ready guide and confidant who helped him sail through any crisis. Nevertheless, there was only one condition; he demanded complete truth from him. Needless to add, Subbudu had suffered all his life for being so outspoken.

Kumar was uninitiated in classical music and dance and therefore his method of appreciating Carnatic music often clashed with the views of Subbudu and Ragini. Whenever they discussed the performance of a particular artiste, Kumar discovered Subbudu a bit more. He soon realised that he was obsessed with facts. He also felt that Subbudu could separate the celebrity from his/her art and then examine the performance. When Subbudu got embroiled in lawsuits, these facets about his personality helped Kumar to defend him.

A year or so after Ragini's marriage, Subbudu's assistant V.V. Subramaniam was transferred to the Madras branch of the Excise Department in the Finance Ministry. Interestingly, Subbudu's devotee, Kanda-swamy was working in the same department but when Subra-maniam joined the Madras office, Kandaswamy was shifted to Delhi. As luck would have it, Subramaniam had to come to Delhi for some office work where he met Kandaswamy and the two got talking. The moment Subramaniam told him that he was Subbudu's assistant in Delhi, Kandaswamy could not believe his ears. He told Subramaniam how much he loved his writing style and also described his first meeting with him. Ever since Subramaniam had moved to Madras, Subbudu had been without an assistant. Subramaniam hit upon an idea and asked Kandaswamy to accompany him to Subbudu's place.

It was 1982, Kandaswamy met Subbudu for the second time in his life and he had little idea of what was in store for him. Subramaniam offered Kandaswamy to Subbudu and he took him under his wing. That was the beginning of a long and enduring relationship between the two. The same year, the title "Vimarsiana Sudharnva" was bestowed upon Subbudu in recognition of his exemplary contribution to the world of criticism, by Dr. Balamurali Krishna.

Subbudu speaking at a dance performance in Bombay presented by noted Bharatanatyam Guru Kadirvelu

Sometimes he likes music, sometimes he likes artistes, sometimes he likes both, sometimes he likes none.

— Dr. Balamurali Krishna on Subbudu's style of criticism

Subbudu had two yardsticks for the artistes. One for the upcoming and the other for the established. If he could spot a spark in a youngster, he took it upon himself to polish and guide the artiste through his writings and personal interactions and as long as the young prodigy responded with an equal artistic energy, he kept up his momentum of praising him/her at every opportune moment. This remained the case till the artiste managed to attain a certain professional status after which, Subbudu held himself back to see where he/she was headed. If the young star lost his/her kinetic energy, he shred him/her to pieces in print, often reflecting his own frustration at the amount of time he spent in moulding him/her. But, if that artiste could pass his incisive eyes, he changed the configuration of the relationship. From guide then, he became an adviser and seeing him/her on the correct path, he slowly distanced himself further, ensuring the talented artiste, his/her own well-deserved fame and glory with Subbudu taking a bow as a well-wisher.

In 1982 itself, Subbudu discovered one such prodigy and promptly became his mentor. He had so much faith in his protégé's talent that during the Madras season of 1989, he dared artistes to better the 19-year-old's feat on the mandolin and swore to shave his head if anyone could beat the genius at his game. At 35 today, mandolin maestro U. Srinivas, popularly known as Mandolin Srinivas still trembles with nervousness at the mention of Subbudu.

During the December season in 1982, at the age of twelve, Srinivas was invited to play for the afternoon session at the Indian Fine Arts Society. Veena S. Balachander presided over the festival that year. As the curtains came up, Srinivas saw Subbudu sitting with T.N. Seshagopalan and Veena S. Balachander. It was Srinivas' first performance under a *sabha* patronage and for him the biggest moment of his life had been affected by the presence of a no-nonsense critic who could destroy a mediocre talent. After his performance ended, Balachander came on the dais and spoke highly of the young boy's performance. Meanwhile, Seshagopalan was so impressed with the child prodigy that he gifted him his gold ring. Two days later, Subbudu wrote a long article on the gifted child's artistic prowess. Srinivas did not know that he had written an article on him until his friend came running carrying a copy of the paper and shouted excitedly, "Look what Subbudu has written about you." Srinivas began to sweat and finally read the article only to cry with joy. The critic had firmly thrown his weight behind him.

That day onwards, whenever Mandolin Srinivas performed during the season in Chennai or in Delhi, Subbudu made it a point to attend each performance and gave him his frank opnion. Right from asking him to be more demonstrative about his art before the *rasikas* to egging him on to play popular *ragas* while continuing his flirtation with new *ragas*, Subbudu gave him a piece of his mind after every concert — good, bad or ugly.

Mandolin was honed by him to play for the audience, to treat them with respect and dignity because they and not the critics like him, were the real patrons, the king makers.

He is my Bramha Rishi.

— Mandolin Srinivas on his relationship with Subbudu

The same year when Subbudu spotted Mandolin Srinivas, a silk cloth business magnate was introduced to the critic. He had been drawn to the performing arts two years ago when he bumped into Doordarshan Natarajan. Nalli Koppuswamy Chetti, the owner of Nalli Silks had gone to request veteran nagaswaram player Namgiripettai Krishnan to play at his daughter's wedding. The artiste turned out to be Doordarshan Natarajan's father-in-law. Though Nalli had absolutely no interest in music, his friendship with Natarajan ensured that he attended the *kutcheris* of the famous artistes.

Once he happened to read a review of a *kutcheri* which he too had attended. Finding the style riveting, he asked Natarajan if he knew the writer. Natarajan smiled and told him that he knew Subbudu very well and when the two men met, Nalli was impressed by Subbudu's knowledge and humour.

While Doordarshan Natarajan was one of the reasons for Nalli's curiosity in music and dance, Subbudu's articles enlivened his interest. Slowly, Nalli started collecting his articles, especially the ones that appeared in *Dinamani Kadir*. Later he met a family friend and was amazed to find that he had also collected Subbudu's articles in English and Tamil. The interesting fact was that this friend did not live in India but in the USA.

Once while talking to him, Subbudu casually remarked how it was so tough to get a cup of coffee early in the morning. Nalli requested his sister Pankajam who lived near Woodlands Hotel to deliver a flask of coffee to the hotel every morning and so Pankajam's husband, Keshavam started delivering coffee to Subbudu's hotel every morning. Subbudu was extremely touched by the gesture and that day onwards, Nalli became a part of his extended family.

In 1983, Subbudu's younger son Ravi married Sujata. In the following years, Sujata and, Sriram's wife, Jayshree discovered that Subbudu and Chandra were very non-interfering in-laws. With Ravi's marriage, Subbudu and Chandra were finally eased of the burden of getting their children settled.

In 1984, Subbudu took Kandaswamy to Madras for the first time. V.V. Subramaniam was extremely disappointed when he came to know that Subbudu preferred Kandaswamy to him. However, Subbudu knew that Kandaswamy was a better time manager and Subramaniam respected what he thought. For the next two decades, Kandaswamy was going to strictly adhere to time management for Subbudu.

That year itself, M.L. Vasanthakumari introduced Subbudu to her disciple Sudha Raghunathan. Sudha started training under Vasanthakumari on a Central Government Scholarship in 1978 and the beginning of the 80s saw her Guru encouraging her to grow out of her own shadow.

Sudha's voice captivated him, so much so that Subbudu was going to write in the coming years that he had to listen to Sudha twice, once as a critic and once as a *rasika*. He felt that just as her guru, Sudha could also challenge any male singer with her gusto power. Every December season review by Subbudu helped her move up the ladder.

These days, whereever she gives concerts, she is introduced by the speakers in Subbudu's famous words, " If I am marooned on an island and if I am granted permission to bring along with me three things I like a lot, I would list the following: (1) an audio visual cassette of Sudha singing, (2) Betel leaves and tobacco and (3) Poet Kannadasan's works."

Most artistes found it surprising that Subbudu could afford to be extremely gentle to some while being harsh to others. Once at a festival, Sudha sang Hamsanandi *raga* and followed it up with a Pushpalatika. The *raga* does not have much variation to it. Sudha sang it a little longer to which Subbudu observed, "Sudha must learn to sing in the right proportion." Unlike with others, Subbudu did not tear Sudha to pieces and did not offer any explanations for his gentle behaviour. However, Sudha's Guru Vasanthakumari's death in 1990 greatly affected her career.

Subbudu always considered Vasanthakumari to be one of the finest individuals he had the chance to meet. He remembers, once when he visited her home in Madras, he was amazed to find her house bustling with children. Having held strong views against Gurukulam himself, he was overwhelmed at the sight of little girls stretching their voices, some out of passion and others out of competition. He asked Vasanthakumari about them but she changed the topic. It was only later that he discovered, that Vasanthakumari never charged anything from the girls, who used to come to her home early in the morning and used to leave her house only after dining at her place.

During her last years, Vasanthakumari was unable to drape a *saree* and therefore preferred to stay in her nightgown. When Subbudu went to meet her, she felt terribly embarrassed. In his own way of making her comfortable, he said, "Do not worry, this gives you maximum coverage", thereby making her laugh. She hadn't laughed like that for a long time. But while narrating the incidents, Subbudu's choked voice betrayed his smiling face.

Few people know that before she died, Vasanthakumari told Subbudu to take care of Sudha. From that day onwards, he became one of the most influential figures in her career and his writings became cues for Sudha to grow in the right direction. Subbudu considered himself fortunate because he got a chance to serve three generations of Guru-Shishyas, beginning with G.N. Balasubramaniam and ending with Sudha Raghunathan.

The year 1984 was the watershed year in the history of Indian dance because Chandralekha returned to dance after a self-imposed exile of nearly a decade, at the East West Encounter, held between January 22nd and January 29th, jointly organised by the NCPA and the Max Mueller Bhavan in Bombay. Her presentation and ideas on dance confronted top starlets, among them, Padma Subrahmanyam and Yamini Krishnamurthy. She was labelled maverick for the way she thought and a year later at the Second East West Encounter, Chandralekha proved just that with her seminal production *Angika*. Incidentally, India's first professional Sikh Bharatanatyam dancer, Navtej Johar was part of the premiere performance of *Angika*. On her part, Rukmini Devi had allowed Chandralekha to use four dancers for reviving her production *Tillana* at the East West Encounter 1984. The festival had thrown open the doors of communication and confrontation between the dancers of various nations. The energy of the festival was reminiscent of East West 64, a festival of music held by the ICCR and the SNA exactly two decades ago.

Meanwhile, Chandralekha's ideas and views on dance were highly appreciated by Shanta Serbjeet Singh and Sunil Kothari. Her entry on the dance scene was crucial because it further divided dance criticism in India. Subbudu and later K.S. Srinivasan and V.V. Prasad tore apart Chandra's *Angika* and later her controversial work, *Primal Energy*.

As Rustom Bharaucha presented Subbudu's and Shanta's reactions at different points in Chandralekha's biography *Chandra-*

lekha, Woman, Dance, Resistance — Subbudu accused Chandra of "assiduously trying to go back to the stone age on the pretext of harnessing primordial energy through the dance forms". He added, "one hopes she does not revert to raw meat". Subbudu did not relent there and wrote that he would have "preferred the originals in their natural habitat or as an alternative a visit to the zoo". As opposed to Subbudu, Shanta appreciated Chandra's work and tried to recreate the impact through her words. She felt that there was, "a rolling off first of the false layers of sentimentality and religiosity, then a slow and measured unfolding of the strength and the sheer beauty of Bharatanatyam underneath it all."

Angika received the kind of publicity which leading artistes could only dream of getting. There was an eight-page spread in *India Today* on May 15, 1985 co-authored by the current editor of *The Indian Express,* Coomi Kapoor and critic Sunil Kothari, with photographs by Raghu Rai. The entire world of dance seemed to be in a frenzy waiting to see what was going to happen. *Angika* was staged as part of the Nritya Natak festival as well. Subbudu again trashed it by saying, "there has to be a core theme for the dance to bring out the drama — not merely an elaboration of the body dynamics..."

Angika and *Primal Energy* antagonised Subbudu no end but his critics accused him of having a coterie who saw to it that Chandra was damned.

She should be driven out of the city.

— Subbudu expressing his anger against
Chandralekha before Anita Ratnam

Chandraleka's presence in the dance world was discomforting for most dancers not only because of the tension she created by just being there, but also because through her productions like *Primal Energy*, Chandra shocked the audience with her "bold representation of the *yoni/lingam* interaction and assertion of the female energy principle." Meanwhile, the Indian government decided to hold the Festival of India in the Soviet Union. Every artiste of repute wanted to be a part of the celebration of Indo-Russian ties.

In order to be invited to the festival, the artistes had to display their works first. Chandralekha presented *Angamandala* in which she added *Primal Energy* to lengthen the production, an attempt which received lukewarm response. Subbudu witnessed the programme and wrote, "The exhibition of this pot-pourri might make our reputation go on deputation. At this moment the government has entered into a historic treaty with Russia and nothing should be done to change our relations."

Chandra's friends and well-wishers launched a diatribe against Subbudu, chiefly among them, journalist and partner Sadanand Menon. He accused Subbudu of creating a vocabulary of dance criticism which reduced female dancers to mere anatomies to be admired or detested.

On her part, Chandra retaliated by writing in *The Times of India*: "You can count the critics who are scared of work on your finger tips. Two, three, four — I can almost see this clique operating in sheer panic. They don't have the necessary refinement. Their criticism operates in total vaccum. I can have no respect for these commercial columnists who have the power of their column and nothing else. They write for bylines and then they get drunk on those bylines. And they come with their measuring tapes wanting to measure everything and collect vital statistics." A section of the media and artiste community flayed Subbudu for his sexist writing. But Subbudu stood strong and violent.

You are a brave girl. Keep it up!

— Subbudu congratulating the Deputy Editor of Sruti, S. Janaki for ripping apart one of Chandralekha's performances

It was interesting and ironic to notice that while on one hand Sadanand chose to attack Subbudu because he found his writing style suffering from the male gaze especially since he thought that Subbudu dwelled more on the vital statistics of the dancers than their talent, on the other hand, Subbudu could not tolerate the bold, uninhibited fixation for literally depicting love and lust between a man and a woman by those who he claimed had avoided the rigours of classical format because they lacked discipline. In spite of the growing criticism by the new breed of contemporary dancers, Subbudu has held on to his views. He still defines Chandralekha's work as a dance of pornography. That, she is also known as an iconoclast by an entire generation of modern dancers is a different matter.

However, as dance critics were busy decoding and recoding their idea of dance, based on its dynamic nature, Subbudu fell out with most of them. He flatly refused to recognise the new voices in dance and held onto the belief that till the time you are not a master of the field, you cannot experiment with it and if you want to, then you must be in a position to define its structure and must give it a different identity. He repeatedly said, "Don't sell crass in the name of Bharatanatyam."

His colleagues felt that Subbudu had begun to represent the puritanical branch of criticism. While it could have been true at a given point, Subbudu's decision transformed him into becoming a saviour of the classical dance, since he did not allow any artiste to address herself/himself as a classical dancer casually. Ironically, the critics in our times, who either hate or fail to understand contemporary dance force themselves to write a good review in fear of being labelled conservative and myopic. For some, giving a clean copy means making friends in the business, where a bad review means making more enemies.

Nearly two decades later after his controversy with Chandralekha, while giving a keynote address at a Dance Symposium on Choreography in 2003, organised by Sri Shanmukhananda Fine Arts and Sangeet Sabha, Subbudu forcefully declared that Anita Ratnam and Padma Subrahmanyam were the only Bharatanatyam dancers who did not deviate from the basic form but evolved it through their research and practical experiences. He added that these dancers were sensitive enough not to label their dance as Bharatanatyam and proclaimed them the only choreographers worth their salt in India.

Anita was stunned when she heard Subbudu's remarks because in her entire career as a dancer she yearned for a passionate review from him but never got one. It was revealed later that Subbudu had been following her work after she returned to India. She had begun experimenting with other classical and folk disciplines and had confessed that even if she wanted she could not return to Bharatanatyam, because her body had adjusted to her new dance techniques. For Subbudu, Anita's commitment to modern dance and at the same time, her sensitivity to the fact that she was not practising Bharatanatyam *per se*, was gratifying.

While taking a dig at those who had declared that Bharatanatyam would have died but for Chandralekha, Subbudu, while reviewing Valli's benefit performance for the construction of a wing of the Tamil Sangam in Delhi, wrote, "A hundred Chandralekhas cannot dethrone classical Bharatanatyam from its traditional greatness by their fangled enthusiasm to update it. This was proved beyond measure… by Alarmel Valli…"

In later years, he went on to even mention Western critcs, who had lavished praise on Valli's Bharatanatyam. Subbudu quoted a German critic, Jochen Schmidt who had witnessed Alarmel's and

Chandra's performances. He wrote, "The traditional dance of Alarmel Valli is so full of art and rich in nuances, that Chandralekha's lean modernity seems poor and antiquated by contrast."

It was an interesting point in Subbudu's life. At the beginning of his career he had questioned the knowledge and the commitment of foreign critics who covered Indian dance and now he had devoted an entire article quoting another Western critic. Aware of the dichotomy of the situation, Subbudu comforted himself with the idea that he did that to save Indian dance from losing the battle against the Culture Nazism. He was stung by Chandra's audacity to call Bharatanatyam a dance of the Mylapore *mamis* on one hand and her desire to use Kalakshetra trained dancers on the other. Moreover, he was concerned that the modern choreographers had been labelled elementary by the people in the West. It was therefore important that only those dancers who stuck to an Indian structure of dance were promoted and not those who passed "titillation as tradition" from the Land of Kamasutra.

However, Subbudu was not blind to the decay that was affecting Bharatanatyam. In the 1990s, he created a hornet's nest by saying that the more he saw Bharatanatyam, the more he was convinced that the *devadasi* system should be revived. He clarified that he wished the dancers to have the same kind of knowledge. Unlike the dancers of today, the *devadasis* had to master Tamil, Telugu, Sanskrit and Kannada. They had to learn vocal and instrumental music, and master the Puranas so that they were consummate dancers.

Subbudu's point of argument was that it is the dancer and not the dance which should be damned. Much as Subbudu mocked Chandralekha's choreographic works, he also took two top rung Bharatanatyam dancers to task on different occasions. While one of them, danced to "Brova Baarama" (Am I a burden to you, O!

Rama?) by keeping her hands on her head and making three pirouettes, the other dancer depicted "Kanmani" (Darling) as Kan-Mani (eyes and bells).

After asking the former dancer to relearn her basics in *abhinaya*, Subbudu wrote, "I am only a reporter, but only today I realised that she is a porter."

> ***"Subbudu berates older artistes for putting road blocks before younger ones, without pausing to extend the same logic to himself as a writer."***
>
> — *Sadanand Menon, The Chennai Season, An Orchestra of Opposites, The Indian Express, December 31, 2000*

From the mid-80s onwards, *sabhas* underwent tremendous changes. Before leaving for the USA, Kamala had complained that the growing number of young mediocre dancers had flooded the Chennai season. As a senior dancer she had every reason to demand her price but she found that leading *sabhas* refused to grant her concerts because they could book two or more dancers for the price of one. With more dancers joining in and audiences continuously dwindling, some *sabhas* began to charge money from the artistes themselves for concert space.

As a Madras-based dancer informed, the price at that time was anywhere between Rs. 3000 to Rs. 5000 but these days, young dancers need to shell out anywhere between Rs. 15,000 to Rs. 20,000 to get a decent platform to perform. The stories of fly-by-night operators, who act as culture *dalals* and fix programmes for a percentage commission, are well known now. Today, there is an audience only for the top artistes and the situation has deteriorated so much that organisers now ask the artistes to bring fifty people at least if they want to participate under the banner of a given organisation. Incidentally the proliferation of the *sabhas* and the rise in the number of artistes participating and thronging the Madras season further increased Subbudu's importance and his power. There were two reasons behind it. Firstly, Subbudu had a history of being a bold and fearless journalist and therefore second generation artistes, needed his approval to be invited by the leading *sabhas*. Secondly, with a number of talented artistes vying for the same platforms, Subbudu's negative comments could destroy their careers.

> ***Today, there are 1200-1300 concerts that take place but there are no audiences and now there are only NRIs and outsiders who hold the centre stage in Madras.***
>
> *— Prof. Anuradha Venkatachalam on the changing face of the Chennai season*

In 1984 and 1985, Subbudu discovered two talented Bharatanatyam dancers, Urmila Satyanarayan and Srekala Bharath. Both were students of Guru K. J. Sarasa. On separate occasions, he told them, "As soon as you arrive on the stage you have to capture the audience. Before you dance, your looks, figure and smile create an impression. Beyond that your costumes get noticed and at the end of it all, dance comes into the picture." Subbudu's mantra was that the dance, which is the last thing on the mind at the beginning of the recital, should entice the mind completely leaving no scope for anything to influence it, by the time the recital ends.

The same season, M.L. Vasanthakumari specially invited Subbudu for her daughter Srividya's Bharatanatyam recital. In spite of the fact that he shared a warm relationship with Vasanthakumari, Subbudu did not mince words while criticising Srividya's physical appearance writing that "If only she could reduce the circumference of her waist, she could circumvent the world." The following day, Vasanthakumari, her husband and Srividya visited Subbudu and Vasanthakumari told him that some film producers willing to sign her daughter had backed off, probably after reading his review.

But she and Subbudu ensured that one sentence about Srividya did not create a wedge between the two. Vasanthakumari was not the only mother who sought Subbudu's blessings for her daughter. There were others too who however lacked her grace and wisdom.

Srekala Bharath had re-entered the professional space after going through a brain tumour surgery. It was a personal victory for her and her passion for dance. Understandably ambitious about her career as a dancer, Srekala was advised to get a review from Subbudu, if she wanted to be taken seriously. Soon, her well-wishers and friends, inundated Subbudu with numerous phone calls. In 1986, after much dilly-dallying, he saw the young dancer's recital and was pleased with himself for having discovered yet another star in the making. He wanted to refine Srekala and guide her till

Chandra, Srekala Bharath with her student and Subbudu

she could be on her own. During the December season of 1987, when Srekala gathered courage to meet Subbudu, she was surprised beyond belief that he could recall that she had performed Purvikalyani Varnam a year back. Subbudu immediately demonstrated to her the way Valli should have looked at Murugha to win his heart. He told her, "Next time do this."

Srekala and Subbudu became particularly close after she suffered another setback in 1990 and was diagnosed with Myasthenia Gravis. She battled it for over three years and eventually emerged victorious. Almost immediately Srekala went back to her guru. Her performance at Nungambakkam Cultural Academy in 1993 was one of her most memorable moments. When Srekala reappeared, no one had to make an effort to call on Subbudu. He was already there, aggressively promoting her this time.

In his review, Subbudu wrote, "In Srekala's performance, one could see all the *rasas.*" Subbudu made sure that he mentioned her battle with serious ailments in every review. He even went ahead and told her mother-in-law, who is a Carnatic singer, that she could have come up if she was as determined as her daughter-in-law was — so much for playing the role of Sage Narada between the two.

Meanwhile, Subbudu decided to bring down the curtains on his drama troupe South Indian Theatre in 1984. Though there were no more rehearsals at home, his habit of ordering cups of coffee and snacks did not stop. But now Chandra had her daughters-in-law and her grandchildren to hear her plight. Even then, she was mild in her criticism. She would say, "Appa does not realise whether we have anything at home or not. We should stock the food items because one never knows when he gets visitors."

Subbudu's grandchildren grew up under the halo of their grandfather's name and struggled to maintain their own identity. Except for his granddaughters Purvaja and Swetha, none of them pursues dance, singing or writing and have set their eyes on professional careers. Though Ravi's elder daughter Divya is an exceptionally brilliant Western singer, she avoids the limelight.

Needless to say, all the children dote on their grandfather, who according to them, is the best storyteller in the world but they recall that they grew up discovering the critic in their grandfather by interacting with the world outside.

As his eldest granddaughter Swetha wrote recently, "As a youngster, I was gently interrogated by visitors as to who was my guru, which type of music I pursued, etc. I would reply immediately, "I don't sing." The ensuing silence used to be deafening. "Then, do you dance?" "No". Silence. Then would come the penultimate question or rather statement, "How come being Subbudu *mama's* granddaughter, you can't sing or dance?"

There were occasions when Swetha and her cousins were angry and embarrassed. She says, "To be very frank, I haven't inherited anything more than some wit and a ruddy complexion from my grandfather. His encyclopedic knowledge of *ragas, layas, taalams* and other musical paraphernalia used to make us feel awed and proud but he has never forced any one of us to learn music or dance."

However, as she was forced to believe that the music was in her genes, Swetha gathered enough courage to learn music from a Hindustani guru. She recalls the episode in her characteristic humour, which she insists, she has got from her grandfather.

"I thought I could sing *ghazals* and light music if not *thumris* and *khayals* but my guru thought otherwise. He felt Subbuduji's granddaughter was capable of much more and started me off on hardcore Hindustani music complete with harmonium *et al.* In my first class, I serenaded up and down on the *sa re ga ma* scale. I do not know to this day whether the guruji complimented me on merit or because of my grandfather but whatever it is, all he said was music to my ears. However, that evening turned into a musical nightmare for me. Armed with my grandfather's harmonium, I assumed my position on the *divan.* No sooner had I started, than my grandfather said, "That is not the correct style of singing. And the positioning of the fingers on the harmonium is also wrong. Let me show you how to play it." That was Swetha's first brush with Subbudu the critic. A few more such evenings followed where she learnt something in the class and then unlearnt the same at home.

"Guruji maintained that my grandfather's tips were useful but quite Carnatic in nature. Thus torn between the South and the North, I kept learning only *sa re ga ma* the whole month."

Swetha felt that her knowledge was so perfect that she could write a thesis on "Differences in rendering '*Sa Re Ga Ma*' in Hindustani and Carnatic style". Finally she decided to stop her music tuition. She thought that her decision could disappoint Subbudu but he replied in his indomitably witty style, "You made my job easy. It would have been difficult to be critical of my beloved granddaughter. You have a ear for good music and that is all that matters."

In the late 1980s, Subbudu discovered that like him, his eldest granddaughter had a way with words. By the time she reached her teens, Swetha started accompanying her grandfather to concerts. Subbudu encouraged her to speak her mind about the performances she saw with him. Then one fine day, he asked her if she would be interested to pursue writing seriously. She knew that her grandfather was going to stand by her decision to become a writer.

He asked her to write the beginning and the end of an article on the recital she had watched with him. Swetha wrote so well that Subbudu told her he was going to use her beginning and ending for his article. Getting praise from her grandfather meant a lot to her but Swetha realised that she had a special flair for humorous satirical writing. The world of dance and music criticism was not her first love and she was too aware of the inevitable comparison with her grandfather's knowledge and style of writing.

If I can be half as famous as my grandfather is, it will be worth it.

— Swetha Sundar, on her ambition to be as renowned as Subbudu

Subbudu's idea of puritanism in music and dance remained same, be it his grand daugther or leading artistes. While fighting for the sanctity of style, Subbudu also had issues with leading Bharatanatyam dancer and guru, V.P. Dhananjayan. He felt that in spite of being a good dancer and one of the most respected gurus of Chennai, he was unable to free himself from Kathakali dance which affected his style of Bharatanatyam. During his training at Kalakshetra, Dhananjayan was trained both in Bharatanatyam and in Kathakali. Subbudu believed this was the reason why Dhananjayan's Bharatanatyam had elements of Kathakali. While both agreed to differ on this point, Dhananjayan nevertheless valued Subbudu's observations. For him the biggest compliment was when during one of his recitals, Subbudu came backstage and wept with joy on seeing him and his wife Shanta perform.

If I may say so, whoever Subbudu has liberally criticised have become better known artists than whom he praised sky high.

— V.P. Dhananjayan on how Subbudu's negative criticism helped him

By 1986, Kandaswamy had adjusted himself to Subbudu's routine in Madras. Since the number of *sabhas* and concerts had increased, his routine had become strenuous. His day would begin at 6 am with a hot cup of coffee. Since the canteen of the Woodlands Hotel used to open after 6 am, Kandaswamy had to get coffee for Subbudu from a coffee stall adjacent to the hotel. After drinking his cup of coffee, Subbudu asked for the day's newspaper. If it contained the article, he would make Kandaswamy read it first and then they discussed the performances reviewed in the article.

Each time Subbudu covered an artiste's recital, he expected him or her to call him and acknowledge his work. It did not matter if they hated his work but he could not afford to be ignored.

After reading the entire newspaper except for the business page, Subbudu would perform yoga for 45 minutes which was followed by a quick bath. After his bath, he would rush to Swami Haridas Giri's Harikathas at Krishna Gana Sabha. Such was Subbudu's relationship with Swamiji that he never sang during the Madras season without Subbudu accompanying him on the harmonium.

After attending the Harikatha, he would walk back to his hotel and again ask for a cup of coffee and then rest for fifteen minutes. During this time, Kandaswamy had to deal with hordes of visitors waiting, to meet Subbudu, be it to invite him, thank him or curse him. Whether there were incessant knocks on the door or innumerable phone calls, Kandaswamy had to ward off any danger which threatened to disturb Subbudu's sleep.

By the time Subbudu used to wake up, Kandaswamy would rummage through the list of invitations and the programmes appearing in the newspapers. While doing this, he had to keep track of all the important people who called on Subbudu.

Whenever Kandaswamy used to feel that Subbudu was getting disturbed he took the receiver off the phone. And each time Kandaswamy did so, he knew, he had booked himself for a huge argument with the Hotel authorities. That's because people would start abusing the hotel operators if they could not connect them to Subbudu. "Sir, please put the receiver back", Kandaswamy had grown old hearing that comment from the staff of the Woodlands Hotel.

Kandaswamy would select six programmes per day which included, a lecture demonstration at the Krishna Gana Sabha every day at 10:30 am, two concerts by stalwarts, one from music and the other from dance and the concerts of three middle level, up-coming or fresh artistes. These three concerts had one dancer and two musicians, one vocal and one instrumental. Even though sometimes the schedule was changed, Subbudu never missed the lecture demonstration every morning. He believed that a lec-dem gave an insight into an artiste's growth not only as a performer but also as a potential guru. Whether the artiste chose to be one or not is a different matter, what Subbudu wished to spot was how far the seeker had become a giver. He also felt lec-dems gave him a chance to know things he may not have otherwise in a normal proscenium set up. He had come a long way from his experience of attending the lec-dem of the dancer who tried bribing him in the early 70s.

After attending lec-dem, Subbudu used to witness afternoon concert at 1:00 pm. Post-concert, his visit to the *sabha* canteen use to be a public affair. His sojourn at the canteen was punctuated by his fans and well-wishers, telling him how they loved his writings. Dressed in spotless white *dhotis* and rich kanchipurams, men and women would prostrate themselves before him leaving him embarrassed.

The canteen owners also used to add their word of appreciation. They liked Subbudu, not only because he wrote well but also because his presence signalled a busy afternoon in the canteen. Since he was someone who kept a low profile, there was always a level of curiosity to spot him. And meeting him in an informal environment was like a dream come true for most artistes, their peers and parents. However, even here, Kandaswamy acted as a radar and deflected any mental torture or physical danger.

As Subbudu grew old, he became more dependent on Kandaswamy but he never used his clout over the man in getting a favourable review for a particular artiste. If at all he did anything, it was just to recommend someone, and knowing Kandaswamy, Subbudu trusted him to be true to him like his own sons were.

Interestingly, wherever Subbudu went, people did not allow him to buy tickets. However, if they received bad reviews later on, those very people tried to stop him from entering a *sabha* hall later on forcing him to tell them that he had purchased a ticket and it was his fundamental right to attend the programme. Nonetheless, having Subbudu at one's performance was an honour and the relatives of the artistes were often busy spotting him in the audience. Some of them tried to keep a tab on their watch to know how long he stayed and after which item he left. Those sitting next to him or around him could never know what he noticed about the performance. Generally people sitting next to a critic strain their necks to see what he/she is jotting down on paper. But with Subbudu, it was never meant to be. On an average, he would attend five to six performances but would never take notes himself nor would Kandaswamy.

Subbudu made sure that he sat at the end of the auditorium when attending the concert of a popular artiste. Kandaswamy would select the cornermost seat in the auditorium so that he could leave whenever he wanted to without creating a ripple.

After attending the last programme, he used to visit the canteen at the Narada Gana Sabha where the canteen manager kept curd rice especially for him. After having his food, he used to sit in the *sabha* office and discuss the day's programmes with Surya Narayan, his brother R. Krishnaswami and others present there. They would discuss everything, from the mistakes made by a reputed singer during the *gamakas* to a dancer bloating out. Subbudu would become a *rasika* while discussing the programmes and would leave the place only when reminded by Kandaswamy that he had another busy day ahead of him.

Those who felt that Subbudu was a no-holds-barred writer probably did not know that when Subbudu spent hours discussing day's performances, he was more vocal and critical. However, when he wrote his reviews, he was more cautious and conservative in his criticism. Moreover, if any artiste approached him to know how he/she perform, he came across extremely polite and docile.

While walking back to the hotel, Subbudu used to invariably tell Kandaswamy that he had forgotten everything. He would worry endlessly about what to write for his column. After reaching the hotel room, he would have tea with biscuits. As the city prepared to sleep, he used to ask Kandaswamy to cut betel nuts for him. Around 12:30 am, he would ask Kandaswamy if he wanted to sleep. A loud "No" from him used to prompt him to tell him to get ready. Every night, he dictated in English first because his reviews were carried in *The Indian Express* daily. As soon as Kandaswamy finished writing that, Subbudu used to look at his watch and once again ask him if he was willing to work for another hour. As always Kandaswamy agreed. He enjoyed Subbudu's Tamil write ups more because of the colloquial richness of the language and his play with words. After taking dictation, he used to put Subbudu to sleep.

And every day, while doing this he prayed fervently that Subbudu should remain healthy. After ensuring that he slept peacefully, Kandaswamy used to collect the pictures of the dancers and the musicians reviewed by Subbudu and would write their names and styles on the back of the photographs. Having cross-checked the names and spellings, he would hit the sack as well but not for long. Around 4 in the morning, a postman from *The Indian Express* used to knock at the door. Half-drowsy, Kandaswamy would hand him the reviews written at night and take from him a copy of the day's edition. Each time, Kandaswamy spotted someone's review in the morning papers, he invariably thought the critic had been strongly inspired by Subbudu's verdict on the artiste. While Subbudu preferred not to believe in Kandaswamy's inference, he made sure that he read the reviews of the other critics and gave them his feedback.

However, when it came to his reviews, Subbudu sent Kandaswamy to the tea stalls to hear what people felt about his writings. He gave more credence to what the common man thought because at the end of the day, artistes and even Subbudu could be made and unmade by the masses.

Even though Kandaswamy was his eyes and ears, he did not take offence whenever Subbudu asked him to stand out sometimes when an artiste visited him, even though he had become his shadow. Kandaswamy did not allow him to move away from his sight for even a few minutes. At times when Subbudu took longer to bathe, he would begin banging the door.

Loyalty means Kandaswamy.

— Subbudu on what he thinks of Kandaswamy

A. Kandaswamy, Subbudu's assistant

Over a period of time, Subbudu had begun to feel that there was a discrimination against South Indian artistes. He therefore went out of his way to help the artistes from the South seeking to create a space for themselves in Delhi. Such was Subbudu's commitment to the cause that he was the only one who provided staunch support to the annual Thematic Festival of Carnatic Music, which was organised by T.V. Gopalakrishnan to showcase the upcoming talent from the South. Artistes like Sudha Raghunathan, Soumya, Kadiri and Unni Krishnan were some of the talented youngsters who performed at the festival. In spite of being close to TVG, Subbudu maintained his distance from him while reviewing his performance. In the 1980s, TVG organised the annual AIMA Festival which was held in the Woodlands Hotel for several years.

Once at the festival, TVG sang a song in Nata Bhairavi *raga* which had been rarely used in Carnatic music. Subbudu did not like the *raga* and criticised him for having attempted it. In fact, he could not speak to TVG for the next six months. When they finally met, Subbudu asked him if he was upset with him for having written that way. Demanding a great personal equation irrespective of their professional relations, was something peculiar to him. For him, what mattered between him and the artistes was in public view, in terms of performances and his reactions. But beyond that, he and the artistes were human beings involved in the common objective of enriching the arts.

Once, his review of TVG's performance prompted the secretaries to debar him from performing at the Music Academy for the next two years.

In the late 1980s and early 90s, Subbudu also noticed that almost all the established second-generation Carnatic singers had begun taking a keen interest in their film careers as playback singers. Subbudu believed that if a Carnatic singer turns to playback singing, he has to train his voice to suit that medium. As a result, most of the artistes did not want to risk their voices on Carnatic music.

In fact, Subbudu's suggestion that, leading Carnatic singer, Jesudas should temporarily suspend his film career and reorient his voice to suit the concert platform escalated into a huge controversy.

Subbudu felt that during his concert at the Mylapore Fine Arts Society, Jesudas showed little involvement in the songs he rendered and concluded that singing in chaste Carnatic style required an assiduous practice and that cooing and crooning would not do. If at all, he wished to, then Jesudas should just forget singing improper classical discipline. Jesudas was furious after reading the review because he felt Subbudu had questioned his freedom as an artiste.

Meanwhile, people close to the artiste misinterpreted the review and he ended up saying, "Subbudu is an ignoramus. His knowledge is *shoonyam.*"

Subbudu replied, "I take it as great honour because *shoonya* is the essence of the arithmetic."

Though Subbudu firmly believed that whatever Jesudas does is his business, he felt that since the artiste became great because of his art, he owed it back. For him, film music represented a world of impurity where talent was sacrificed at the altar of commercialism. Incidentally, Subbudu also expressed his frustration after Unni Krishnan had started singing for films but celebrated his return to the classical fold in the mid-90s.

Meanwhile, three days after the review appeared, Jesudas had a performance at the Narada Gana Sabha where the number of people witnessing his performance was drastically reduced. It is believed, Jesudas told the Secretary of the Narada Gana Sabha, R. Krishnaswami that he would not sing if Subbudu attended the concert. Krishnaswami told Jesudas that if Subbudu was willing to attend the concert, nobody could stop him and if he was uncomfortable singing in the *sabha*, he could make arrangements for him somewhere else. Meanwhile, Subbudu chose not to attend the concert on his own.

Soon after the Jesudas controversy, Subbudu visited Cochin for a music festival organised by the All India Scouts Association. Balamurali Krishna participated in the festival as well. It so happened that Dr. Krishna was approached by Jesudas' self-professed fans who wished to meet Subbudu to teach him the lesson of his life. Apprehending a danger to his life, Balamurali prevailed upon the crowd and ensured Subbudu's safety.

As soon as Subbudu came clean from the Jesudas controversy, he locked horns with talented musician Illayaraja. Subbudu had been uncomfortable with Illayaraja composing the *kritis* sung by the trinity in *ragas* different from the ones in which they were originally composed. So while appreciating his intelligence, he wrote that he had no business to change the *ragas* of the *kritis*. Subbudu felt that the *kritis* were composed in a certain mood and hence they should not be tampered with. He also told him that while indulging in folk music, Ilayaraja should use Indian drums. "Do not use bands," he wrote appearing teacher like. Illayaraja got angry and shot back.

The exchange continued for some time, till Illayaraja wrote, "Please leave me alone. I am indulging in child's play." A few years later, when he invited Subbudu and Chandra to his place, he was surprised to see Subbudu's deftness on the harmonium. They discussed his criticism of his work and the critic explained exactly what he was trying to say. On the other hand, Subbudu also looked at the work done by the artiste and admired him for his talent. Later Illayaraja wrote in *Ananda Vikatan*, that he had misunderstood Subbudu and the meeting between the two had enabled him to understand that he only wanted him to improve himself. The moment Subbudu and Illayaraja raised white flags, the veteran critic found fault with yet another Carnatic musician. All these incidents, it seems, kept him in good humour.

In the late 1980s, after witnessing a fusion recital spearheaded by Maharajapuram Santhanam, at the Narada Gana Sabha, Subbudu began his article by writing that he was sleeping when a dream came to him that he and Kandaswamy go to a hotel where they bump into Adi Shankaracharya in a spotless *dhoti kurta*, having *masala dosa*. Subbudu had driven home a point. He soon found Maharajapuram knocking on his door and asking Kandaswamy for an appointment with the bizarre writer. He did not allow him and instead said that whatever his grudge was, he should share it with the Editor of the paper.

The fact that Subbudu had become synonymous with criticism was underlined when, in 2002, he was requested by film director and actor, Parthiban to play the role of a music critic in his Tamil feature film, *Ivan*. Parthiban believed that no actor could

Subbudu with Parthiban

Giving a shot in the movie ***Ivan***

have fitted the role as well. Illayaraja had set the music score of the film.

Since 1984, Kandaswamy had to endure the howling of a woman who wanted Subbudu to just see her daughter's performance once. While Subbudu could not manage time that season, Kandaswamy ensured the lady that the next season, Subbudu would surely see her daughter's recital. Eventually, the lady waited for three years and finally her dream of having him at her daughter's performance came true. Subbudu attended the recital and wrote a scathing review on the dancer's performance. He was more indignant because the dancer was not only shoddy but also ambitious. Once she read the review, she never returned to Subbudu or ever invited him for any of her future performances. So much so that once, when Subbudu was waiting outside the Narada Gana Sabha for a lift, Kandaswamy overheard the young dancer asking her mother to drive from a different route as the "Old man would come running for a lift".

Even though Subbudu had touched seventy, artistes cared a little before physically assaulting him. Much as we get to hear from the same artistes that Subbudu did not matter or had an impact, it baffles one's common sense, why these people used to get enraged and attack the seemingly harmless old man?

Once during the December season, Subbudu criticised senior musician, B. Rajam Iyer. But his criticism against the man did not end here. Subbudu went a step further and wrote that Rajam should not have taken music as his profession. As expected, the artiste felt he had been ruined because of Subbudu's damaging write up and he chose to avenge himself. The same evening, he caught hold of Subbudu in the foyer of the Music Academy and before anyone could know what was happening he tore Subbudu's shirt and tried to hit him. Immediately Kandaswamy sprang to Subbudu's defence and other people gathered around to protect Subbudu. Rajam Iyer was asked to leave the venue. T.S. Parthasarthy, who was one of the secretaries of the Academy asked Subbudu why he criticised an artiste so much to invite their wrath. Subbudu had a simple answer, "If their art is not good to my ears and eyes, my words can never be good to their heart and mind." Parthasarthy remained the Secretary of the Music Academy for two decades from 1979 to 1999.

Around the same time, Bharatanatyam dancer, Devyani criticised Subbudu for having used her car and still writing a negative review. Subbudu countered Devyani by saying that he did not use her car and reached her venue on his own. Moreover, he told her that if artistes sent cars to pick him up hoping they could get a favourable review, then they were sadly mistaken.

> ***In the South, artistes live like frogs in the well. There is no live and let live policy.***
>
> — *Subbudu on the politics of Madras*

Subbudu had his share of troubles with instrumentalists as well. Some front ranking *mridangists* in dance came under his line of fire when he found them performing in an inebriated state. While one held him by his collar on one occasion, the other threatened him with dire consequences. There were many occasions when the artistes' fans encircled Subbudu and demanded an apology from him.

Whenever there were arguments during the day, Subbudu had disturbed sleep. Sometimes, it made him wonder, why he should even bother about serving the arts. Hadn't he done enough? But, whenever he saw artistes and their parents putting their fate in his hands, he could not afford to say no.

Mama taught me simplicity, humility, honesty, integrity and forced me to be a good administrator.

— Kandaswamy, on what he learnt from Subbudu

In 1986, Subbudu wrote a comparative analytical piece on Tyagaraja and Muthuswami Dikshitar where he reasoned how Tyagaraja's compositions were not only popular but more spontaneous as well. He maintained that his compostions addressed to Lord Rama were based on incidents and therefore helped the masses connect with it. On the other hand, Dikshitar was like Beethoven. He added that Tyagaraja had over a hundred disciples and he participated in *bhajans* regularly whereas Dikshitar who went to Benaras, was credited with composing songs in Drupad style. Moreover, Dikshitar had only five disciples, the Tanjore Quartet and a *devadasi*, Kamalam Ammal. And while Tyagaraja's students took it upon themselves to propagate his work, Dikshitar's disciples attached themselves to the Tanjore court and codified Dasiattam.

Dikshitar's devotees were shocked to read Subbudu's article. Letters were written to the Editor of *The Statesman* demanding an apology from him but the man stuck to his guns.

Years ago, Subbudu was involved in a controversy with Justice Venkatarama Iyer which had its genesis in Dikshitar's *kritis*. A legal luminary par excellence, Justice Venkatarama Iyer was passionately involved in popularising Dikshitar's works. Eminent musician, S. Rajamaiyar helped Justice Venkatarama Iyer in this endeavour. Both of them did extensive research before they gave a proper form to Dikshitar's compositons. When musicians came to know of this, they started learning Dikshitar's *kritis* from Justice Venkatarama Iyer notably, D.K. Pattammal. However, Madurai Mani Iyer could not learn the *kritis* from Justice Venkatarama Iyer because he had some physical disability.

Incidentally, when Justice Venkatarama Iyer presided over one of D.K. Pattammal's performances, he took a swipe at Madurai Mani Iyer's style of singing and made some unsavoury remarks about his strange mannerisms on stage.

However, he praised D.K. Pattammal profusely and at length explained a Pallavi which she rendered in *Sankeerna gati* (or nine counts). Justice Venkatarama Iyer erred and said the Pallavi was performed in *Mishra gati* (or seven counts). Subbudu was extremely annoyed with the renowned judge's conduct because he had criticised Madurai Mani Iyer in absentia. Later he wrote in *The Statesman*, "Rarely do Delhi's Carnatic *rasikas* get an opportunity to hear concerts from great musicians and therefore, it is unwise to inflict long speeches on them."

Justice Venkatarama Iyer was upset after he read the review because he thought it was because of him that the "audience was able to comprehend the intricate nuances of Pattammal's concert".

On reading his review Justice Iyer's fans and well wishers, criticised Subbudu for ridiculing him. In fact, Justice Iyer's nephew

Balasubramaniam wrote a strongly worded letter to the editor of *The Statesman*. His letter was published with Subbudu's rejoinder in which he wrote, "It was sheer humility that compelled me to avoid pointing out the grievous error in the speech of the great luminary. He had said that the Pallavi was in *Mishra gati* whereas it was in *Sankeerna gati*."

As Subbudu later revealed, "If I remember, Justice Venkatarama Iyer never came to preside over any concert in Delhi."

The following year during the December season, people hounded Subbudu for writing against Dikshitar but he maintained his line of argument often asking historians to correct him.

Meanwhile, on December 25, 1987, another star was born in Subbudu's eyes and within a year, that young girl, discovered by him, became one of the most sought after artistes in Madras. Before he located her, she used to draw a motley crowd of 15 to 20 people and post Subbudu's blessings, she had nearly a thousand people attending her concert. She was Bombay Jayshree.

It so happened that all the *sabhas* decided to mourn M.G. Ramachandran's death. The most influential non-Congress politician, and former Chief Minister of Tamil Nadu, MGR was a patron for a host of artistes in Madras. One of the most popular Tamil actors ever, he was a dominating figure behind the rise and fall of many artistes. Understandably, his death sent shock waves throughout the country. While it impacted national politics on one hand, it also affected the fate of a young Carnatic singer whose concert was pushed to the evening slot after an artiste backed out. Like other *sabhas*, the Nungambakkam Culture Academy had also sold its tickets in advance. Fearing the loss of audience, the *sabha* organisers decided to allow junior artistes to perform in prime time slots, so that the audience had at least something to listen to. To make matters worse, it was raining heavily that day. As such the organisers expected a thin crowd but because it was one of the very few sabhas, holding a concert that day, Subbudu decided to go visit it.

By the time he and Kandaswamy got off the cab, they were completely drenched. The very next moment, something hit Subbudu and he was swept off his feet. It was the voice of young pétité singer.

As his practice was, Subbudu entered the auditorium and chose the seat next to the exit door so that he could leave the auditorium when he had his fill. However, he was so impressed with the young singer that he stayed on till the end of the programme and later introduced himself to Bombay Jayshree. Two days later, she found a half page review in *The Indian Express* and in the weekend, she found herself covering an entire page of *Dinamani Kadir*. Subbudu had placed his bet on the young girl's talent and had predicted that the young girl was destined to become one of the best voices of the generation. Over the next three years, he did not miss a single opportunity to praise her and ensured that she was a sell out artiste in every season. Jayshree could not believe herself when she read the review for the first time. She read it repeatedly and still couldn't imagine that the man who she had grown up reading and hearing about from her parents, had approved of her.

A day after the review appeared in *Dinamani Kadir* and in *The Indian Express*, Jayshree went to Woodlands Hotel to meet Subbudu. Seeing her, his face lit up. He blessed her and told her that she need not worry about her future because she was a genuine artiste. Later when Bombay Jayshree went to give a recital at the Spirit of Unity concerts in Delhi, Subbudu compared her to Steffi Graf, who was the new sensation in the world of tennis in the late 1980s.

Interestingly, Subbudu later discovered that he had known Jayshree's mother from the time she helped his drama troupe in Calcutta by reciting a prayer at the beginning of the show after rehearsing it for merely an hour.

While the young crop of musician embraced Subbudu as their patriarch he played his part as a watchdog to perfection when despite his close friendship with M.L. Vasanthakumari for accepting yet another award. This time from the Indian Fine Arts Society. He observed that if awards and titles had any meaning and credibility, senior musicians should impose a self-denying ordinance to avoid proliferation of titles. Essentially, he was bemoaning the fact that so many titles and awards had been instituted that they had lost their value.

With Bombay Jayshree

Around the same time Subbudu also made a career shift and decided to snap all ties with Manian. Though *Idayam Pesukirathu* closed down after Manian's death, Subbudu's departure from the magazine in 1986-87 had sounded its death knell. He decided to leave the magazine after a controversy on the payments of his hotel bills took place in December 1987. Subbudu had to suffer embarrassment before the hotel authorities over the non-payment of the bills before the matter was sorted out.

Meanwhile, he had became sure that newspapers and magazines invited him only to increase their sales and after they reached a particular target and managed a loyal readership, they showed him the door because absolutely no one could afford to ruffle feathers with the top artistes for long.

Even though Manian throve on controversies, he could not possibly tell Subbudu to tone down against certain artistes, who had befriended him. His reasoning was that he had to survive in Madras while Subbudu could call the shots because he was in Delhi.

Among other things, when newspapers and magazines wanted to get rid of Subbudu, they started editing his copies and he hated that.

> ***Mr. Subbudu is pouring hot water on the roots of young saplings.***
>
> *— Manian indicating to a friend that he had become uncomfortable with Subbudu's writing*

But the fact that Subbudu meant sales was comforting enough for him. He had learned the hard way that truth cannot be tolerated and it destroys everything, if used powerfully.

In 1988, K.V. Ramanathan joined Indian Express as its resident editor. A seasoned bureaucrat, he invited Subbudu to start writing for *Dinamani Kadir* again since he was already writing for *The Indian Express*. Ramanathan gave complete freedom to Subbudu to write the way he wished to. The impulse and passion of his writing style seemed a refreshing change to him from the tentative behaviour of most critics at that time. Here was a man, nominating new *darbaris* of his *darbar* every year during the one month season of music and dance.The man who was forever old for the second generation of Bharatanatyam dancers and Carnatic singers and the man who was in love with beauty in any shape and form. Ramanathan fell for Subbudu's impulsive writing style. He poured his heart out when he wrote and not many could do that, either out of fear of falling out of those they criticised or due to the pure inability to experience the intensity of the moment. As he started interacting with him, he felt that Subbudu had this desire to appear anti-establishment which he was in more ways than one. By the end of the 80s, when criticism as such was on wane, Subbudu was still selling and hurting well.

Subbudu continued writing for *Dinamani Kadir* till 1997 after which he shifted to *Ananda Vikatan* again.

At that time, his professional shifts were equally matched by fiery exchanges with the top artistes. During his last years Veena Maestro, S. Balachander was involved in one of the most bitter fights with Subbudu over the authenticity of Raja Swati Tirunal as a composer. Balachander was sure that Swati Tirunal had not composed any of the *kritis* attributed to him. Interestingly, Veena Balachander also said that if M.S. Subbulakshmi goes to Tirupati, lights a camphor and blows it off with her hand, he would accept Swati Tirunal as the composer. Subbudu in one of his riveting write-ups, asked MS to exactly do the same for the benefit of the music world. By saying so, he ridiculed Balachander's observations on Swati Tirunal and trivialised the entire matter. Moreover Balachander's remarks created a rift between him and Semmangudi, especially because Semmangudi's major contribution had been in reviving and popularising the compositions of Swati Tirunal, not only as a master vocalist but also as the Principal of Swati Tirunal College in Kerala.

Balachander was so upset with Subbudu's article that he is said to have sent threatening letters to the Editor of the *Idayam Pesukirathu* at that time, which the paper refused to publish. Unwilling to give up, he took the matter to the Press Council of India accusing Subbudu of defaming him. While the Press Council observed that Subbudu's freedom to write could not be challenged because of lack of mala fide intentions, the Council directed the magazine to publish Balachander's reply to his write up. Though Subbudu was able to prove his point, Balachander ended up calling him names. Subbudu could never forget and overlook his remarks. Perhaps, it was the intensity of the moment in which Balachander ended up accusing him in uncharacteristic fashion, but the critic ended his relationship with the musician and decided to move on with life.

> ***He is 30 per cent critic, 30 per cent cynic and 40 per cent purchasable commodity.***
>
> *— Veena S. Balachander, at his vitriolic best*

The Twists of Paradox

Commenting on the dance scene of the 1980s and 90s, Subbudu felt that *babudom* got the better of the arts. In India, like elsewhere in the world, art and artistes have survived because of the sustained patronage of kings, queens, clergymen, religious heads, *sabhas*, aristocrats and the general public. Also, it was an accepted truth that artistes did share a special relationship with their patrons, which often blurred the definitions of morality in the age of survival. While the organisations serving the arts have often come under fire for glaring discrepancies, Subbudu's decision and desire to stay out of the mess was the result of his experiences with the Audition Boards of All India Radio and Doordarshan. Not much is known about the current state of affairs, but he left the boards after he found that the pressure tactics could twist the board's sense of judgment.

Yamini Krishnamurthy recalled that during one of the audition sessions held to grade the dancers, Subbudu was extremely impatient and had to be stopped from telling the dancers to get out. He could only tolerate mediocrity if he was able to vent his anger on the artiste.

Yamini was honoured with the title of Nritya Choodamani in 1988. However, it is believed that before finally accepting the award, she sought Subbudu's advice on whether she should accepte the award or not. He told her that he felt that a dancer who had been honoured with a Padma Shri at the age of 28 in 1968 should refuse the award. However, a few weeks later in Chennai, Yamini accepted the title of Nritya Choodamani. Dancing on the occasion, she performed a 13-beat *Alarippu*, which Subbudu felt did not come to *taala*. While reviewing her performance, he criticised the item and also described the dancer's dance movements during her *varnam* as akin to manual deforestation.

Yamini was understandably upset after reading the review and met K.V. Ramanathan, the then Editor of *The Indian Express* who stood by Subbudu and told Yamini that if she did not agree with the critic's viewpoint, she could write a letter to the Editor which he promised to publish in the paper. But that was not to be.

On his return to Delhi, Subbudu in his article "More than a music festival" for his column, expressed surprise at Yamini's decision to accept the award. Incidentally, the award had been won by a mix of young and old dancers like Padma Subrahmanyam, Chitra Vishveshwaran, Alarmel Valli, Dhananjayan and Lakshmi Vishwanathan among others. In hindsight, both Yamini and Subbudu crossed the mutually acceptable boundaries, she in seeking an official reprimand for him and he, in stretching the argument on how Yamini probably felt guilty for receiving the award "rather late in the evening of her life".

However, the real winner at that time was *Ananda Vikatan* which published Subbudu's and Yamini's interviews in its back-to-back issues of February 5, 1989 and February 12, 1989. Though the interviews ensured rocket sales, they made the situation messier. Ironically, while Subbudu did not level charges against Yamini in his interview, the dancer decided to launch a direct attack on her critic.

The biggest shock for Subbudu came when *Ananda Vikatan* published Yamini's interview where she addressed him as "Sakunithanam Pannugirar Subbudu" or Shakuni Subbudu. The controversy did not end there. On March 11, 1989, her lawyer served a legal notice on him, the Editor, the Publisher and the Printer of *The Statesman*. Subbudu was accused of "criticising the dancer with mala fide intention with a view to discrediting the said prominent dance personality for no reason other than personal prejudice and vendetta". Letters written by dance and music scholars on one hand, and self-professed Secretaries of the Yamini Fans Club, thickened the plot.

Everyone had a point to make against Subbudu, from accusing him of mentioning living people as dead ones, to suspecting if he sometimes reviewed a performance while sitting at home. The charges against him, except his self-confessed technical mistakes in print, were baseless and beyond a point ridiculous; it did little to affect his credibility.

The legal notice sought a written unconditional apology from him and also demanded a compensation of Rs. 50 lakhs from all the three accused parties for irreparable damage to the name, fame and image of the internationally renowned danseuse.

Subbudu's son-in-law, lawyer Krishna Kumar filed a rejoinder in which he answered each charge levelled against him and in turn demanded an unconditional apology from Yamini and the Editor and the Publisher of *Ananda Vikatan*. He began by asserting that the dancer had telephoned him and sought his opinion on whether to accept Nritya Choodamani or not.

He also challenged Yamini to present the letter which was allegedly written by him to Yamini's nattuvanar Devanathan. He further questioned the motive behind Yamini's interview which was printed "maliciously, recklessly and without ascertaining the authenticity of the facts" and which went "against the standards of journalistic ethics and/or public taste". Subbudu also accused Yamini of quoting things out of context. His lawyer further wrote that these acts had "brought about disrepute and defame" and that Subbudu, "had been brought into public odium and contempt" and had suffered and was still suffering from such humiliation.

Moreover, Subbudu also told Kumar that he wanted to debate with Yamini on a public forum so that no one could doubt his integrity as a critic. Krishna knew that Subbudu was not lying. He further told him that when he criticises someone for a dull performance, the artiste must not forget that he/she is a public figure. The fact that artistes perform for the public and get paid for it cannot be disputed. Since the public pays for the performance, the artiste has to be accountable. Krishna followed it up by writing in his legal notice, "If you are being paid more and you do not perform your services, it amounts to deception."

Yamini and her lawyers did not file the charges and Subbudu too decided not to proceed further.

Regardless of what happened between them, Subbudu maintains that after Bala, Yamini was the only natural dancer. For him, she is not a woman but just dance.

He is like Nature, unpredictable yet powerful.

— Yamini Krishnamurthy, on what she thinks of Subbudu

Though Subbudu had been honoured by the state government of Tamil Nadu way back in the 1970s, the Delhi government woke up in 1989 when he received the Parishad Sammaan from the Sahitya Kala Parishad, New Delhi for his overall contribution to the performing arts. It was a reminder to him that he had worked enough and that perhaps he was getting old. But Subbudu felt, he still had a few years to survive. Sixteen years have elapsed since then.

In 1989 itself, during the Madras season a dancer-choreographer, who had come to Madras from Lucknow, sought Subbudu's attendance at Maris. She was Saraswati. Now a close confidant of

At a gathering to honour Subbudu
(From left to right Doordarshan Natarajan, Nalli Kuppuswami Chetti, Subbudu, Dr. Balamurali Krishna and Dr. Saraswati)

Dr. Balamurali Krishna, Dr. Saraswati went on to collaborate with Subbudu on a number of dance productions and events, notable among them, ICCR productions.

For a number of leading artistes, it was difficult to understand, why Subbudu supported Saraswati, even though the popular impression was that she was not a mainstream dancer. For him however, Saraswati was the only dancer who did not seek his guidance and friendship because he was a renowned critic. Be it her student's *arangetrum* or her performances, she always told him that she did not require a review from him at all. She was aware of the fact that very few students were willing to take up dance professionally because of the generally depressing trend. On top of it, Subbudu's remarks could potentially kill their interest to learn dance. It is a different matter that he was exceptionally lenient towards young artistes. Beyond that, as he was growing old, she was one of the very few artistes, who supported him in his creative endeavours. He asked her to do a ballet on Kamakshi of Kancheepuram and Goddess Saraswati's pride. The ballet was called Vipanchi and it was a huge success.

Subbudu has also been grateful to Saraswati for her support in overhauling the Tyagaraja Aradhana Festival. He did not want television to show the face of the musicians when they sang in high pitch. More than that he wanted the Tyagaraja *kritis* to be sung by leading musicians in different format, musical, instrumental and chorus singing in the form of an opera. Along with this he also wanted a neat presentation of *panch ratna kritis*. His desire to have a dance production based on Tyagaraja's *kritis* was fulfilled by Saraswati.

By the time Subbudu entered the last decade of the 20th century, the pressure tactics on him and on his fellow critics had ended. It happened for two reasons. Firstly, the space for criticism began dwindling and so artistes, in need to be covered and have publicity turned soft on their critics. Secondly, the critics themselves, were now old faces of the organisations and therefore, nothing bothered them. The Editors on their part had begun losing their interest in performing arts criticism because of the controversies attached to it.

As India opened its doors to cable invasion and economic liberalisation, the Indian mindset had begun to change as well. Over the years, consumerism and competition became the buzz words. Profit was dictated by advertising and sales and they in turn were driven by the moods of the masses. And the masses, were intoxicated by the West which beckoned like never before, because it reached the private spaces of Indian homes through television. The culture had shifted and critics and the artistes found the arts becoming less and less significant. From centre spreads, arts coverage had come down to a page and new battlelines were drawn to fight for weekly column space. Subbudu was the only critic, whose importance and space in *The Statesman* remained unassailable. For the rest, the sun had begun to set on the horizon. The third generation of critics, chose alternative careers, as culture commentators, dance historians, communication experts and still some chose to continue being performers. Around the same time, *The Times of India's* Executive Editor told a young critic, known for his caustic remarks and honest writing, that dance criticism was a dying job because it just catered to a constituency of two thousand only. Meanwhile, *The Statesman* told Subbudu that he could continue *sine die*. Till today, *The Hindu* and *The Statesman* are the only two papers that have a page devoted to the arts and review.

The turn of the decade also brought new disciples in Subbudu's Gurukul! Though the lawsuit controversy became a turning point in Subbudu's and Yamini's relationship, the beginning of the 1990s saw Subbudu become a mentor to one of Yamini's best disciples, Rama Vaidyanathan. Subbudu and Shanta who witnessed the magic of Yamini through the 1960s and 70s confessed that they had to bite their tongue to believe that they lived in that era. Rama, who is one of the best bets in Bharatanatyam today, witnessed only Yamini perform for the first ten years of her training. As someone who learnt to absorb by observing, Yamini exposed her to the madness of her dance.

When Rama came into the Vaidyanathan household, the first thing that her mother-in-law Saroja Vaidyanathan told her was that she should not be bothered about the critics. Moreover at that time, her relationship with Subbudu was rather strained because he was not kind to her while reviewing her performances. The turnaround happened when Subbudu noticed Saroja's contribution as a teacher.

Rama did not invite him for the first few concerts because she was not confident about her prowess. Since he was related to Saroja, he was extremely cordial and warm at the family functions but it was just that. Finally she invited him in 1990 to her first performance. Understandably nervous, she was glad to know that he gave her a descent review. He felt that she needed to work on *sancharis* and basic dance postures to embellish her performance which otherwise was well above average.

Later when people read the review, they called Rama to congratulate her on getting a positive review from the old man of Indian criticism. But Rama knew the areas where she had to improve and so she worked herself to perfection to win his admiration. Over a period of time, Subbudu became close to her, so much so that by the end of 1994 during the Madras season, he recommended her name to various Sabha Secretaries including the Krishna Gana Sabha and the Narada Gana Sabha. But by then Subbudu had started to become overworked. Most artistes who travelled to the 1994 Cleveland Festival, held in honour of Lalgudi Jayraman and himself, felt that Subbudu was extremely humble but he did show signs of fatigue. Subbudu also participated in the Toronto Festival and visited New York , New Jersey and Chicago. He fell in love with the awe-inspiring temple complexes there. Incidentally, Subbudu was reluctant to go abroad for three reasons. One, he ate *paan* and felt he did not have the luxury to spit anywhere he liked. Two, he was a complete vegetarian and was weary of the food served abroad and three, he did not want to leave his wife alone. The organisers decided to sponsor his wife's ticket and convined him to travel to the USA.

On his return, Subbudu hit upon a brilliant idea to make documentaries on the twelve singing giants of Carnatic music. The series was known as the Great Masters of Carnatic Music. He wrote a letter to the then Director General of Doordarshan and put the idea before him. N. Krishnaswamy, who was on the panel

K. Suresh, N. Krishnaswamy, Anu Gopal, the team of Great Masters of the Carnatic Music series

of producers was given the task to make the documentaries with Subbudu's help. Initially, the documentary series featured six musicians. However, because of its success, six more artistes were canned. The documentary series was so popular that it was dubbed in Tamil and relayed at the Madras Doordarshan later.

Meanwhile Subbudu continued mentoring Rama. As with other artistes, Subbudu also told Rama to be more demonstrative by informing her that he found the entire argument that dance is spiritual and it comes from inside, extremely ridiculous. "If it comes from inside then it should only remain inside." When you are on stage, you are dancing for the audience and that is the most important thing.

Subbudu's idea of criticism was extremely personal and he shunned anyone trying to influence him. Once watching Rama's performance, he found that a *jati* did not come to *taal*. Incidentally, Rama did not realise this while performing and when she reached home, she received a call from a fellow dancer who told her how one of the *jatis* did not fall in place. Unfortunately, the dancer called up Subbudu and told her about the error in Rama's performance. She was completely flabbergasted when Subbudu turned around and told her it was none of her business and asked her how she could dare to try and influence his judgement. In the article, Subbudu mentioned Rama's error but he told Rama to be cautious of such 'well-wishers'. Meanwhile, the other dancer visited Subbudu and apologised profusely for her misadventure.

Today, Subbudu's relationship with Rama is more of a father and a daughter but that hasn't stopped him from critcising her whenever she has gone off track. However, unlike with other dancers, Subbudu has reserved his criticism for her only over the phone. She offers an interesting explanation, saying that if he had advised her through his column, people would have said that She was following Subbudu's diktat.

Once while performing a Kamas Varnam, "ra ra ra enmate," Rama depicted a *nayika* who invites Shiva to come to her. She prolonged the *sancharis* by repeating the invitation in various ways. Subbudu was so put off by her depiction that he told her over the phone that, "You were busy saying, "Come, Come Come and Shiva came and also went away."

While he continued to hog the limelight, there were other critics too who were making serious critical interventions in the field of dance. Senior critic Leela Venkataraman of *The Hindu*, who made her foray years ago, recalled that once she overheard the two *rasikas* talking about his review of Ravi Shankar's performance. Apparently, Subbudu had inadvertently mentioned a *raga* which the sitarist had not played. While there was considerable furore by his critics, the two men were completely unfazed by it and one said to the other in Tamil, "It does not matter whether he played the *raga* or not. What matters is that Subbudu mentioned he played the *raga* and what he mentions, matters." Leela was amazed to see the faith a common man had in Subbudu's writing. With such confidence anyone could have an expanding ego but she remembers that when Subbudu started reading her articles, he made it a point to call her and tell her, " You write extremely well. Keep it up." Even though he has considerably withdrawn himself from the world of dance and music, Subbudu gives his feedback to all the critics, young and old, even today."

The place at the top is very lonely and there are occupational hazards.

— Leela Venkatarman on what it takes to write when influential artistes try to manipulate the press aggressively

Since the late 1990s, his decision to go to Madras has been influenced by his health. Whenever he wished to go, he implored Chandra to accompany him. Moreover, his friends in Madras prodded him to visit the city. Each time Subbudu told them that he was planning to stop writing, his friends asked him how could he do so. Invariably the only question running through the minds of his family members, during the month of December every year, was — should he or shouldn't he? However, he went each time primarily because Chandra agreed and also because he knew he could trust Kandaswamy to take care of him.

In fact, Kandaswamy had gained notoriety for not letting Subbudu's family members meet him. When in Madras, he took complete control of Subbudu and forced him to follow his strict schedule. He was not allowed to meet anyone at the cost of his sleep. His afternoon nap was extremely important and he had clear instructions that Kandaswamy should not allow anyone to disturb him. Kandaswamy had a record of completely disowning his

Subbudu with long time associate R. Krishnaswami (second from right) on the occasion of the former's 81st birthday

family and his work whenever Subbudu happened to be in town. Subbudu has not gone to Madras after Chandra's death.

During the interactions, Subbudu often recalled that every time Chandra came back from Madras, she had her list of complaints. She felt that he completely ignored her and never used to ask her if she wanted to go shopping or meet their relatives. Their grandchildren invariably hauled up Subbudu for not keeping Chandra in good humour. His arguments had gone dry. "She has the car and the money. She can do whatever she wants to do."

But Chandra reasoned that Subbudu had always been like this and it was impossible to change him now. On his part, he wished Chandra to be with him so that if anything happened to him he would have his wife beside him. At his level, his biggest concern was Chandra's health. When Chandra experienced water retention in her lower legs, she found it difficult to even walk properly. Gradually, the problem affected her feet making it impossible for her to wear normal slippers. When Subbudu noted this, without telling anyone, he asked his friend in the Bata Shoe Company to send someone who could take measurements of her feet and prepare a special pair of shoes for her. Chandra never made demands and Subbudu never flaunted his gesture to claim that he loved her.

Since she spent more time with her grandchildren, they became her messengers to Subbudu. Whenever she could not tell him anything directly, she asked them to tell him. She knew that he could never refuse his grandchildren anything they asked him to do. Chandra and Swetha also discussed the way Subbudu wrote about a dancer or a musician's physical appearance. In fact, Swetha chided him for writing in such a manner but he always found an easy passage by saying that his readers wanted such comments.

"What is wrong in that?", he asked whenever someone cautioned him. "This is how I look at an artiste and his/her work. If somebody does not agree with my outlook he or she can always throw me out of the paper or the magazine. Since I still write, it means they want me and I have to write the way they want me to write. Fortunately, this is how I want to write as well." Subbudu's prepared answers were born out of struggle and his need to assert himself.

Having lived his life with gusto and passion, Subbudu began showing signs of weariness. He told Chandra that he wanted to go before her. He knew he could not take care of himself.

In 1999, Subbudu's love for *paan* and *supari*, which he had got from his mother landed him in hospital. Doctors told Chandra and their children, that he required a cholostomy operation otherwise his condition could deteriorate. The monsoon was on the verge of hitting Delhi. Subbudu and Chandra had completed 61 years of matrimony a month ago and now the doctors appeared grim about his prospects.

The man himself was least bothered for Chandra was still alive. On the day of the operation, when he was being taken to the

Operation Theatre, Subbudu held his son-in-law's right hand tightly. The doctors thought, he was getting nervous. Little did they know, Subbudu was comforting his family.

Subbudu had become a spectator of the *tamasha*. He could distance himself from the world and laugh at its ironies. He knew, Chandra was alive and she could take care of everything.

One of the doctors told Subbudu not to worry. "There will be no problem", he said in a practised tone. Subbudu looked at him and then looked at his son-in-law and then he glanced back and smiled at his sons standing a few feet away. He told the doctor, "If I come back, there will be no problem to anyone. If I don't come back, I will still have no problem, but they will have problems."

At a time, when the doctors had hinted that anything could happen, Subbudu managed to retain his wit and his capacity to mock death.

Fortunately, his operation was successful and he came back. He told Chandra, he was not going to leave her so soon. Though mentally, he had convinced himself that he would die before her.

Two years later, he noticed that the Madras season was taken over by the third generation of musicians nurtured by him. Mandolin Srinivas, Sudha Raghunathan and Bombay Jayshree led the change, while Subbudu congratulated himself and bid farewell to the second generation of artistes.

His big moment came in 2002 when his 85th birthday was celebrated in Madras and New Delhi with much fanfare. In fact it became one of the most well-attended events of the year. Two anthologies of Subbudu's writings in Tamil, published in various magazines in the 1980s and 90s entitled *Subbudu's Durbar* were released. Sponsored by his friend and admirer Nalli, the book release function and anniversary celebrations had their high point when Subbudu's favourite dancer Rama Vaidyanathan performed one of his compositions. He had composed a *Valachi varnam* cen-

PH. : 379 43 66
FAX : 301 49 25

5, SAFDARJUNG ROAD
NEW DELHI - 110 011

R VENKATARAMAN
FORMER PRESIDENT OF INDIA

26th November, 2001

Dear Shri Subbudu,

Your review of Kalakshetra festival is superb (as usual). I entirely agree with you that certain scenes need to be pruned. I have been insisting on this for the several years but the Old Guards are reluctant to change even a coma of Rukmini Devi.

I plead guilty to the lapse in the case of Kamala Rani. She was not in the group of other accompanying artists.

Your shrewd eyes have noticed it.

With best wishes,

Yours sincerely,

R Venkataraman

(R Venkataraman)

Shri P V Subramanian
C -104, Pushpanjali
Delhi - 100 092

Shrewd at 84.
R. Venkataraman's letter to Subbudu on reading his review

tering on Devyani and Valli's fight. He asked Rama to choreograph the compositions. What impressed Subbudu most was the fact that she personally came to him and sought his interpretation of the *varnam*. Her superb rendition on the day of his 85th birthday celebrations was followed by his incisive remark, "You performed so brilliantly because you came to me and sought my interpretation of the *varnam*."

Rama Vaidyanathan performing at Subbudu's 85th birthday celebrations in Chennai

His birthday celebrations in Delhi were courtesy G.S. Rajan and Anjana Rajan, the talented musician-dancer couple. Rajan's web portal Art India sponsored the event, which was presided over by former President, R. Venkataraman. Fellow critics Shanta Serbjeet Singh and Leela

Subbudu with Rama Vaidyanathan

Anita Ratnam honouring Chandra for being Subbudu's better half

Subbudu with Anita Ratnam

Signing copies of his collection of Tamil writings ***Subbudu Durbar*** *for Parthiban as Chandra looks on*

At the release of Subbudu's works Nalli Kuppuswami Chetti, Chandra, Subbudu, Anita Ratnam, N.N. Vittal former CVC , Justice Bhaktavatsalam, Doordarshan Natarajan, Parthiban and Mr. Murali of Krishna Sweets

For Subbudu

To Sir with love, from those who err with love

Samuel Taylor Coleridge, great poet of foreign shores,
Once wrote a song of fantasy, (as poets are wont to do)
He wrote of Kubla Khan, who escaped from mundane chores,
By decreeing a stately pleasure dome in a place called Xanadu.

Here in our land of Bharat-varsh, we do have our share of surprises,
Like fork-tongued folks and chameleons who talk, but we have no Xanadu
Yet there is no reason to feel ashamed, for among our truly great prizes,
Is a wonder who writes as none other can write, and his name is Subbudu!

A scholar who knows, a musician who plays, a reviewer who needs no aid,
He understands his subjects well and calls a spade a spade.

So those who blow and key and strum,
Those who bow and those who drum,
Those who dance and those who sing,
All of them fear that pen with a sting.

We find at times a silver spoon, in the mouth of some lucky men,
But Subbudu's case is a class apart — he was born with a pun in the pen!
So even his scathingly pointed critiques, will elicit some loud guffaws,
Because of the jokes that pepper the piece, and enliven the list of flaws.

And it's not as if he only knows about the performing arts,
He's also privy to inside yarns and hush-hush goings-on,
He knows that spirituality can be hawked at roadside marts
And the different masks for different tasks, that people tend to don.

So when he considers it necessary
He'll come out with the right repartee,
Since the knowledge stored in his memory,
Is as good as an armoury.

Since I can't match his pun command,
With anything of a similar brand,
I've racked my brains and used this time,
To pay tribute to him in rhyme.

Now we must bring this to a close, resisting the urge to be verbose,
About one who likes things short and sweet, finding in length no special treat.
To Subbudu then, this toast we have raised
May he and his arts live long and unfazed!

A poem written and read out by Anjana Rajan at the function

Venkataraman and dancers, Sonal Man Singh and Swapnasundari too spoke on the occasion. Rama also danced in Delhi for the occasion. Subbudu took a bow. He felt that he could die peacefully now.

He will be the Dhruvatara for the art of music criticism...

—N. Vittal, former Chief Vigilance Commissioner while presiding over Subbudu's 85th birthday celebrations in Chennai

But he didn't know, he had still to wait and die many times. Subbudu lost his grandson Tejasvi on May 10, 2003 in a brutal road accident. That day, Tejasvi's mother and Subbudu's daughter Ragini lost all faith in God. The young teenager's death was the first blow to the family. Chandra took her grandson's death to heart. Subbudu trusted God with his decision but could not convince himself.

Everything paled before his grandson's untimely death. While the family was trying to come to terms with the catastrophe, another tragedy struck the family. Chandra who suffered from chronic blood pressure suffered a massive heart attack and died on April 4, 2004. She had been in hospital for two weeks and died just a day before the doctors were going to discharge her. Two days before she left Subbudu, she held his hand and told him not to bother their daughter-in-law Jayshree and to cooperate with her.

When he was told that his wife had died, Subbudu's first reaction was of relief. He had seen her through excessive pain in the last few days. During her funeral, as he sat beside her, he caressed her head as if putting her to sleep. A sixty-eight-year relationship had come to an end. Later Subbudu told Kandaswamy, "She got the boarding pass first."

The last time Subbudu visited Chennai with Chandra, he met M.S. Subbulakshmi. That was going to be their last meeting. Ever since Sadasivam had died, MS had stopped singing.When the couple met her, they were so overwhelmed by the moment that tears welled up in Subbudu's and MS' eyes. Subbudu and Chandra did a traditional *namaskaram* to MS and sought her blessings, even as she told them not to embarrass her. As they took a trip down memory lane, MS confessed that she felt bad when Subbudu criticised her but she reasoned to herself that she knew he was correct. She thanked him for checking her and encouraging her. Subbudu was humbled by the enormity of the moment and chose to remain silent and smiled.

But Chandra's death ended everything in his life. When he was told that the Sangeet Natak Akademi had decided to honour him for his lifelong contriution to the arts, Subbudu shrugged his shoulders. Chandra was not going to be there to see him receive the award.

He was fortunate to have Chandra because she did not misinterpret his lack of interference in household chores as neglect of duty. It was rather easy for her to adjust to him because she knew that she had married into the family which had a great passion for music and theatre. The atmosphere at her in-laws' place was no different and Subbudu was only following the family tradition.

Meanwhile, at the Sangeet Natak Akademi's awards ceremony, the President, A.P.J. Abdul Kalam walked up to congratulate Subbudu after the function ended. His gesture touched his heart and made him realise that life, till it lasts must be lived. Even though the feeling remained with Subbudu temporarily, the interest shown by the President, in his health and his activities, made him feel important and appreciated.

Later the President called him to praise him for his writings in *Subbudu's Durbar* and sent in a letter of appreciation. Subbudu

Subbudu receiving the award from the President Dr. APJ Abdul Kalam as former SNA Chairperson Sonal Man Singh looks on

convinced himself that it was because of Chandra that all this was happening to him.

> ***Going to a party means spending Rs. 300. Who has money for all the humbug?***
>
> *— Subbudu on why he hates attending parties*

A.P.J. Abdul Kalam

Rashtrapati Bhavan
New Delhi - 110004

டிசம்பர் 9, 2004

திரு. சுப்புடு அவர்களுக்கு,

வணக்கம்.

தாங்கள் திருமதி பத்மா சம்பத்குமரன் மூலம் கொடுத்து அனுப்பிய 'சுப்புடு தர்பார்' இரண்டு பகுதிகளும் கிடைத்தன. தாங்கள் பர்மாவிலிருந்து அகதியாக கால்நடையாக இந்தியா திரும்பிய அனுபவத்தையும் இந்தியசுதந்திரப்போரின் உச்சக்கட்டத்தின்போது தாங்கள் தலைநகர் தில்லியில் 'கள்வனின் காதலி' நாடகம் நடத்திய அனுபவங்களையும் ரசித்துப் படித்தேன். வீணை வாத்தியத்தில் புதிய சிந்தனைகள் புகவேண்டியது பற்றி யதார்த்தமாக எழுதியுள்ளீர்கள். வீணை காயத்ரி பற்றிய விமர்சனத்தில் தங்களது எழுத்தின் வீச்சு என்னைக் கவர்ந்தது.

பகுதி ஒன்றில் பக்கம் 268-ல் தாங்களே எழுதியுள்ளதுபோல தாங்கள் நல்ல உடல் ஆரோக்கியத்துடன் எல்லாவளமும் பெற்று நீடுழி வாழ இறைவனை பிரார்த்திக்கிறேன்.

உங்களுக்கும் உங்கள் குடும்பத்தவர்களுக்கும் என் வாழ்த்துக்கள்.

அன்புடன்,

(ஆ.ப.ஜெ. அப்துல் கலாம்)

திரு. சுப்புடு,
C-104 புஷ்பாஞ்சலி
தில்லி - 110 092.

A letter from the President A.P.J. Abdul Kalam

The Cross and the Crossroad

As Carnatic singer Sudha Raghunathan, gained fame in the music world, she became busy with her career. A few year ago, Subbudu composed a *Vallachi varnam* on Devyani, Valli and Murughan. He told Sudha that he wanted her to record it in her voice. Somehow, she could not do that.

Recently, he wrote a letter to her saying, "I know you are a very major singer. If you recall, I had given you a cassette which had a *varnam* composed by me. I had requested you to record it in your voice. If you think that the composition is not worthy of you then you can tell me and forget it." Sudha felt extremely humiliated. Ever since she read that letter, she has been unable to sing the *varnam*. She knows time is running out and she has to do it but the sense of shame for having let her own mentor down weighs heavily on her heart.

Today when Sudharani misses Subbudu, she takes out his reviews of her performances and every time she reads them, she finds something new to learn and understand. His reviews breathe, she says.

Madras Misses Subbudu

— T.V. Gopalakrishnan, Sudharani and Anita Ratnam concluding their separate interviews with the same phrase

As Subbudu started attending fewer programmes because of ill health and old age, he revisited incidents of his life and began to mull over the areas where he had failed. Even though he wrote with a sense of dharma and ripped endless artistes, he began to feel that perhaps he crushed some genuine talent down the years. He was harsh, he felt and that he was responsible in a way for destroying those who needed his protection. Subbudu realised that when those who were torn to pieces by him continued to respect his verdict and were reduced to being second rate artistes because they did not have his stamp.

Without such artistes ever saying anything to him, Subbudu felt guilty whenever he heard the stories of their struggle. He shared his thoughts with his son-in-law, who told him to take satisfaction in the fact that he could realise what he had done and was trying to come to terms with it. Subbudu knew that himself but like always he needed an assurance from his loved ones.

In recent years, it was felt that Subbudu's crisp objectivity had begun to crumble. Mediocre artistes began to receive his praise. There were accusations that he had grown lenient with the artistes. Anyone who fell at his feet was guaranteed a great review.

Once after reading a review written by him, Sudharani asked Subbudu, "*Mama* you know jolly well that the dancer who performed was nothing but mediocre. Why did you then extol her?" Subbudu's reply brought tears to her eyes. He said, "Sudha my child, I have been scolded so much all my life. I am growing old now, so I need flattery too. If someone comes and says pleasant things to me, I write well for them. Am I doing wrong Sudharani?"

That day for the first time in the thirty-five-year-old friendship, Sudharani saw the man behind the critic and therefore forgave him for his misgivings. Subbudu had the courage to accept the clout of time. He had loosened the reins. Instead, he turned to his wife. As his interest and dominance in the world of criticism lessened, his interaction with his wife improved a great deal. From discussing the serials on TV to worrying about their children and grandchildren, Subbudu grew old to turn into a family man, a husband and a father.

In our times, critics have their own agendas since they arrive with preconceived notions. While on one hand it reduces the standard of criticism, on another, it gives the artistes an opportunity to influence them. This could not happen with Subbudu because of his knowledge. The interaction with critics, which began some time in the 70s, reached its crescendo in the late 80s after which there has been a steady downfall. With a generational change happening in the world of the performing arts and also in the world of criticism, the dialogue has become faint, almost mute.

Young artistes know little about the difference the first and second generation critics brought to the life of the performing arts. Young critics can be easily influenced by the greatness or the lack of it, of the seniors in the field of the performing arts. It is little surprise then that artistes can bend the press these days and the press crawls.

Keeping that in mind, Subbudu's unscrupulous way of expressing things and his longevity have been two remarkable features, at a time when, the new generation of artistes and critics have taken their positions. But his world and his kingdom is part of a bygone era.

From being a father figure, Subbudu has become a printed name, leading the pack of critics, who appreciated an artiste's work over the years. Perhaps, artistes usually moved ahead after Subbudu stamped them. They remained indebted towards him but the ambition to pursue their careers made it increasingly difficult for them to keep in touch with him. Till Subbudu had the stamina and the desire to plough the land for the new crop of artistes, he did not have time to think about the generation of dancers and musicians, he had mentored and destroyed. He tended the plants and when they were able to grip the earth and capture the sunlight, he left them alone. By that time, new saplings were ready and required his care. This trend continued for decades till he decided to slow down his pace and stopped attending to the newer saplings. Time moved for the plants and they became trees while Subbudu in his eighties decided to rest. He did not require fruits but sought the shade of the trees he had tended. Did he get that?

Today, his words of praise are mentioned while introducing an artiste to the audience but artistes rarely call on him. Even as Subbudu assumes an air of bravado and says it does not matter, his family knows how much he is hurt when he comes to know that artistes visit and leave the city without having the courtesy of making a two-minute telephone call.

> ***I do not think, a writer can be too far from the person. The work reflects the man who has neither served himself nor the king.***
>
> *— Shanta Serbjeet Singh on Subbudu's passion and lack of personal ambition*

Subbudu now lives to see his granddaughter Purvaja establishing herself as a competent Hindustani singer. But he has not done anything to promote her. In fact, he has had the most bitter arguments with her whenever she has told him that she wants to be a dancer. Purvaja has won the national finals of the Boogie-Woogie dance competition on Sony television. Much as Subbudu takes pride in his grandchild, he has made it known to her that he will not be happy if she decides to become a professional dancer. He knows that the life of a dancer is extremely tough. It demands complete sacrifice and he does not want his granddaughter to be in that situation. He is only too pleased listening to her sing Hindustani Classical melodiously.

If you want be a dancer, remain single.

— Subbudu, indicating that dance demands complete devotion.

In one of the most poignant moments of his life, he witnessed his granddaughter getting an award for excellence in Indian music from her college in 2005. As he saw Purvaja ascending the stage, he crushed Kumar's hand and tears streamed down his eyes. When Purvaja was young, Subbudu had predicted that the young girl would do what no one else could. He always considered his eldest sister Rajeshwari as the best singer and Purvaja reminded him of her.

When I am alone, I cry.

— Subbudu on life without Chandra

As Subbudu has grown old, Purvaja has become his confidant who scolds him everytime he goes into moments of extreme sadness. She knows her grandfather is not the Subbudu her eldest cousin Swetha had known when she was of Purvaja's age.

Subbudu has surely changed. He does not need these artistes any more. He misses his wife and when his health permits, talks to her portrait kept in the drawing room before going to sleep. As his daughter-in-law scolds him for thinking negatively, Subbudu reminds her that he does not take offence to her scolding because Chandra told him not to bother her.

I am only a critic not a man at all.

— Subbudu

Subbudu and Chandra

Visitors still come, artistes still pester but Subbudu can see through them. The world does not inspire him, he does not care what people think and how history will record him. He knows, his children have stood by him, his grandchildren look up to him and that he loved and was loved unconditionally by his wife. The world of dance and music, the adulation and the criticism pale before his family's love for him. The warrior now rests in his shell, convinced that there is nothing more left to conquer, nothing more left to lose. He looks forward to the next life when he will come back as a musician, who will seek another Subbudu to examine him. That musician will be there but will there be another Subbudu?

I will come back.

— Subbudu, on what he thought of life after death

Select Glossary

Aalapana	Exploring the Raga through improvisation in such a way that its structure and form is revealed
Arangetrum	The first solo performance by a dancer.
Avataar	Incartion
Bhagavatar	Musician
Darbar	Court
Devadasi	Temple Dancer
Devamritham	Nectar
Gamakas	Continuous tone or ornamentation of Indian melody
Ghatam	An earth ware pot
Ghazal	A Persian form of verse limited in the number of stanzas with a recurring rhyme. Also known as Persian love song.
Gotuvadyam	A string instrument. It is Veena minus the frets and the waxy ledge.It is played by gliding a piece of cylindrical wood over the strings.
Gur	Jaggery
Jati	Complex rhythmic patterns in a unit of time

Jatiswaram	An item of pure dance in which a dancer shows the versatility of movements on a basic musical composition sans lyrics.
Javali	In Tamil it means, a song of erotic nature
Karam Bhoomi	The place of work
Karanas	Temple sculptures, which according to Padma Subrahmanyam are actually movements in space and not merely static poses.
Khayal	Standard classical vocal form in Hindustani music
Kritis	Songs
Kutcheri	Music concert
Laya	Tempo
Mama/Mami	Uncle/Aunt
Mridangam	Double sided drum instrument
Mudras	Hand gestures
Nandanar	A *harijan* or an untouchable devotee of Lord Shiva.he is one of the sixty three devotees of the Lord who is worshipped in all Shiva Temples.
Natya Shastra	A treatise on dance,music,drama.
Nritta	Pure dance
Paan	Betel leaf
Pallavi	It means a combination of Padam(words), Layam(rhythm) and Vinaram (improvisation)
Raga	Modal scale
Rasa	Enjoyment
Rasika	Audience
Sabha	Cultural Organisation

Sanchari In dance, it means delineating a line of lyrics and in Carnatic music it would delineating a structure of a raga in different ways

Slokas Hymns

Sringara Love

Sruti Musical microtone

Swara Musical note

Talam Time cycle

Tanam Improvisation originally developed for the Veena,Tanam consists of repeating the word Anantham (endless) in an improvised tune. The name tanam comes from false splitting of anantham repeated.

Teeramanam Teeramanam in Varnam is a long jati that is set to drum syllables in a given time cycle.

Terai chelai Curtain

Thani Avartanam Solo sequence with an accompnist in Carnatic music concert

Thumri Common style of light classical music

Tillana A nritta item.The finale of Bharatanatyam repertoire.

Varnam Central piece of Bharatanatyam repertoire in which equal importance is given to pure dance and expressions.

Veena A string instrument

Vibhti Sacred ash

Vidwan Scholar

Viraha A feeling which comes out of the separation from the lover.